FRENCH ENTRÉE 3
NORMANDY

A **P & O European Ferries** guide

3rd edition

Patricia Fenn

Quiller Press

Chateau de Quinéville

First published 1985 by Quiller Press Ltd
46 Lillie Road, London SW6 1TN

Revised edition 1985
Second revised edition 1987
Third edition 1989
Reprinted 1989

Copyright © 1985, 1986, 1989 Text: Patricia Fenn
Illustrations and maps: © 1985 Quiller Press Ltd
Wine Section text: © 1985 Jancis Robinson

Line drawings: Ken Howard
Area and port maps: Paul Emra
Cover design: Peter Hurst and Kate Hughes-Stanton
Book design: Jim Reader
Design and production in association with
Book Production Consultants, Cambridge

ISBN 0 907621 47 3

Printed in Great Britain by
Billings, Worcester

Contents

Notes on using the book – and an appeal

1 The area maps are to help the reader to find the place he wishes to visit on his own map. Each place is given a reference on the relevant area map, but they are not designed to replace a good touring map.

2 A number in brackets at the beginning of a telephone number is the area dialling code, used when making calls from outside the area.

3 o.o.s. stands for 'out of season', Other abbreviations such as f for francs, are standard.

4 L, M or S in the margin stand for 'L' = Luxury, 'S' = Simple and 'M' for those in between.

5 H stands for Hotel; R for Restaurant and C for Chambres d'hôte in combination with 4 above, ie (H)S, (R)L etc.

6 stc means service and taxes are included (*service et taxes compris*).

7 The ▶ symbol means the establishment fulfils exceptionally well at least one of the author's criteria of comfort, welcome and cuisine – see also pages 24–5.

8 P stands for parking.

9 Credit cards: 'A' = Access, 'AE' = American Express, 'V' = Visa 'DC' = Diners Club, and 'EC' is Eurocard.

10 ¶⊞¶ means Hotel of the Year.

11 ⬛ and ⬛ stand for readers' reactions, for and against.

Prices have not been updated since the first edition, so at *least* 20% should be added to your expectations throughout.

Author's appeal

In order to keep *French Entrée* up to date I need all the latest information I can get on establishments listed in the guide. If you have any comments on these or any other details that might supplement my own researching I should be most grateful if you would pass them on.

Please include the name and address of establishment, date and duration of visit. Also please state if you will allow your name to be used.

Patricia Fenn,
c/o P&O European Ferries P.R. Dept.,
Channel House,
Channel View Road,
Dover, Kent

Introduction

When I embarked on *F.E.1* it was the only guide to the Channel ports and their hinterland; even its limited range of recommendations within 100 km was welcomed by travellers, seasoned and uninitiated. 'More,' said the readers, 'further'. So *F.E.2* expanded the range to 100 miles. But other guides were quick to follow and now there are shelvesful, covering the same region in various ways.

So . . . we decided that rather than outline a large area sketchily, we should concentrate and consolidate. One province at a time should be intensively researched, so that almost every village, every hotel, every restaurant, every reader's recommendation could be considered and given space if found valuable.

The arrows are the ideals. They are awarded for various virtues – good food, comfort, welcome, situation, good value. A list is on p. 24 giving the reasons for their selection.

So . . . here is *French Entrée 3 – Normandy,* which I hope will be half as pleasurable to read as it has been to write. Its research has taken me deep into the core of that rich and diverse province. Its furthest point, some 200km south from the Channel ports in the *département* of the Orne, has been one of the most fruitful discoveries; in the north, old friends have been revisited and new ones made, with the aid of readers' advice. I believe I'm a pioneer again in claiming to be the only author to have visited every single entry personally (excepting those in italics, from readers) and can freely share this delightful experience. I now feel I really know and understand Normandy (understanding the Normans may take longer).

But although the area has changed somewhat, the principles behind the recommendations have not. As before, I look for good value in each of the three categories: L (for Luxury), M (for Medium) and S (for Simple). To define them:

The Luxury recommendations follow the value-for-money criterion, too. Some obvious omissions are because the price is too high for what's on offer. Standards here are quite different from those applied to the S or M categories; it is as irrelevant to complain of the charges being high as it is to grumble that there's no haute cuisine on the 35f menus.

There are few typical luxury hotels in Normandy. The Château de la Salle at Montpinchon is recommended as much for its restaurant as for its rooms, some of which are decidedly spartan. *F.E.2's* 'Hotel of the Year', the St-Pierre at La Bouille, I chose because of its fabulous situation and unusually comfortable bedrooms, but no one could describe it as sybaritic. Compare their charges – from 200 to 350f for two people, or that of a gourmet meal – from 120f, with the English equivalent, and the deal looks a bargain.

The M range are where the majority of French would normally eat. A greater part of the Frenchman's budget is allocated to food than would be the case with his British counterpart. He and his family will eat out regularly and know (and discuss) the merits of all the local eateries. They will take several generations to their favourite for Sunday lunch and spend three or four happy hours there indulging in their national hobby – eating – while the Englishman cleans his car, plays a round of golf, goes to the pub or digs his garden. *Chacun à son goût,* and the Frenchman's *goût* is for the best restaurant he can afford. In this category you can hardly go wrong. For between 65f and 150f a substantial three or four course meal of good-quality ingredients is guaranteed. With luck it might be prepared by a young chef, not quite at the top yet, giving of his best in his quest for recognition. The décor may not be lavish but it will be 'correcte'. I would single out Le Village at Jullouville (see p. 130) as an example in this bracket. At restaurants like this you will find wonderful meals in unassuming surroundings.

The M hotels will be safe. Perhaps they lack the refinement of the L grade, but for 100–200f for two people you will get clean, well-equipped rooms in pleasant surroundings with friendly management.

Some readers, for reasons of economy or inclination, will only be interested in the S group. Recommendations here are for the young, the hard-up, and those, like me, who like a bargain. Don't expect the Ritz and you won't be disappointed. You can bank on clean beds but not bathrooms en suite. I always rate friendly, helpful managements as important, but never more so than here. Invariably they will be family-run concerns, father cooking, mother welcoming, often second generation are concerned too. Food will be simple but wholesome, preferably from fresh local ingredients; if you suspect your dinner is out of a tin, please tell me and I guarantee deletion of culprit. (Letters from S discoverers outnumber all others. Is this, I wonder, because it gives so much more satisfaction to unearth an unassuming bargain?) Amazingly, it is still possible to find good three-course menus for 35f and a clean room for two for 60f.

This guide's all about what pleases *me*. So readers will have to accept that it is biased and egocentric, and allowances will have to be made for personal prejudices. They are: a long-standing love of France in general and more recently of Normandy in particular, a passionate interest in the art and skills of cooking, and a preference for the colourful to the anonymous. If a list of safe, plastic-boxed hotels and middle-of-the-road meals is what you are looking for, *don't buy French Entrée* (or rather, buy it and give it to an intelligent friend).

If I seem to give undue space to Michelin ratings it is not because I always agree with them. However, it cannot be denied that their assessment, along with that of their rivals, Gault-Millau, can literally make or break a restaurant. The award of a rosette can have many effects. At best it can give encouragement to a young chef to realise he is nationally appreciated and urge him to achieve a second star. At worst it can breed complacency and arrogance, especially after several years of star-rating; prices will go up, standards down. The rosettes are neither awarded nor removed lightly and several years may elapse before justice is served.

Introduction to third edition

It is now four years since *FE3* was published, and a quick flip through the pages will indicate how quickly and frequently changes take place in the catering world. Even in France, with its tradition of family continuity, some come, some go, many change.

Unfortunately, for obvious commercial reasons, the text of a modestly-priced paperback cannot be altered. The options are to go on reprinting new editions which are identical with the original, or to try and squeeze in at least some modifications into the margin.

I have chosen the latter, lesser of two evils, alternative, but am well aware that the prices are now hopelessly out of date, and would recommend allowing around 20% on top of those I have quoted for 1985. Regrettable, admittedly, but just compare what's on offer with back-home equivalents. Particularly for a double room, the bargains are still there. Wine is too expensive in restaurants, breakfasts continue to decline, and fresh vegetables to disappear, but not a single reader says he wouldn't go again. First-timers are still bowled over and become faithful converts.

A thumbs-up 👍 or thumbs-down 👎 symbol has been used to indicate readers' reactions. Where opinion has been eloquent but divided, both signs appear. Where there is no sign, there have been no letters.

Several arrows have bitten the dust, either because they have sadly closed, like the Hôtel de la Risle at Pont Audemer, or changed hands, like Le Relais de la Diligence at Carolles and La Divette at Cherbourg, or because current opinion is divided to say the least, like the Simon at Le Havre and Le Plouc in Cherbourg. However, there are some new luminaries to take their place, whose files are bulging with enthusiastic recommendations. If I had to award double arrows they would go to the Château de Maleffre, at Alençon the Family Home at Bayeux the Auberge Vieux Donjon at Brionne and Le Donjon at Conches, Le Phare at Granville, but top of the pops undoubtedly are still those two wonders at Hambye, L'Auberge and Le Restaurant. This means that they are full of Brits undeniably, but what discerning Brits!

New arrows are:

La Bouille – Hotel de la Poste (HR)M good value.

Caen – La Bourride (R)L The best cooking in Normandy.
Honfleur – Le Belvédère (HR)M At last – a good reasonably priced hotel in this popular town.
Putanges Pont Écrepin – Le Lion Verd (HR)M Wide popularity.
Quinéville – Le Château de Quinélle (HR)M Arrowed for good-value rooms and lots of character. Question-mark food.
Les Vertus – La Bûcherie (R)M–L Sustained excellence.

There have been so many intriguing readers' suggestions for new establishments that it has been impossible to list them. They will have to wait until next year when I plan to investigate them all personally. That is not to say 'Enough' however. On the contrary, the more the definitely merrier. Please keep the ideas and reports, favourable and otherwise, rolling in. They should be addressed to:

Patricia Fenn,
c/o P. and O. European Ferries P.R. dept.,
Channel View Road, Dover, Kent

Recent publications in the French Entrée series have been *FE6 Boulogne, Pays d'Opale, Somme, Picardie* and *FE7, Calais, Champagne, Ardennes and Bruges*.

FE8 – The Loire will be published in March, 1989.

Patricia Fenn.

New Discoveries

Map 4D	**BÉNOUVILLE** (Calvados) 10 km from Le Havre; 128 km from Cherbourg

Le Mycene
(R)S.
(31) 44.62.00.
Closed Tue.

A good place to stop for a drink at a table overlooking the canal and the historic Pegasus Bridge. Several new restaurants have opened up to cash in on the opening of the port of Ouistreham, and the natives regard most of them with deep suspicion. Not so here. Micel Harivel's modest restaurant meets with general approval and you have to be quick off the mark to get a Sunday lunch table.

The 49f menu buys mussels or a good, rich fish soup, then trout with sauce normande or rabbit cooked in cider, cheese/salad/pud. But invest another 11f and you get eight oysters or an assiette de fruits de mer, followed by haddock in sorrel sauce, superb lamb or a brochette of monkfish with a sauce made from lobster coral, with modest cheese or desserts. *See also main text entry for Bénouville.*

Map 3E	**LE BREUIL-EN-AUGE** (Calvados) 69 km from Le Havre

Le Dauphin
(R)M.
Route de
Deauville.
(31) 65.08.11.
Closed Tue.
lunch, Wed.,
Oct., 2 weeks
in March.

Breuil-en-Auge is a boring little village on the main road, but its star, Le Dauphin, has already put it on the map. Ask any local with gastronomic pretensions where to eat in the region, and he will say 'Forget all the chi-chi-ness of Deauville and make for the Dauphin'. Fame, alas, is already beginning to affect the prices, but the youthful and ambitious Régis Lecomte has resisted the temptation to smarten up his charmingly rustic little roadside restaurant. Gault-Millau, always quick off the mark to spot a winner, gives him two red toques, but the more cautious Michelin, never happy with shooting-stary chefs, sticks with one set of crossed forks that indicates the simplicity of the building but tells you nothing about the brilliance of the food.

The lunchtime 76f menu is a bargain still. Just four courses are offered in each section, such as sauté de spaghetti aux cêpes parfumés au basilic, followed by ris de veau et escargots à la giboulée de legumes and excellent desserts like a strawberry *soupe* with fresh mint. Expect a bill of 250f, including modest wine, if you eat à la carte.

Certainly one to watch – M. Lecomte is clearly after his first Michelin star, and probably deserves it, but there's a danger of excessive adulation leading to disillusionment.

Map 3E	**COLLEVILLE-MONTGOMERY** (Calvados) 3.5 km W of Ouistreham

Le Ferme St Hubert
(R)M.
(31) 96.35.41.
Closed Sun.
p.m., Mon.
o.o.s.,
Christmas–mid
Jan.

Madame Famin has returned from running a Paris restaurant to her home base and serves some of the local dishes she knew as a girl. Nowadays her son and daughter-in-law help out. Don't expect anything too rustic – the 'ferme' is a substantial modern building, set in the middle of nowhere, with a few rafters and a log fire to set the scene.

Every day there is a 'suggestion du jour' on each of the menus, from 65–180f. I recommend the 90f version for its interesting gratin de moules – mussels cooked in a winey sauce with leeks for texture contrast, then a choice of good fish. The tarte Tatin wasn't special – go rather for the home-made sorbet au calva, and the well-chosen cheeseboard.

Map 1G   DIEPPE (Seine Maritime) 11 km from Le Havre

L'Armorique
(R)M.
*17 quai Henri
IV.
(35) 84.28.14.
Closed Sun.
p.m., and
Mon., 1/6–15/
6, 15/10–31/10,
EC V.*

The difference in price between this professional and elegant restaurant and that of the other quayside restaurants, usually full of straight-off-the-boaters is minimal; the difference in the quality of the food considerable. You won's get a cheap menu, which would probably include commercial ice cream and plastic cheese, but you will get one or two perfectly cooked dishes, served with style.

Bag a table by the window if possible, to get the best of both worlds – a good view of the quayside activity and the benefit of the calm and order within.

Downstairs is a selection of the fish available from the day's catch. Scallops are particularly good, served in a variety of guises, as is local sole, including one dish with a light creamy curry sauce. There are few meat dishes for the fish-allergics, and a definitive plâteau de fruits de mer to kill a wet afternoon. No eyebrows were raised when I ordered for a light lunch just a bowl of moules. They were 'extra' – for 23f.

Desserts are well worth leaving room for here, especially the fruity ones, such as a peach sorbet with strawberry sauce or since this is Normandy, a feuilleté of apples with an apricot sauce. Muscadet sur Lie is 58f. Expect a bill of around 120f. *See also main text entry for Dieppe.*

Map 2F   FÉCAMP (Seine-Maritime) 40 km from Le Havre

Le Grand Banc
R(S).
Quai Berigny

A recent discovery on the less-frequented stretch of quay, but only to be recommended for those who don't mind sitting stuffed cheek by champing jowl, with an entirely French clientele, at ten tables squeezed miraculously into a tiny step-up-from-the-street room.

The 58f menu offers several house specialities as well as the usual excellent moules, à la crême or marinière, and straightforward fish dishes of raie au beurre noisette, or sole mennière. Hareng farci, coquilles mayonnaise, terrine marcassine, and maquereau à la moutarde are first-course alternatives, followed by filets de St. Pierre a l'oseille, morue a la crème or foie de genisse. Add to this an unusually delectable tarte Tatin, fraises Chantilly, or good cheeseboard and a litre of house wine at 16f and you have a very good deal indeed.

The service by the new young owners is as cheering and unpretentious as the food. *See also main text entry for Fécamp.*

Map 3F   HONFLEUR (Calvados) 57 km from Le Havre

**Au P'tit
Mareyeur**
(R)M.
*4 Rue Haute.
(31) 98.84.23.*

A most welcome newcomer to the depleted Honfleur scene. The pretty little navy-blue and white restaurant is in the misleadingly named Rue Haute (i.e. at the bottom of the town) and specialises, as well it might, in fish fresh from the morning's catch. Its owners, Chantal and Christian, commendably exploit local produce from field as well as sea and try to promote regional specialities.

The three-course 66f menu is high quality and good value; the four-course 86f version includes oysters in its first choices, and variations on the fishy theme, such as nage de raie aux amandes.

An almost certain arrow I believe, subject to a few more confirmations in addition to those I already have from local customers. *See also main text entry for Honfleur.*

| Map 3E | **PIERREFITTE-EN-AUGE** (Calvados) 67 km from Le Havre |

Les Deux Tonneaux
(R)S.
(31) 64.09.31.
Closed Wed.

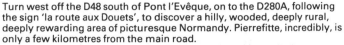

Turn west off the D48 south of Pont l'Evêque, on to the D280A, following the sign 'la route aux Douets', to discover a hilly, wooded, deeply rural, deeply rewarding area of picturesque Normandy. Pierrefitte, incredibly, is only a few kilometres from the main road.

For jaded appetites and pockets. This is the kind of unspoiled, *temps-jadis* over-the-top picturesque village tabac/bar/bistro that it's hard to find anywhere in the North of France, let alone so near the autoroute.

A visit to Pierrefitte, which must qualify as one of the prettiest villages in Normandy, is alone good reason enough for the detour, but a Deux Tonneaux omelette made from the eggs of 'poulets libérés' will set tired tastebuds atingle. They determinedly stick to what they do best – a menu collation du pays – rillettes, omelette, salad, cheese – for 25f; the deux tonneaux – the two barrels from which the cafe gets its name – dispense good farm cider, one sweet, one dry, for another 12f a pichet. Order ahead if you want a plainly roasted farm chicken, plumply yellow, or try their home-smoked ham. Crêpes are reckoned to be the best in the region, so this is the perfect choice for a lunchtime escape, even if only to read the hilarious English menu. I urge you not to miss this one.

TELEPHONING
Most of the public telephones in France actually work. You put your 1f piece in and watch it roll down for starters, then as many more pieces as you estimate you will need. If you over-estimate, out it all comes at the conclusion of conversation.
To Dial Great Britain:
Wait for the dial tone then dial 19; wait for second tone then dial 44; pause and dial British code and number, omitting the initial 0.
To Dial in France, for the same area:
Wait for dial tone, then dial local number (8 digits).
To Dial in France, from province to province:
Wait for dial tone, then dial the 8-figure number (this is arrived at by adding the old 2-digit area code to the existing 6-figure number).
To Dial Paris from inside France:
(The code for Paris is 1. All Paris numbers now start with the figure 4. For the outskirts of Paris, the prefix number 3 or 6 should be added to the 7-figure number.) Dial 16, then the 8-figure number.
To Dial France from Great Britain:
Dial 01033, then the 8-figure number.

Tips for Beginners

1. Planning

Michelin maps are cheaper in France – about 6f – but on the other hand
you may well decide to buy them before you leave home in order to plan
your route ahead, and certainly half the fun of a holiday can be in its
anticipation. I recommend strongly the purchase of 52, 54, 55, 59, 60
to cover individual areas of this book or 231 for the whole of Normandy.
They will add immeasurably to the pleasure of discovering some of the
less obvious countryside .

Unless you are in a hurry – and that would be a great pity in such a
limited area – use the white or yellow roads wherever possible. They are
usually the prettiest and always the least crowded. Some of the red
main roads are nightmares.

The green Michelin guide to Normandy will help fill in any details of
particular interests. I never travel without it.

Other guidebooks to consider: the red Michelin guide to hotels and
restaurants is the eating man's bible and a very sound investment.
Gault-Millau, now in English, is more interestingly eccentric and
describes its recommendations in more detail, but is nowhere near so
comprehensive. If you buy only one, it must be Michelin.

Do make use of the French Tourist Bureaux in London and in France.
You can leave the 178 Piccadilly offices armed with free maps,
brochures and advice on special interests. Have specific questions
prepared before your turn comes at the desk, or the queue behind you
will tut.

This is also the address of the Gîtes Ruraux office, where you can find
out the details of the admirable scheme of renting carefully-vetted
country cottages at the kind of prices that make a family holiday in
France a bargain, especially out of season. There are many such
possibilities in the north of France and we have used the organisation on
several occasions, with the greatest success.

An early visit to the local tourist bureaux is recommended. They will
not only advise on accommodation but actually make the booking for
you, so if it's out of season and your French is shaky, it might well pay
off to let them do the telephoning for you.

2. Choosing an hotel or restaurant

There are various chains of hotels and restaurants throughout France
and if you have been pleased with one example you may wish to look for
others within the same organisation. They all publish their own guides.

The grandest is the Relais et Châteaux chain. These hotels are
situated in buildings of outstanding interest – châteaux, manor houses,

mills, etc – which have been adapted to the most luxurious standards. They are well advertised all over the world and usually booked well ahead. Some of them will only accept a booking for a room if dinner is taken as well.

In the medium price range look for the green and yellow badge of the Logis et Auberges de France chain. These are unpretentious hotels outside the big towns, which emphasise that the welcome – *accueil* – is as important as comfortable bedrooms and good food. They are generally reliable and inexpensive and it is well worth acquiring their annual Guide free from the French Government Tourist Bureau in Piccadilly to direct you to the logis in an unfamiliar area.

Rock-bottom prices for rooms and meals are what you may expect to pay at a café bearing the red and blue Relais Routiers sign. This chain was originally organised along the main roads to suit the tastes – copious helpings at modest prices – of the long-distance *routiers*, or lorry drivers. Nowadays they welcome all travellers and have extended their coverage to include minor roads. Average menu price is around 35f. However, they are better for the famished than the faint-hearted. Your money goes where it is considered by the French most needed – towards the food and not to waiters, paint, linen or loos.

3. Booking

It is often advisable to book ahead in the better-known restaurants and almost essential for Sunday lunch. If you don't speak telephone French, the best bet is to ask someone in your hotel to do it for you. There is a list of gastronomic terms at the back of this book, which I hope will help with menu translation.

When it comes to booking an hotel, my advice would be the same. If in doubt, write in English or get a French linguist to write for you. Even small hotel managers in the north of France are quite capable of dealing with letters in English from their clients.

I have noticed recently an irritating tendency for hotels in all price ranges to insist on demi-pension and many letters confirm how often this leads to misunderstanding. I find it particularly annoying if I want to stay more than one night and to sample another restaurant. No solution can I suggest except to establish firmly at the time of booking if demi-p. is *obligatoire* and move elsewhere if this is not acceptable.

Another new hassle is the increasing demand for a deposit on a phone booking. My method is to send the hotel an English cheque, which they seem to accept quite happily, either returning it when the bill is paid or converting it into francs and deducting that amount from the total.

4. Opening hours

Closing hours and days need to be considered when eating or shopping in France and I have listed these very carefully. Rage and frustration are guaranteed when a special journey to a mouthwatering restaurant ends with a notice on the door announcing '*Fermeture Hebdomadaire*'. The different weekly closing days are a good idea in that they ensure a whole town is not shuttered for one whole day, but it always seems to be the day you choose that is barred. Do check before you venture.

Dates of annual holidays are always announced ahead by the hoteliers and restaurateurs and I have listed these too. In an area as seasonal as the Manche, hotels are often closed for the entire winter.

Many a careless Englishman has been caught out by disregarding French feast days (*fêtes*). No one can conceive the degree of chaos that these holidays – some of them strange to our calendar – can bring about until he has tried to get into a hotel without a reservation, or not allowed for the delays that the traffic jams will undoubtedly cause. Our Bank Holiday rush to the coast has nothing on a French holiday, when the entire population seems to be on the move. Hotels and restaurants are booked weeks ahead, so be warned. Sleeping in the car is not necessarily a joke that only happens to other people. Take note of public holidays:

New Year's Day
Easter Sunday and Monday
Labour Day, 1 May
VE Day, 8 May
Ascension Day
Whit Sunday and Monday
France's National Day, 14 July
The Assumption, 15 August
All Saints' Day, 1 November
Armistice Day, 11 November
Christmas Day

5. Exchanging money

If you haven't done it before leaving home, or on the car ferry, you have the choice of banks, big hotels (where the rate will certainly be low), or *bureaux de change*. The latter stay open after the banks have closed, and the tourist office will supply their addresses.

6. Buying

Unless you are (a) going across for a very short time or (b) exceedingly greedy, it is wiser to think in terms of concentrating on one large meal a day and economising on either lunch or dinner. A picnic in France has the double pleasure involved in both eating and shopping.

Mass-marketing has arrived there too and very popular with the housewives it is. Hypermarkets thrive and there is no doubt that they have some advantages (petrol is often cheaper in their garages, for example). But even here the national priorities are evident. No one could confuse a French hypermarket with an American version. The French conception is more like a covered market, with pre-packing kept to a minimum and the housewife's right to select for herself exactly which is the freshest fish, the ripest cheese, the bloomiest peach, upheld as a matter of course. The street markets and the small, family-run specialist shops survive and flourish in spite of the giant's onslaught and in them shopping becomes a pleasure, an art, a social occasion. It seems to me that the combination of efficient hypermarket and colourful 'local' is the best of all possible shopping worlds.

I love being able to shop in the evenings – 7 p.m. is usual closing time – but regularly get caught out at midday when the shopkeepers put up the shutters and go home for their main meal of the day, usually for two and sometimes three hours. A decision to have a picnic has to be made early in the day.

Wine is an obvious choice to bring home, and the present allowance is well worth shopping for. Hypermarkets score here because of the vast range they carry and because their adjacent car parks obviate lugging heavy bottles too far. 4.50f buys a litre of red, white or pink plonk for instant quaffing; expensive wines need more careful thought and are often cheaper in England, both in shops and in restaurants.

Other buys depend on how quickly you can get them home. I always buy fresh fish if I can have it in my fridge by the same evening, and quantities of fresh vegetables and early fruit. Cheeses and pâtés are not much cheaper, but in infinite irresistible variety and good condition. Coffee is a good buy, and I usually manage to find some item of kitchen equipment I covet, because it's cheaper or unobtainable at home. Olive oil is a must. Even if you don't use it yourself, the gift of a bottle is the nearest way to a keen cook's heart.

7. Petrol

Even at the hypermarket petrol is more expensive in France, so aim to arrive with a full tank and leave with an empty one. If you have to buy 'essence', ask for 'le plein' if you want to fill up, or wave whatever size note you think appropriate.

8. Take with you

Soap (only the grander hotels supply it). A comforting bath-towel is not a bad idea (handkerchief-sized and bald is not uncommon). If you can't live without cereals, decent tea, orange juice, Marmite, marmalade, take them too. They are either expensive or difficult to locate in France.

9. Breakfast

Can be expensive if you order extras like orange juice. Generally if you ask for 'café crème complet' you will get jugs of good coffee, milk (often sterilised and/or cold), a croissant if you're lucky, some fresh bread, butter and jam, increasingly prepacked. If the last two items come in dishes, not plastic wrappings, you know you're on to a good thing. (Tell me.)

Guides, maps and advice are excellent stimulants, but even greater satisfaction will come from making your own discoveries in France. I am well aware of the gaps I still have to fill and of the endless possibilities waiting to be explored.

I hope readers will feel prompted to share their French experiences with me, that I shall have many new entries to record in subsequent editions, and that F.E.3 will indeed prove to be an entrée to France.

Introduction to Normandy

I can think of no other French province that offers such a variety of landscape and interest as does Normandy. Even within each of the five *départements* there is contrast:

Seine-Maritime With modest old-fashioned family resorts like Étretat only an hour's drive away, its capital, Rouen, likes to think of itself as sophisticated. (Its rival Caen, might say *nouveau riche, parvenu*.) Certainly it is increasingly influenced by Paris, thanks to autoroute proximity.

The high chalky plateau of the Caux region, windswept villages visible for miles over the flat cornfields, slides down into the deep ravines of the Seine, hiding little Norman towns like La Bouille. Dieppe, one of its main ports, is at heart still a fishing harbour, Le Havre, second most important port in all France, is totally industrialised; abbeys like Jumièges remain mysterious, spellbinding, castles like Les Andelys make jolly family outings.

To cross into this area of Haute Normandie from **Calvados** is like going abroad, say the natives of its neighbouring *département*, across the natural division of the all-mighty Seine. Here the contrast is pointed within a few kilometres. Turn your back on the glossiness of Deauville and lose yourself in the sleepy Norman villages, careless of the great autoroute that bounds across their country lanes.

Great rivalry exists between their capitals, Caen and Rouen. Caen has the prestige of the university, founded by Henry IV in 1432, and the bones of the Duke of Normandy, but is considered by the aggressive Rouennais as a provincial backwater. Rouen had all the luck in the wartime devastation, but Caen, of all cities, has set about its rebuilding intelligently and profitably. How can you compare Rouen's magnificent cathedral with Caen's magnificent St-Étienne? But they do.

Honfleur is a smaller fishing port than Dieppe, but more picturesque, more self-contained. Lisieux is another entity, ugly but dignified with a great (ex) cathedral and the centre of the rich farms of the valley d'Auge, their black and white timbering and brown and white bespectacled cows part of the archetypal Norman landscape. Bayeux is Bayeux is the tapestry.

Crippling battles swathed a vast slice out of the heart of Calvados, with most poignant reminders of human lives lost in the landing beaches and cemeteries along the coast. Only those with long memories fully appreciate what was lost in terms of Norman heritage, but the new concrete villages soon merge with the ultra greenness of the *bocage* that flummoxed the enemy, and the surviving old manor houses and châteaux, built from the local stone, are so much a part of the scenery that they seem naturally rooted, not imported.

The river Orne is as deeply peaceful as ever it was. Its valley extends south into the *département* of **Orne**, with some exquisite market towns like Mortagne and Alençon, or Sées, with its landmark of a cathedral beckoning the traveller on the 20th-century *route Nationale* seven centuries backwards in time.

The royal hunting grounds of the forests of Écouves, Perseigne and Andaines and the aristocratic studs of the Perche country in the south contrast with the peasant dairy farming land around Vimoutiers, further north, home of France's most famous cheese, the Camembert. To the west the artificially manicured spa of Bagnoles, defending modern livers and veins against 20th-century perils, is sandwiched between the 11th-century fortifications of Domfront and Carrouges.

The *département* of **Eure** crosses the Seine to include favourite towns like Les Andelys, with its unforgettable site and dominating castle, and Vernon, Manet-famed, up to the forest of Lyons, a rural retreat for the Rouennais. Evreux, the capital, has the most notable cathedral of the

Normandy

département. Highly industrialised and rather unpleasant around Louviers, boringly flat over the Neuborg plain, then deeply rural and unspoilt in little towns like Conches-en-Ouche, looking down on a deep valley, surrounded by forests rich with game – the variety is here too. On the *département*'s southern border is another favourite town – Verneuil-sur-Avre, to whose residents the weekly market is of far more import than all the northern factories' outputs. To the north, Pont Audemer, another market town, popular with British visitors, on the river Risle, whose delightful valley bisects the *département*.

The Manche is neatly contained within the Contentin peninsula, with a bulge eastwards to include St-Lô. More contrasts within its small area – the untamed rocks of the north-west, with the highest cliffs in Europe around La Hague, softening into the flat dunes of the west, where the family holiday resorts cluster, past the busy harbour of Granville, down to what is the most marvellous (and I use the word carefully) sight in all Normandy – Mont St-Michel. The cathedral at Coutances surviving the holocaust, the entire town of St-Lô razed, the uplifting abbey of Lessay wonderfully restored. The prettiest villages like St-Vaast-la-Hougue and the sad memory and wind-swept beaches of Utah, Omaha. Avranches on its hill looking westwards across the racing tides, Carentan on its flat eastern pastures and sluggish marshes. Remote little villages of stone grey houses, lost in time, a few miles from the huge nuclear power station on the north-west tip.

And my *Hotel of the Year* – the Auberge de l'Abbaye at Hambye (see p.108), chosen partly because of its situation, in the heart of Norman countryside, near a Norman river, hard by a Norman ruin.

These are the highlights but there are many many more, or perhaps that is the wrong word, for the treasures of Normandy are not showy. They appear as though the landscape had grown around them when they weren't looking. Best to come upon them as if by chance (but wisely guided, I trust).

The people who live and work in this heterogeneous assembly of town and country, city and village, are not really foreigners to the British. No volatile Latin blood disturbs the order of their calculated days. They share with us a Viking heritage and for nearly 400 years after the Conquest, a political union, 'William, Duke of Normandy, King of England' are the priorities on the slab in St-Étienne. But the English colony proved more than a territorial asset; the exchanges, cultural and financial, were two-way and the links are many. No wonder the creamy Caen stone looks so familiar to anyone who knows Canterbury cathedral or has seen the grime of the Tower of London cleaned away to reveal the same material. Bec Hellouin provided us with bishops and an archbishop, and the architecture of many an English village church 'Norman' is shared with that 'Romanesque' across the narrow strip of water that divides us in language but not in heritage.

FOOD AND DRINK

Sailors and farmers by tradition and inclination are these Norman cousins, and fishing and farming are still two of the province's main occupations. No surprise to find that Norman cuisine centres around these two richnesses. A first plâteau de fruits de mer is an unforgettable experience; nowhere are they better than in Normandy and Brittany.

Simple, fresh, local is the key.

Perhaps it is the very abundance of prime ingredients that hinders Normandy from ranking as a top gastronomic province. If there were but one goat grazing on the hill and thin vegetables fighting through barren soil, anything that moved or grew would be pressed into imaginative culinary service, but when the Norman larder overflows with tender lamb from the salt marshes, thick yellow cream from the indulged Norman cow, with lobsters from the Cotentin rocks fit for the best tables in Paris, and sole brought flapping from the Dieppe catch, and if the cauliflowers and artichokes and baby beans proliferate in this natural market garden (where they say a stick poked in the ground will burst into leaf overnight) and a surplus of apples and pears plop to the ground for want of picking, there can be little temptation to conjure and scrape marvels of gastronomic improvisation. Escoffier had no need to preach 'Faites simple' to the Normans.

The products of cow and apple – butter, cream, cider and Calvados – appear repeatedly (some might say monotonously) in the cooking. Sauce normande literally covers a multitude of sins. At worst it can be merely cream sloshed indiscriminately with no attempt to blend and enhance, at best an unctuous glossiness made by whisking the cream and butter into a cider sauce and used to coat, not drench, the vegetables or, with fish stock added, the fish.

The fecund Pays d'Auge gives its name to a sauce combining cream and apple. The two most common bases are chicken and veal escalope, but turbot vallée d'Auge is a traditional dish for first communion celebrations around Étretat. The Caux area of upper Normandy is potato country and you can expect to see them included in any dish labelled Cauchoise, along with the cream. A simple but perfect Salade Cauchoise is made by dressing the freshly boiled potatoes with vinegar and seasoning while they are still hot and tossing them in creme frâiche, with additions like ham and celery to make a substantial meal.

Crème fraîche, an unknown quality still to most British shops, is a key ingredient to Norman cooking and always top of my French shopping list. It has a slightly fermented tang, too sour for some tastes, but I much prefer its slight tartness to sweet cream. It also has the added virtue (or vice) of a high butterfat content that naturally thickens any sauce made from it and can be boiled to a wonderfully concentrated reduction if required. It keeps well too – up to three weeks for savoury dishes, though best used fresh and light for desserts.

A familiar sight in the apple orchards is a fat pig happily rootling amongst the windfalls. When his time comes to be despatched by the local charcutier, some of his more obscure parts will go into a variety of sausages, like the smoked andouilles from Vire, or the boudin noir, coloured with blood and enriched with cream. Butchers from the North of England compete in – and sometimes win – the boudin competition held in Mortagne every year. Imagine the scene! I shall go one day. The strong-flavoured liver of the pig goes into terrines, along with the pork fat, their richness spiked with a lacing of Calvados.

From Rouen comes canard rouennais. I don't know anyone in Normandy nowadays who sticks by the rules and smothers the duck so that its blood is retained, but duck presses survive which squeeze the bones to supply the juice to enrich the red wine and cognac (or

Calvados) sauce. The bird should be a special variety, half domestic, half wild, but again the original concept is loosely interpreted. The Hôtel de la Poste at Duclair used to be famous for serving the bird in fourteen different ways, but generally the most you can expect now will be any kind of duck roasted and served with a wine sauce, with luck, thickened with a purée of the duck's liver.

Mussels breed abundantly along the coast and the tiny juicy variety from these cold northern waters are far better than the inflated southern kind. The Norman way of preparing them, of course, is to add cream and kneaded butter to the broth and to serve them 'à la crême'. Very, very good too. If you see 'dieppoise' attached to a dish, it will probably involve the baby grey shrimps hauled in at Dieppe. I prefer marmite dieppoise, a fish stew using white fish, shelled mussels and peeled shrimp, and made piquant with spices (echoes of Dieppe's early eastern seafaring forays) to the over-rated bouillabaisse from the Mediterranean.

Tarte aux pommes is the ubiquitous dessert and comes in legions of shapes and guises. Many is the slice of blackened cardboard pastry topped with thin leathery apple slices I've choked on in the interests of this book. My favourite recipe uses a rich buttery eggy pastry, and tops it with almond cream which browns and bubbles through the fanned apple slices. (The French use dessert apples for cooking, incidentally.)

Crême pâtissière, another base, can be solid yellow plastic or delicately nutmegged creamy 'real' custard. Check the windows of the pâtissier before you buy. Chances are if his custard is synthetic so will be the rest of his products.

Tarte aux demoiselles Tatin is often found in Normandy, but in fact has its origin in the Loire region, where the blessed Tatin daughters accidentally burned and caramelised their sugar and turned their tart upside down to disguise their carelessness. Delicious if well done, but time-consuming to get right and short cuts can be disastrous. Another version purées the apples and covers them with a latticework of pastry. Lovers of apple dumplings will be pleased to find a Norman version, known as 'bouillons'.

CHEESES

To understand why cheeses are at their best at different times of the year one must consider the date when the cows are put out to pasture and the length of time it takes to make the cheese. Just as wine buffs know the soil and microclimate of every vineyard and how long the wine will take to mature, so will the cheese purist know at what season the grass sprouts, not once but twice a year, and when the meadows break into flower. He will know about individual cheese-making methods within a limited area, sometimes no longer than a few fields; vegetation, climate, rainfall, subsoil and breed all add up to subtleties never dreamt of when you ask for a slab of Irish Cheddar in your Co-op, but a Frenchman will reject a cheese because it is not 'in season'.

There are really only four outstanding names in Normandy. However, within these varieties, Pont l'Evêque, Livarot, Camembert and the cream cheeses loosely referred to by the name of the area from which most of them come – Neufchatel, there are many distinctions and it is worth while remembering what to look for. If your restaurant offers a good cheeseboard, ask to try two or three unfamiliar local cheeses, note the names of the ones that please and thus eliminate mistakes in bring-home purchases.

Pont l'Evêque Probably the oldest cheese in Normandy, known in the 13th century as Angelot. Still made almost entirely in the farms of the pays d'Auge, with commercial producers just beginning to try and emulate. Small, square, soft and tender, with golden rind, it has a pronounced tang, should feel supple when pressed and smell 'savoury with some bouquet' as the king of the cheesemakers, Pierre Androuet, puts it. He also says 'avoid one with a cow-barn odour' which shouldn't be too difficult. Also avoid specimens with a hard rind, greyish tinge, grainy texture, leakage (how very unpleasant I'm making this sound).

From the same stable, or should I say barn, comes a larger version, the pavé de Moyaux, which is said to be the ancestor of Pont l'Evêque. It has a brighter yellow rind and a smell of 'cellars and mould'. (If that hasn't put you off, Androuet prefers it to its parvenu descendant.)

The generic name for these square cheeses of lower Normandy is Pavé d'Auge. They are all at their best during summer, autumn and winter.

Livarot Another cheese with a long history, probably devised originally, like so many good things, in a monastery. Considered by some to be the finest of all pungent cheeses, it has a stronger, spicier smell than Pont l'Evêque, due perhaps to its being aged in airtight cellars lined with hay. Production, which is still mainly in farms around the valleys of the Viette and Vie, declines each year and tentative attempts are being made to reproduce commercially the brown-rinded cylinders. If you hear a cheese referred to as a 'Colonel' it will be a Livarot, the five bands of sedge which enclose it evoking the five service stripes.

Best seasons are late spring, autumn and winter. Avoid any with a dry, or sticky, rind, and consistency must be neither chalky or runny. Petit Lisieux is similar.

Camembert Commercial Camembert, produced all over the world, compared with unpasteurised 'fermier' is like chalk and cheese. Sadly, it is not easy to seek out the farm variety, but if you do have a choice, it is well worth the extra money. The best has an appellation V.C.N. (véritable Camembert de Normandie).

Camembert gets its name from the village where a cheese was made to present to Napoleon III in 1855. He is said to have kissed the waitress, but whether this was before, after, or during tasting is not recorded.

Marie Harel is credited with the invention of the cheese in 1791 but it was another hundred years before the familiar little wooden box was thought up by a M. Ridel so that the cheese could be enjoyed at any distance from the farms. Its popularity spread and it is now part of any worthy cheeseboard throughout France and far beyond.

It should have a very even downy white surface with touches of red (mustn't be *too* white nor *too* red). It should feel supple, not soft, and taste mildly fruity.

Smell is a good guide to buying the perfect Camembert (hard to describe smells in cheesey terms – 'like the feet of a god' was one attempt). A tangy fragrance with no trace of ammonia is the best I can do. Correctly it should bulge but not run when cut, but (please forgive me, Messrs Androuet and Olivier) I like mine oozing a bit. Best seasons are late spring, autumn, winter.

The group of cream cheeses loosely termed Neufchatel, after the town, come from north of the Seine in the pays de Bray. They make a splendid sight on the market stalls, in towns like Gisors, in their varying sizes and shapes – hearts, discs, obelisks. Look out for Triple Bondard, supposed to be the shape of the bung of a cider barrel (*bonde*), with a very pronounced fruity flavour. Its best season, like all these creamy cheeses, is late autumn. My own weakness is for Brillat-Savarin, which comes from Forges-les-Eaux, a triple cream with a wicked 75% fat content. This one even looks and smells appealing, which is more than can be said for most, with a downy white rind and delicate creamy nose. An upstart little cheese, invented by the grandfather of Pierre Androuet between the wars, but perfectly delicious.

Cider and Calvados are to the apple and to Normandy what wine and brandy are to Bordeaux. You cannot eat a cider apple – far too mouth-puckering – but you can see the trees throughout Normandy, wizened and bent with their load of tiny red apples. If you explore some of the side roads in the Auge Region you will come across signs indicating *Route du cidre*. There is one from Beuvron-en-Auge, which leads through delightful little villages set on hilltops above the sloping orchards, with *dégustation cidre fermier* signs on every farm gate. Quite an experience to sit in the farm kitchen at the scrubbed table and sample the golden liquid.

In autumn the presses go from farmer to farmer, each extracting from the neat glowing piles the juice which he will then mix with a proportion – usually about a third – of sweet apple juice to make his own blend of 'cidre bouché'. Left to ferment in the bottle, this is the champagne of cider. An everyday version, a kind of cider plonk known as petit bère, is made by adding a lot more water and passing the lot back through the apple pulp again.

Lovers of German *Spatlëse* wines would appreciate that the best cider comes from the latest apples, with a touch of frost to concentrate the flavour.

Like wine-making there is a lot of judgment and a little luck in producing a good vintage, but perhaps in Normandy the farmers attach more importance to considerations like the moon being in the right quarter and the wind blowing from the right direction before perfect bottling can be achieved than would their aristocratic counterparts in Épernay.

Young Calvados is for stronger stomachs than mine. Not for nothing has the glass of the firewater offered between courses been named a 'trou normand'. It may well make room for more food but you can actually feel it burning the hole! However, a mature Calva, stored in oak for ten to fifteen years, is another matter – a smooth, golden, fruity and distinctly soothing digestif. Look for an appellation controlée label as an indication of quality, and don't drive afterwards.

SPECIAL RECOMMENDATIONS

The hotels and restaurants marked by an arrow ▶ have been selected for the following reasons:

Alençon: *Au Petit Vatel* (R)M – Good food in attractive town. p.31.
Hostellerie du Château de Maleffrè (HR)M – comfortable, unusual base. p.30.

Bayeux: *La Rapière* (R)M – Good value food, attractive restaurant. p.45
Family Home (H)S – Comfortable cheap accommodation in town centre. p.46.

Bénouville: *Le Manoir d'Hastings* (R)L – Superb food. p.49.

Beuvron-en-Auge: *Le Pavé d'Auge* (R)M – Good food in exceptionally attractive village. p.51.

Beuzeville: *Le Petit Castel* H(M) – Popular, comfortable accommodation. p.51.

Boucéel: *La Ferme de l'Étang* (HR)S – p.52.

La Bouille: *Le St-Pierre* (H)M (R)L – Outstanding position, exceptionally comfortable rooms, good food. p.52.
La Maison Blanche (R)M – Outstanding position, good food. p.54.
Hôtel Poste (HR)M – New arrow. p. 55.

Brionne: *Auberge Vieux Donjon* (R)S – Popular, good value, good food. p.59.

Caen: *La Bourride* (R)L – New arrow. p. 64.

Carentan: *L'Auberge Normande* (R)M – Outstanding food. p.68.

Carteret: *Hôtel Marine* (HR)L – New arrow. p. 69.

Clécy: *Le Moulin du Vey* (H)M (R)L – Outstandingly attractive site, comfortable rooms. p.78.

Conches-en-Ouche: *Le Donjon* (HR)S – Good value, good food, friendly proprietor, in pleasant town. p.81.

Conteville: *Auberge du Vieux Logis* (R)L – Outstanding food. p.81.

Ducey: *Auberge de la Sélune* (HR)S – Popular, good value, attractive hotel. p.94.

Goupillières, Halte de Grimbosq: *Auberge du Pont de Brie* (HR)S – p. 104

Granville: *Le Michelet* (H)M – Comfortable hotel in popular resort. p.106.
Le Phare (R)M – Best fish restaurant. p.105.

La Hague: *Auberge des Grottes* (R)M – Outstanding site, popular, good food. p.107.

Hambye: *Auberge de l'Abbaye* (HR)M – F.E.3's Hotel of the Year. Attractive site, excellent food, good value, friendly proprietors. p.108.
Restaurant de l'Abbaye (HR)S – Attractive site, good food, outstanding value. p. 109.

Le Havre: *Le Cambridge* (R)L – Best fish restaurant. p.117.

Honfleur: *La Belvédère* (HR)M – New arrow. p. 127
Château de Prêtreville (H)M – p. 128.

Jullouville: *Le Village* (R)M – p. 130.
p. 168

Jumièges: *Restaurant du Bac* (R)S – Outstanding value on attractive site. p.133.

M. Regis Chatel – p. 131

Marigny: *Restaurant de la Poste* (R)M – p. 139.

Montpinchon: *Château de la Salle* (HR)L – Outstanding food, some attractive luxury bedrooms. p.143.

Putanges-Pont Écrepin: *Hôtel Lion Verd* (HR)M – New arrow. p. 161.

Rouen: *Le Beffroy* (R)M–L – Outstanding food in outstanding city. p.168.

Bertrand Warin (R)M–L – Outstanding food in outstanding city. p. 168

Sainte Adresse: *Hôtel des Phares* (H)S – p. 173.

St-Aubin-du-Perron: *Château du Perron* (H)M – Elegant unusual surroundings, inexpensive. p.175.

St-Vaast-la-Hougue: *Hôtel France et Fuchsias* (HR)M – Outstandingly popular, attractive hotel, excellent food, in attractive port. p.180.

Verneuil: *Hôtel du Saumon* (HR)M – Pleasant hotel, good value, in attractive town. p.194.

Le Clos (HR)L – Attractive rooms, excellent food, good value in luxury bracket. p.194.

Les Vertus, Offranville: *La Bûcherie* (R)M–L – New arrow. p. 196.

Veules-les-Roses: *Les Galets* (R)L – Outstanding food. p.196.

Villequier: *Hôtel de France* (HR)S – Good value, attractive site.

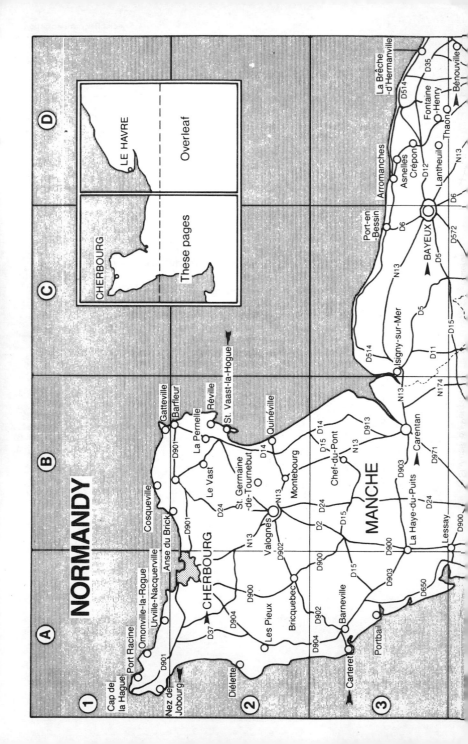

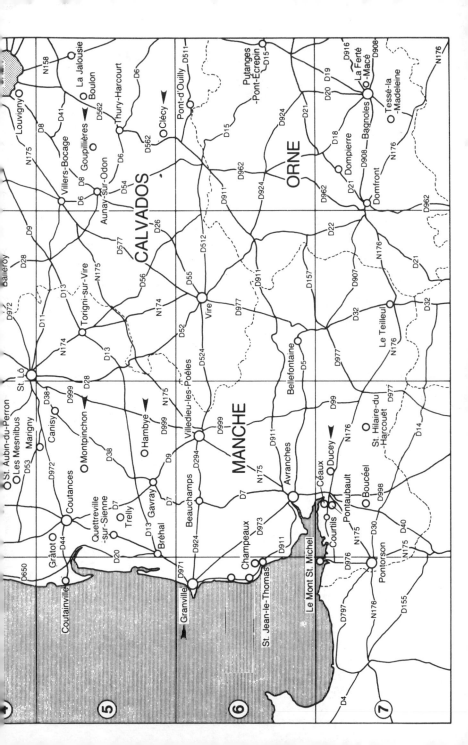

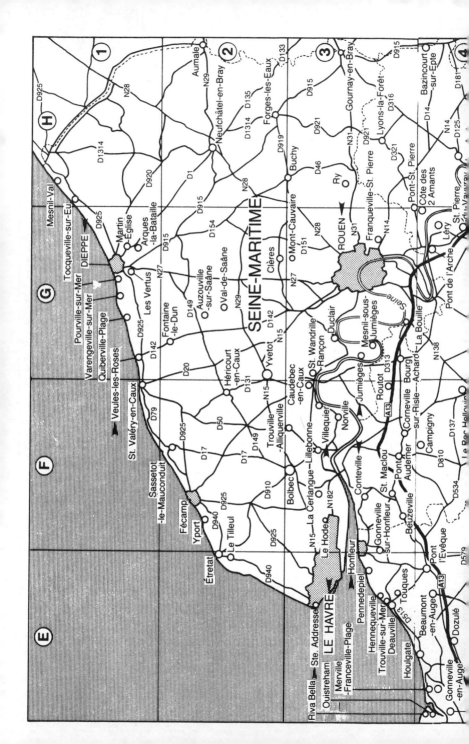

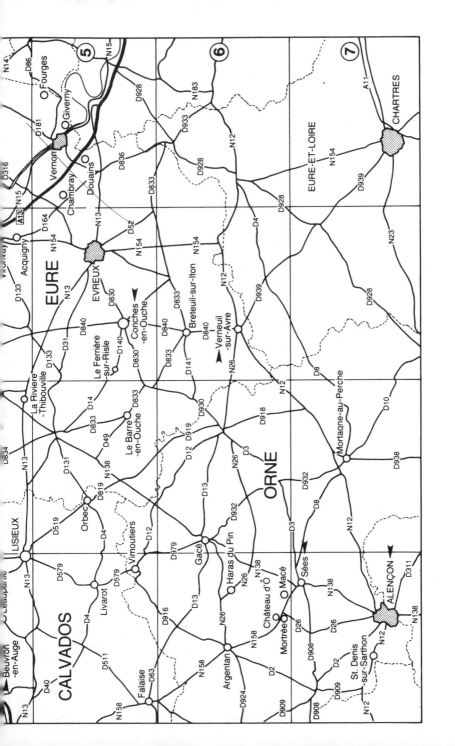

Map 7 E   **ALENÇON** (Orne) 220 km from Le Havre

A delightful old town, of manageable size. Narrow, ancient, cobbled streets, mellow stone courtyards, black Norman timbered houses, window boxes full of geraniums, splashing fountain (modern – hideous) in the main square, pedestrianised centre, all guarded over by the massive cathedral, make it a very agreeable place to pass an hour or so.

The Information Bureau is now agreeably sited in the 15th-century Maison d'Ozé, whose colourful garden makes a serene retreat in which to study maps and ideas. Perhaps a visit to the École Dentellière might appeal, to see the delicate Point d'Alençon lace. The school in the rue Pont Neuf, is open 10–11.30, 2–5, except Sun. and Mon. The art of lace-making is dying, alas, and now a scrap of the intricate work costs, if not a king's ransom, more than a tourist's. The State keeps the school going more for prestige than as a commercial enterprise. Some of the lace is exhibited in the Musée de Beaux Arts in the 18th-century Hôtel de Ville, whose somewhat mixed collection of paintings includes a Ribera – 'Christ Bearing the Cross' – and a Géricault – 'Naufragé'.

Nôtre Dame is one cathedral that I prefer to view from the outside (preferably sitting at the café in the square). The flamboyant porch is the best bit. Inside interest centres on the chapel to St Thérèse, who took her first communion there, and the 16th-century stained-glass windows in the nave.

Alençon makes an excellent touring centre, from which to explore lower Normandy, especially the *Perche* region, with delightful little towns like *Sées* and *Mortagne* within easy reach. It is set between the forests of *Écouve* and *Perseigne*, with the *Alpes Mancelles* (the name is grander than the Alpes) and the newly designated *National Park of Normandy-Maine* to the west. *Châteaux d'Ô*, (p.147), *Médavy* (p.147) and *le Pin d'Haras*, the national stud and stunning 18th-century château, are pleasant drives to the north. I thoroughly recommend a stay here, particularly combined with:

►**l'Hostellerie du Château de Maleffrè** (HR)M *Arconay, St-Paterne (33) 31.82.78.*

What a gem! One learns, with experience, to read between the Michelin symbols and I had picked it originally because it was outside the town and boasted a 'parc', but the location – on the main Le Mans RN 138 – and its modest rating – one turret, nothing in red, no rocking chair – caused me grave doubts on a hot, dusty July day when I craved calm and greenness and a cool shower. Was this going to be another rundown 19th-century château-folly with lorries under the windows? I needn't have worried. The park proved to be a respectable sixty hectares and the château a perfect little dolls' house, originally 14th-century but elegantly restored and looking very French, with its white shutters and tall slate roof. OK, so the lorries' progress is still all too obvious, but the length of lawn and the density of the lime avenues buffer the fret.

Before my car had stopped, out popped the rotund and jolly M. Gaetan de Nanteuil to direct me to shaded parking, to welcome me and ask how I had found him. He was born here at the château and has been running it as a hotel for ten years. His visitors' book is full of enthusiastic testimonials to his friendly hospitality.

'Could I please have some tea on the terrace?' 'Pas de problème,

Madame'. In fact nothing seems to be a *problème* chez Gaetan de Nanteuil – you have but to ask.

The bedrooms are charming. I would find it hard to choose between 'La Bleue', 'La Rose' and 'La Jaune'. Some have twin beds, some baths, some showers; some are for families, some are 'mignonne' singles at 75f, and the one in the delightful annexe is self-contained, sleeps four, has its own bathroom and kitchen for picnics, all for 250f. Expensive flowery wallpapers throughout and spotlessly clean everywhere. The lovely old wooden floors and staircase gleam with polish and the sunshine pours in but fails to expose any dust.

Why the poor Michelin rating and why only one NN star rating? I asked. Because the rooms don't have private loos and telephones, is the answer. In my book that's good news. I am quite happy with a loo next door and a telephone downstairs for a bedroom (turquoise) as nice as mine – 140f for twin beds and a good bathroom.

From Monday to Thursday there is a table d'hôte dinner served at a long communal table in the dining-room. For 110f, including as much wine as you can drink – and Monsieur C. de N. says the English, who 'aiment beaucoup le vin', often have difficulty mounting the stairs after taking full advantage of the good house wine. I was committed to eating at the Petit Vatel, but an English couple told me that the food had been copious and very good, plain but well-cooked and served. They had eaten a tuna-egg salad, roast pork and several home-grown vegs, apple tart and cream and cheese for dinner, drunk deep of excellent red wine, and thoroughly enjoyed their evening, although speaking little French.

A very useful and agreeable stop, bang on the route south, but don't expect to be the only Brit to have found it.

If you prefer to stay in the town itself, both Michelin and Gault-Millau recommend:

Le Chapeau Rouge 🖐
H(M).
*1–3 bd
Duchamp
(33) 26.20.23.*

An attractive little white-painted hotel, but I cancelled my reservation when I found it was on a dreadfully busy corner of the Le Mans exit. It has been recently completely renovated and sound-proofed, and perhaps, for a winter break, it would be no bad thing to stay centrally, but I would not fancy keeping my windows barred against all that traffic in the dog days. Nice rooms from 106f to 202f. No restaurant.

Au Petit Vatel 🖐
(R)M.
*72 pl. Cdt
Desmeulles.
(33) 26.23.78.
Closed
11/2–28/2;
15/8–31/8;
Wed CB, AE,
DC.*

Parking in square outside.

Ten minutes walk out of the town centre, on the Rennes road. A delightful little restaurant, more impressive inside, with its peach and blue décor, than out, and presided over by the genial M. Michel Lerat. Not a great restaurant but a very agreeable one, about par for the course with its one Michelin star.

Certainly the 88f menu is splendid value. For me it offered a selection of three terrines – fish, veg and chicken liver, with a tarragon cream sauce – then trout stuffed with a mousse of monkfish, cheeses and a fresh strawberry charlotte. The selection of sorbets is justly famous, with esoteric flavours like banana and coconut included in the range. Surrounding Frenchmen were tucking into the 120f version – confit of duck, gratiné de fruits de mer, langoustines, etc. – and it all looked copious and good, if a little over-sauced. One determined gentleman demanded melon and a lamb chop and got just that – beautifully ripe and juicy charantais and tender pink meat, so if you don't like rich sauces, say so.

M. Lerat introduced me to a new drink – Le Pommeau – with which he was dosing next door's melon. No prizes for guessing it is made from apples. I thought it delicious, though for my taste too sweet to be taken as an apéritif which is what it is meant to be. M. Lerat gave me the name of the local supplier – M. Préaux, Les Caves de la Rotunde in the Halles au Blé – but I did later see it on sale elsewhere in Normandy, at around 40f a bottle.

Le Grand St-Michel
(HR)S.
7 r. du Temple.
(33) 26.04.77. 🏃

An old-fashioned cheap hotel in a central, quiet side street. Rooms (which were all full, so I could not inspect) are 80–160f for a double, and Michel Canet, the chef, cooks good plain food on menus from 45f.

l'Escargot Doré
(R)M.
183 av. du Général Leclerc.
(33) 26.05.40.
Closed Mon. P.

At weekends, when he serves no meals, M. Gaetan de Nanteuil of the Château Maleffré, sorts out his clients according to what he judges their budgets and tastes to be and directs the prosperous foodies to Le Petit Vatel, the hungry families to a local caff and those in between to l'Escargot Doré, a kilometre or so on the Le Mans route towards Alençon. They do very well there. The restaurant is quite charming – stone walls, rafters, good linen, a pleasant garden for drinks, and a huge charcoal fire, over which the speciality grills are prepared. Menus are 85, 115 and 140f, but you can just have one very good piece of meat, like a côte de porc, for 35f or a chateaubriand steak for 67f.

Map 4H **LES ANDELYS** (Eure) 115 km from Le Havre

The town with everything. Away from the industrial sprawl, near the autoroute to Paris, sheltered from the north and east by the jagged white escarpment sliced by the ever-fascinating Seine, and dominated by the impressive Gaillard Castle, its setting is probably the most attractive in the Seine Valley.

Richard the Lionheart, King of England, Duke of Normandy, thought so too. He built his fortress here in 1196, high on the commanding cliff-top and successfully barred the way to Rouen from the French King Philippe-Auguste. So massive was its foundation, so formidable its site, that it held Philippe at bay for seven years, by which time King John had succeeded to the English throne. Philippe assembled all his forces and eventually the castle yielded to his battering.

I would rate a visit to the ruins top priority in a visit to this area. The view from the summit is literally breathtaking, no matter whether you approach it by a long puff up the hill behind the Tourist Bureau or by car, 3 km via Le Grand Andelys. Far below the loops of the Seine lie shining, to left, to right and to centre; Le Petit Andelys nestles in the crook, and the river barges passing slowly in and out of the range of vision, as though pulled by an invisible string, add animated perspective. A couple of hours could pass by very easily here, walking, clambering, photographing, picnicking. Don't miss it.

La Chaine d'Or
(HR)M.
27 r. Grande.
(32) 54.00.31.
Closed 1/1–1/2;
Mon. p.m.; Tue.

A fine 18th-century building, peacefully established on the banks of the river.

I notice subtle changes since I last wrote about it, in that the Foucaults' regime has obviously proved successful and both they and the hotel now seem more prosperous, more sophisticated. Definitely no longer 'S'. And the prices have gone up accordingly.

However, it is still an outstandingly attractive hotel, and I think some of the bedrooms are among the most attractive I have found. Mine, No. 11, with tall windows opening on to the Seine was unusually spacious and well-furnished, with elaborate marble fireplace and large double bed; with generous modern bathroom, it costs 200f. No. 1 is even larger, with an extra double bed, and now costs 240f. The cheapest is 80f.

Les Andelys

Menus are 55f and 85f during the week, rocketing up to 150f on Sunday when French families for miles around converge to enjoy the food and the view from the attractive dining-room's windows and it is essential to book in or out of season. Wines are not cheap.

However . . . more than one reader has found the welcome less warm, the desire to please less obvious, than previously, and, reluctantly, I have to agree. Very disappointing because I thought here I had found the perfect hotel. The arrow has to go for the time being.

Map 2B **ANSE-DU-BRICK** (Manche) 10 km from Cherbourg

Take the coast road (D 116) east of Cherbourg, signposted not very clearly, near the terminal 'Anse du Brick', and you will get out of the town almost immediately and enjoy a peaceful and attractive ride, sea views to left and rolling Norman countryside to right. Michelin calls it the Fermanville–Bretteville Corniche, which, it says, 'should be taken slowly to be appreciated'.

You can visit the lighthouse at Cap Levy, where 113 steps to the top will reward you with a spectacular view of Cherbourg and as far west as Cap la Hague.

Above a beautiful bay, rocks, and sandy beach stands:

L'Auberge du Maison Rouge (R)M. *(33) 54.33.50. Closed Mon.*

Pink rather than rouge – of tablecloth, curtain and wall – with a pleasing view over the water. If I were looking for one memorable meal within a very easy drive of Cherbourg I might well choose a lobster, snared on the rocks below, and eaten here for around 180f (ample for two).

For the same price you could have a vast plateau de fruits de mer, including half a lobster, or the 120f gastronomic menu again features that same popular crustacean.

But you don't have to be in the lobster class to eat here. The 60f menu is excellent value, with four generous courses, including lots of fish and home-made patés served in individual terrines. The Auberge has become very popular recently and it would certainly be necessary to book at busy times.

There are rooms, at 80f, but I met my match with the very bolshie Madame who was not prepared to let me look at them if I had no intention of staying there that night, so I cannot report.

Map 6E **ARGENTAN** (Orne) 177 km from Cherbourg; 226 km from Le Havre

---

For a rebuilt town, Argentan is not bad, deriving what character it has from being hilly and flowery, but I didn't find anything there which would merit a special visit. If an overnight stop were indicated, I think the best bet would be:

La Renaissance (HR)S.
20 av 2ème.
(33) 67.16.11.
Closed Sun. AE, DC, V.

M. Moulin, the *patron*, is a *traiteur* who smokes his own meat. His menus start at 48f and rooms (which I have not seen) are from 83f.

Map 1G **ARQUES-LA-BATAILLE** (Seine-Maritime) 114 km from Le Havre

---

From Dieppe I suggest you head for St-Aubin on the D1 and the Manoir is on your right, near Martigny. If you get lost, it's no great hardship, since the forest of Arques is delightful, with narrow lanes cutting through the beeches, and the D 56 to St Nicholas is pleasure all the way.

I thought I had found a treasure here in the *Manoir d'Archelles,* a beautiful small manorhouse which has been restored and modernised, with a bright and cheerful interior. It would, I thought, make the ideal base to explore the region round Dieppe, so strangely lacking in places to stay; it was not expensive (rooms now 90–150f) and is a Logis de France, which is usually good news. But reports have been strangely unforthcoming and one reader writes that the food was 'uneatable', so I think it can only be suggested for emergencies. I would like to know more, though.

Manoir d'Archelles

35

| Map 3D | **ARROMANCHES** (Calvados) 100 km from Cherbourg |

They say that this little town is a tourist trap in the summer, or more particularly around the time of the D-Day landings in June; I have only been there out of season, when I found it unexpectedly delightful. Admittedly the D-Day museum does dominate the seafront but the rest of the town retains a lot of its old character and there is a very pleasant little beach.

A visit to the excellent museum is a must, not only for the veterans who remember, but for subsequent generations who cannot fail to be moved by this unique slice of history vividly recaptured. Climb the hill above the town and look down upon the caissons that formed part of the astonishing Mulberry Harbour. A substantial portion of the original 8 km stretch still remains. The *table d'orientation* clarifies the differing landings and the tourists seem strangely quiet, as the impact of just how it must have been hits them.

Back in the town for:

Hôtel de la Marine
(HR)M.
(31) 22.34.19.
Closed
5/11–15/2.

Lots of praise for this little hotel, set on the quayside, with a splendid view over the port. M. Verdier is a very friendly host and doesn't seem to have allowed the easy custom that comes with such an eminent position to spoil the atmosphere of a simple French hotel. The rooms are clean, smallish, comfortable, many with sea views from 110 to 170f, and the food is very good, with menus at 47 and 80f. Private parking too.

Just in case Arromanches does prove to be too crowded, one reader has suggested a nearby alternative. Mr D. G. Pinder recommends the **Hôtel/restaurant Skania**, pl. Alexander Stanier, at Asnelles, which is 2 km east of Arromanches. More reports welcome.

| Map 2H | **AUMALE** (Seine-Maritime) 122 km from Le Havre; 156 km from Calais |

Right on the Normandy border, 22 km east of Neufchatel, where the D 316 crosses the N 29. An important dairy-farming centre. The little hotel Dauphin was the one I had ear-marked, because of its Michelin red 'R' but my spies tell me the food is better at:

Mouton Gras
(H)S (R)M.
2 r. de Verdun
(35) 93.41.32.
P. AE, DC, V.
Closed
16/8–10/9;
Mon. p.m.; Tue.

An attractive Norman building, two centuries old. Rooms are 110f. *'A restaurant with rooms, which we found excellent. The food is perhaps the main attraction, since our double room was very small. The excellent "menu touristique" was 90f.' – Godfrey Spence.*

Map 5D   **AUNAY-SUR-ODON** (Calvados) 132 km from Cherbourg; 136 km from Le Havre

The hub of six D roads, roughly south of Bayeux and on the river Odon, this little town was almost completely destroyed in '44.

Le Saint-
Michel
(H)S (R)M.
6 r. Caen
(31) 77.63.16.
Closed Jan.;
Sun. p.m.; Mon.
o.o.s.

I can hardly claim that this is a *French Entrée* discovery, since it features in every guidebook imaginable (and therefore you should book). I like it very much for its honesty and excellent value. The rooms are simple, and have no bathrooms, but at 67f who's grumbling? The menus are amazing value, from 33.10 to 70f, including most interesting specialities, like croustade d'andouillette sauce moutarde, sucking pig (which is quite delicious), good Norman cheeses, and home made pâtisserie. The welcome is friendly and the little dining-room most attractive.

Map 2G   **AUZOUVILLE-SUR-SAANE** (Seine-Maritime) 74 km from Le Havre

One of the prettiest roads in the Caux area is the little D 2, which follows through leggy poplar avenues the valley of the Saane to the village of the same name – Val de Saane (see p.191). This is neat, prosperous, organised countryside, with glimpses of well-tended formal gardens surrounding elegant châteaux – weekend retreats for Parisien aristocracy. The farms are tidier than usual, too, with white-picket fences, timbered homesteads, flowers all the way, clean white chickens and Norman cows spoiled by the abundancy of rich pasture.

We followed it and the D 152 to the coast one Bank Holiday Sunday, listening to the radio reports of traffic jams back home, and congratulated ourselves at having this route to ourselves.

Auzouville is a hamlet in the middle of nowhere, which makes it very surprising that it boasts two restaurants and an extensive *parc de loisirs*. The latter centres on a dammed stretch of river, with pedalos and canoes, and offers the kids an unusually imaginative day out, from swings and greasy poles across the stream (wet jeans guaranteed), to rope ladders, pony and trap rides, heaving inflated moonlands and hosts of other diversions. Disco on Saturday nights. Predictably all a bit seedy by the end of the season, but not really interfering unpleasantly with the peace and beauty of the valley. All three *French Entree 2* recommendations proved very popular.

Au Bord de la
Saane
(R)M.
(35) 83.20.12.

Everybody likes this eye-catching little roadside restaurant – all that a Norman Inn should be, with its black and whiteness, low beams, copper pots and the helpful young Mme Clamaron to help choose the menus. We ate very well from the four course 79f menu. No rooms here but it is only a pleasant stroll up the street to:

Madame Remy Lambert
'Le Teillage',
Auzouville-sur
Saane, 76730
Bacqueville en
Caux
(35) 83.23.80.

I admire the lace bedspreads, wall crucifixes, family photographs, potted plants, allied with a modern bathroom, large sitting-room and Madame Lambert's desire to please her guests. Her shiningly clean little house is newly built on her son's farm, and fresh eggs and butter therefrom feature on the best breakfast eaten in France for many a day. No packaged jam here.

The idea is that most guests like to buy a picnic lunch, which they are welcome to eat in Mme Lambert's pristine kitchen or down by the river that flows through the farm, spend a convivial evening down at either Au Bord de la Saane or the l'Orée du Bois and stroll back to her simple home comforts.

However . . . although the vast majority have been delighted and re-booked on the spot, one reader points out that no basins in the bedrooms are a disadvantage (I agree) and another couple that we met at breakfast did not recommend the barn annexe.

Accepting that it is only b. and b., with attendant limitations, I think for 90f for two, including that sizeable breakfast, it is to be highly recommended.

Auberge de l'Orée du Bois
(R)L.
(35) 83.27.16.
Closed Wed.
p.m.; Thur.

Very agreeable on a fine summer's evening to sip a Kir or two in the well-tended garden overlooking the village, before going inside the very pretty thatched restaurant to sample M. Saumier's specialities.

I revisited it recently to find out if the increased Michelin rating (now three forks) had changed my original high assessment. I found it as recommendable as ever and consider 115f for food and settings of this

Auberge de L'Orée du Bois

standard to be very good value. Marvellous mixed sea and river fish terrine, with a delicate aneth sauce, excellent entrecôte, emincé de morilles. Well worth saving up for a special treat here.

See also Val de Saane, p.192.

Map 6B ## AVRANCHES 134 km from Cherbourg

A lively and colourful town, sited on the main approaches to Brittany and Mont St-Michel and therefore popular for overnight stops; well served with hotels.

In 1944 General Patton launched his victorious 3rd Army attack from Avranches, which got off the mark so quickly that the town escaped extensive damage. American soil and trees were flown over to form a square for the Patton Memorial, which thereby stands on American territory.

On the site of the former cathedral is 'La Plate-Forme', where Henry II knelt to do penance for the murder of Thomas à Becket, which resulted from his exasperated plea for someone to rid him of this insolent priest. Having viewed the little square, walk to the end of the terrace to get a good panorama of Mont St-Michel.

Another good viewing point of the Mont and surrounding countryside, river Sélune threading through, is from the Jardins Publiques above the town. From there you can train a telescope on the distant island and, like a James Bond film, watch unsuspecting figures walking round the ramparts.

The gardens themselves are a blaze of all the unflower-like flowers so dear to French gardeners' hearts. Cannas, cacti, begonias, tortured into unnatural cohabitation, dazzle the eye with their strident orange, purple and fuchsia-pink. Gertrude Jekyll would have turned in her grave at the vulgarity, but the gardens are certainly a cheerful, cool retreat, and the Avranchins are extremely proud of them.

For connoisseurs of the bizarre, a visit to the basilica of St-Gervais might prove interesting. There in the Treasury, rests the skull of St-Aubert, holed by the reproachful finger of St-Michael, grown impatient at Aubert's dilatoriness in building the usual tribute to the saint on the summit of Mont Tombe, later Mont St-Michel.

Croix d'Or
(HR)M.
83 r.
Constitution
(33) 58.04.88
Rest. closed
Jan.

Lovely old building on the outskirts of the town. Beamy, countrified dining-room and attractively-decorated bedrooms in a peaceful chalet complex annexe from 68 to 250f.

The food is excellent – interesting combinations, prime ingredients of fish, meat and vegetables, well presented. Can't say I found the management over-sympathetic and they don't like phone bookings.

Menus start at 70f and include one composed entirely of fish.

Central
(HR)M.
2 r. Jardin des
Plantes
(35) 58.16.59
Closed
14/10–28/10;
Sat p.m. o.o.s. V.

One of my justifications for writing this book concerns hotels like the Central. Michelin and the map will show you that it lives up to its name and is central indeed, and in a quiet side street. What this doesn't indicate is that just opposite, a biscuit toss from my bedroom window in fact, is the fish market; I was lucky – it was non-functional on the day I was there, but I give warning that early morning activity might not please sleepers-in.

The hotel's not bad, but a fairly basic double room and bath is 143f, so with 12f for garage opposite, it's not much cheaper than the Croix d'Or, which, with its pretty rooms, good restaurant and easy parking, is infinitely preferable.

Map 7D

BAGNOLES DE L'ORNE (Orne) 175 km from Cherbourg; 265 from Le Havre

Bagnoles has two moods, closed and firmly closed. Previous visits out of season have left me believing that if only I'd been there last week or next it would all have been happening, but this year I resolutely visited in July and the droopiness was just as depressing. It is pretty, well-manicured, calm, peaceful – and I don't like it one bit. I think if you were old enough to want to stay there you'd never stand the journey! However, although I would never recommend it for a longer stay, 'La Capitale des Veines' might make a pleasant half-day excursion.

No French feeling (far too well-groomed) and no decent restaurants but the lake is pleasant to stroll round and the surrounding Forest of Andaines is cool and green. There are dozens of hotels to choose from; most of them open only in the season, but even then there is no problem about rooms being available, so it would be quite unnecessary to reserve in advance (unless you were aiming at the over-priced and over-publicised *Bois Joli*). A good place, in fact, to make for if accommodation elsewhere became a problem; then wander round and take your pick. I would choose the cheaper hotels since every one in this little spa looked immaculate.

TESSÉ-LA-MADELEINE, the residential annexe, is altogether less artificial and has a market, on the road to the château, on Wednesdays. It has two not-at-all-bad hotels – the **Nouvel** and the **Tessé**.

Take a picnic to the lake at the **Vallée de la Cour**, 5 km out of Bagnoles. There is a hotel/restaurant there whose weektime tranquillity is rudely disturbed by a raucous disco on Friday and Saturday nights, but otherwise is a good choice for refreshment.

Map 4C

BALLEROY (Calvados) 80 km from Cherbourg

This sleepy little village, with its wonderful wide main avenue and market square, leading towards the magnificent 17th-century château, Mansard-designed, Le Notre-gardened, at its foot, has been in the public eye recently, because of the activity of the balloonists who meet in this unlikely setting to compete with their fantastic creations. Most fantastic of all was the exact copy of the château, which, seen floating over the rooftops, could give you a nasty turn.

Château de Balleroy.

Apart from the balloon museum, the interior of the château is well worth seeing, with richly painted ceiling and impressive portraits. Said to be open every day but Wednesday, but don't believe them.

Hotel Des Biards
(HR)S
1 pl. du Marché.
(31) 21.62.05.
Closed Jan.; Feb.; Mon.

I must confess I had some doubts about what kind of reaction this extremely simple old-fashioned hotel, in the corner of the main square, would evoke. I gave it full marks for honest good value in its bracket and the friendliness of the owner, but what would my readers make of its peeling paint and decidedly un-smartness? I needn't have worried. One or two have shied away at first sight, but generally there is unstinting praise:

'An enchanting place and a most sympathetic and delightful hotel. Rooms are still amazingly cheap – 65f for a double with bath nearby. It added greatly to the success of our holiday.' – Ariel Crittall.

'Madame couldn't have been sweeter and packed us off with the remaining croissants from the breakfast table in case we should need them on our journey.' – June Youle.

For those who value atmosphere above gloss, here is undoubtedly a

41

good cheap base from which to explore the Forêt de Cerisy and the Romanesque abbey at Cerisy-la-Forêt. Rooms from 60f. Menus start at 40f.

Map 2B   **BARFLEUR** (Manche) 27 km from Cherbourg

It seems I did Barfleur in general and the Hôtel Phare in particular an injustice. I still prefer the livelier St-Vaast, but so many readers praising the Phare can't be wrong, and I think I must look again.

Hôtel Phare (HR)M. *(33) 54.02.07. Closed 1/1–4/3; Sun. p.m.; Mon. o.o.s.*

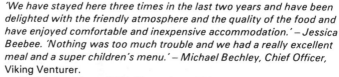

'We have stayed here three times in the last two years and have been delighted with the friendly atmosphere and the quality of the food and have enjoyed comfortable and inexpensive accommodation.' – Jessica Beebee. 'Nothing was too much trouble and we had a really excellent meal and a super children's menu.' – Michael Bechley, Chief Officer, Viking Venturer.

Double rooms are 150f. Menus from 75f.

Take a look at the little harbour, watch the fishing boats unloading, and then perhaps make an excursion along the coast to: **Gatteville** . . .

The famous lighthouse, one of the tallest and most important in France, stands alone on a rocky promontory and you can visit from 10 to 12 and from 2 to 4 and admire the coast and valley of the Saire. Little beaches here, good for picnics since there is little other refreshment offered.

Gatteville is charming, more like an English village in its floweriness. Every cottage has marigolds, roses and candytuft tumbling round it and even the greyness of the church, with its 12th-century belfry, is overwhelmed with the oranges, scarlets and pinks of brimming flowerbeds. Valerian sprouts from the roof of the tiny mariners' chapel next door (Romanesque apse). It's the kind of village that in any other part of France would certainly have a café/bar in the square, but no, here there are only a couple of shops.

The D 116 follows the coast, with narrow lanes leading off to the sea. Deserted beaches most of the year mean few hotels but ideal camping and picnicking.

Map 3A   **BARNEVILLE** (Manche) 38 km from Cherbourg

Barneville and Carteret, either side of the estuary, are often lumped together as one map reference, Barneville–Carteret, but they are very different. Carteret (see p.68) is a lively little family holiday resort and fishing port, Barneville Plage is more staid and residential, and in the middle, inland, is the old market town of Barneville itself, which, I am ashamed to say I had always ignored until a very useful recommendation led me to this modest hotel bang in the centre of the town:

Hôtel de Paris
HR(S).
pl. de l'Eglise
(33) 54.90.02.
Rest. closed
Mon. o.o.s.

'About two miles inland from the more fashionable Barneville, an excellent one-star family hotel. Friendly service, comfortable room with bathroom en suite, five-course meal beautifully prepared and good house wine.' – F. C. Smith.

Madame Poitevin showed me round all the bedrooms, some basic at 70f, some with shower at 120f, some with bath at 165f, some in main hotel, some in annexe (suitable for the handicapped). The vibes were right.

M. Poitevin is the chef and an excellent pâtissier. He makes the pastries and ices not only for his restaurant but for his adjoining shop.

Map 5F   **LA BARRE EN OUCHE** (Eure) 96 km from Le Havre

A hamlet on the D 833, south of Bernay, in a rather dull patch of countryside.

Auberge de la
Route Fleurie
(HR)S.
(32) 44.35.25.
Closed Sun.
p.m.; Mon.

Nothing to look at from outside, but there has been praise for this little Logis, which certainly offers excellent value for money and a good cheap stop.

'We came for one night and stayed for four. Excellent room with our own bathroom for 80f. Good choice on fixed price menus.' – Wilfred Bartlett.

Rooms 59–100f. Menus from 45f.

Map 3C   **BAYEUX** (Calvados) 92 km from Cherbourg

It must be three years since I last stayed in Bayeux and a lot has happened to the city since then. I find it vastly improved. The busy lower half of the main street has been pedestrianised and no longer do you have to walk Indian file on the narrow pavements, shuddering at the proximity of traffic noise and fumes; how much more pleasant it is now to stroll over the cobblestones between the tubbed baytrees and admire the old stone houses and courtyards. A lot of restoration work has gone on all over the place and shabby old 'hôtels' and smaller dwellings have been rescued and spruced up; iron balconies gleam with fresh paint, creamy Caen stone glows grimeless.

Try not to rush Bayeux – its quiet side streets, vast squares , river walks and wonderful old buildings deserve time to be discovered and relished. The city served as a hospital town during the 1944 fighting, was liberated early, and so escaped the devastation that removed so much character from other less fortunate Norman centres.

The tapestry alone takes half a day to do it justice, and the huge cathedral too needs to be admired from afar and near, then to be walked round and in, and through. The graceful east side, buttresses flying, needs a long stand-back, the crumbly little stone figures showing Thomas à Becket's murder, over the south door, can only be identified with close scrutiny.

The original cathedral was completed in 1077 by William's half-brother, Bishop Odo, but now only the façade towers and crypt are that old. In the 13th century the towers were buttressed to support Gothic spires surmounting them. The 'bonnet' on the central tower was added in the 19th century, 'most regrettably' as Michelin so rightly says. Distinctive is probably the kindest word for it.

Inside, the nave is surprisingly light and the whole cathedral provides a wonderful opportunity to compare and contrast the slender Gothic (three-storey chancel, nave, vaulting) with the robust Romanesque (carved nave arches). Try and picture the effect of the entire nave being draped in the glowing tapestry showing William's conquest of England!

The Tapestry of Queen Mathilde:
About three years ago the city fathers obviously realised that their biggest and unique asset, the tapestry, was not being seen to advantage. At that time it was housed in the Maison du Doyen beside the cathedral and it was almost impossible to see it without peering over burly German shoulders or shuffling round in a slow gaggle of Japanese. A huge work of restoration has since developed a 'cultural centre' in an old seminary and signs all over the city persuade you in that direction. 14f now to get in, but you get an awful lot for your money. Don't think of trying to fit it in in less than two hours, and that's pushing it.

On the first floor is a mock-up of every detail of the work and a clear description in English and French of what is going on. The critical scenes – Harold's oath, Edward's death, Harold's coronation, the Norman invasion, William's bravery, Harold's death – are all emphasised to make identification easier when you do eventually get to see the actual tapestry. Then there's a 15-minute film, regrettably americanised, and here I would advise a preliminary check of the times of the English version – you could just miss the last showing of the day, or have a very long wait. And then at last into the dark passage where this priceless account of the customs, clothing, food, events of 900 years ago, recorded so unforgettably vividly, awaits you. Don't miss the English moustaches!

The recorded guide costs another 2f and is probably still worth while, but what happened to the cool, cultured Englishman who spoke so wittily and effectively in the old recording? Nowadays it is an inappropriate American.

(An amusing codicil: Little realising what a hornet's nest I was putting my foot in, I showed what I had written about the tapestry to Liz de Mauny, a tireless local worker for its promotion, who seized upon my criticisms as fuel for her pro-British lobby. Thanks to her efforts, the unfortunate American film commentary is being replaced by one beautifully spoken in English by her husband, Erik de Mauny, and two other compats, and there is hope that the ear-phone chat will be similarly improved. Yanks go home. Long live English chauvinism.)

One institution that hasn't changed in Bayeux is:

Hôtel Lion d'Or ⬛🔳
(HR)M.
71 r. St-Jean.
(31) 92.06.90.
Closed
16/12—20/1.
AE, DC, V.

This old coaching inn, recessed in a courtyard, has been the favourite Normandy refuge for British tourists for many years; I had hoped that the awful leopard and ponyskin fittings and furnishings might have gone by now, and that the décor generally would be a shade gentler and more countrified, but no, it all looks exactly as it was on previous visits, the lighting as harsh, the colours as unrelenting (but I am told that some of the bedrooms are being done up).

The restaurant has a Michelin star; I tried the 110f 'régionale' which was a shade dull but tasty enough. The 90f, 'touristique' was probably a better bet, though in both cases the cheeseboard was disappointing and the desserts a disaster. I thought it altogether less inspiring than on earlier visits and do hope tiredness is not beginning to prevail. In fairness, it was Sunday dinner, when French restaurants are never at their best, and readers' letters have been generally in favour. Double rooms are 110–220f.

Guided by a reader, who wrote: 'extremely comfortable and tastefully furnished; management very helpful, with fair command of English; they phoned ahead for us to book other hotels', we chose to stay at a new hotel:

Hôtel d'Argouges
(H)M
21r. St-Patrice.
(31) 92.88.86.

Contrived out of a nice old 18th-century *hôtel particulier*. It is approached through an archway in the pl. St-Patrice and although it has no restaurant, the excellent 'Ma Normandie' is only a few doors away.

The rooms, with their high dormer windows, are simply furnished, the bathrooms work (but the towels are skimpy and scratchy), all is blissfully quiet, parking is free, and the breakfast is good. From 150 to 200f.

Hôtel du Luxembourg
(HR)M.
25 r. des
Bouchers
(31) 92.00.04.

M. and Mme Morel have modernised and restored what was once an old coaching inn and the Luxembourg is now very popular with tourists and locals alike. There is a garden where drinks are served – a great asset in the heart of the city – and courtyard parking. A lively bar and three dining-rooms might be expected to take care of the custom, but on a February Monday they were full up for lunch, which was not surprising when I saw what value the 40f menus offers. Rooms are 150f to 187f, which includes breakfast.

'We decided to take the children to Normandy in the October half-term holidays and, encouraged by the accuracy of your report re our Calais experience, we booked for a whole week at the Hôtel du Luxembourg. We had the largest family room they had and were delighted with all we found. We were given special reduced terms for our long stay and found the service unobtrusive and excellent. The hotel was comfortable and the restaurant was superb value.' Dr R. L. Marcus and family.

Hôtel Notre Dame
(HR)S.
44 r. des
Cuisiniers
(31) 92.87.24.
Closed Sun
p.m.; Mon.; Oct.

Logis de France give M. Hébert's cooking a 'casserole' for excellence, and the locals I asked agreed with that. It is a little hotel just opposite the west door of the cathedral, with a surprising cellar dining-room. Menus from 44f. Rooms are 85f, but it was on a Monday when I tried to inspect, so I have not yet seen them. Readers report well.

▶**La Rapière**
(R)M.
53 r. St-Jean.
(31) 92.94.79.

Another restored old building, in a courtyard just off the main pedestrianised area, recently converted into a charming little restaurant. Stone walls, lace tablecloths, open fire, pink napkins, all very spruce and agreeable. Equally agreeable are the prices. Sticking to the 55f menu (others at 88 and 120f), one of us had six oysters and a huge and juicy charcoal-grilled pork chop, another a generous plateful of crudités, and hake with a good beurre blanc sauce. I chose wickedly garlicky snails and a beautifully fresh truite normande. Then followed a good cheeseboard and an unusually satisfactory apple tart.

Especially useful on a Monday, when, in common with so many French towns, Bayeux dies and its restaurants likewise. An arrow is deserved for good value and delightful surroundings.

Ma Normandie
R(S).
41 r. St-Patrice
(31) 92.09.88.
Closed Mon.

An old favourite family-type restaurant on the market square (and therefore particularly busy on Saturday morning). Excellent value menus from 35f have delighted *French Entrée* readers. *'Greatly added to the success of our holiday – excellent food, especially the quenelles de brochet.'* – Ariel Crittall.

'The 62f menu included 9 oysters ~~NEW MANAGEMENT~~ *starters, then melon in port, a generous-sized fresh cheeseboard and tarte aux pommes – all excellent. M* ~~NEW~~ *locals were drinking cidre bouchée. On a previous visit, with only thirty minutes to eat, I was particularly impressed by the helpful staff.'* – J. C. Baber.

▶**Family Home**
(HR)S.
39 r. Général de
Dais
(31) 92.15.22.

A real find, for which I am indebted to a reader, Mrs K. Thaxton, who had stayed here and enjoyed it enough to write and tell me.

An unfortunate name; in this case 'Family Home' means something between a hotel and a gîte. You may take from it whatever suits you best. It is in a nice old 16th-century house, set sideways on to a quiet street leading from the main r. St-Malo to pl. Charles de Gaulle, i.e. very central. It is certainly the family home of Madame Lefevre, who lets out sixteen rooms, some with cooking facilities, all with washbasins, for 50f per person, including breakfast and baths/showers. As in most homes, the rooms are all different; some with twin beds, some family rooms, those in the older part being the nicest, but all irreproachably clean:

If you do not wish to cook for yourself, Madame prepares an evening meal, which is eaten, *en famille*, round a long table in the old beamed dining-room. Three courses, with wine, cost 40f.

I think this makes an unbeatable base for a cheap stay in quiet pleasant surroundings, in the heart of a fascinating city, with a good deal of flexibility. On those grounds I give it an arrow, to encourage readers to try something different, but I haven't eaten there myself, so any reports on the food would be most illuminating.

Map 4H   **BAZINCOURT-SUR-EPTE** (Eure) 155 km from Le Havre

Take the D 14 north of Gisors.

It had been a great privilege and pleasure to be a guest of Moët et Chandon in Épernay during the vendange and we left Reims on a high. The dreadful N 31, hour after tedious hour through jammed Soissons, Compiègne, Beauvais, blinded by spray from an eternal lorry procession, changed all that, and it was two very late and very fatigued travellers who sought out the Château de la Rapée that night, so maybe judgment was not as impartial as usual. I don't think I would choose to go back, but I write about it because I suppose that others will be encouraged, as was I by the Michelin red rocking chair rating, and might like to know what to expect.

The 19th-century château is a very strange building indeed. As we approached it at last, bumping down an interminable drive, driving rain obscuring everything save the headlight's narrow range, a flash of lightning, bang on cue, illuminated its Gothic towers and turrets. A sinister black-coated butler might well have answered the gloomy door. He didn't – a perfectly normal Madame ended the fantasy – but the strangeness continued inside in that we were the only guests in the echoing building; and hushed whispers seemed appropriate conversation at the table for two, amidst all the other empty ones in the flock wallpapered, tapestried dining-room. The dinner wasn't very good. Perhaps they hadn't felt it worth while to make an effort.

To be fair, the bedrooms were reassuringly 20th-century, with comfortable beds and bathroom, and the breakfast was exceptionally good; a red rose on the tray, real jam, real butter, masses of coffee and chocolate made me hope that, with daylight and sunshine, all would look different. But not really. The situation is undoubtedly quiet – eerily so for some tastes – but the surroundings are pretty drab. So there you are – ugly but peaceful, pretentious downstairs but comfy bedrooms, not very good dinner but superb breakfast and a bill of 600f for two, including dinner. Not the best value for money I can think of.

The real bonus was **Gisors**, 6 km away – a really super little town with a wonderful market filling the square on Fridays. The cathedral and castle ruins with pleasant gardens make a visit well worth while and I liked the look of a little restaurant called the **Hostellerie des 3 Poissons**. Next time I would eat here and try the **Hôtel Moderne**. Reports particularly welcome.

Map 6B   **BEAUCHAMPS** (Manche) 103 km from Cherbourg

Les Quatre Saisons (R)M. *(33) 61.30.47. Closed 25/9–20/10; Mon. p.m.; Tue. p.m. o.o.s.*

On the crossroads where the Coutances–Avranches road (D7) crosses the Villedieu–Granville road (D 924).

Very pretty old building, inside and out, with interesting four and five course menus for 45 and 68f respectively. Friendly proprietors, who speak English. Book at weekends.

Map 4E   **BEAUMONT-EN-AUGE** (Calvados) 70 km from Le Havre

The N 815 from Pont l'Eveque to Caen is a tedious road, giving the impression that the Auge countryside through which it passes is boring too; however, 2 km to the north on the D 58 the scene is altogether different. Quintessentially Norman is the scenery around, with timbered farmhouses set in apple orchards on green cowslipped hillsides, dotted with placid, stumpy Norman cows, or smart studs and frisky elegant horses. The little road climbs to the delightful village of Beaumont and there from the square in front of the church is a splendid panorama of the surrounding paysage.

Across the way is:

l'Auberge de
l'Abbaye
(R)L.
(31) 64.82.31.
Closed Jan.;
Tue.; Wed.

A surprisingly sophisticated restaurant for a sleepy little village, if this were not France, where a restaurant of this standard can attract discerning clients from miles away.

The interior is calculatedly *typique*, beamed and coppery. the dishes are admirably local, like duck cooked in cider, flaky apple tart. It is very good food, skilfully prepared from prime ingredients, in a charming building in an enchanting village, and the locals obviously approve. So why no arrow?

I totally agree with the Gault-Millau summing up: 'it is a pity that the management is not as agreeable as anything else'.

If you feel like braving Madame, the menus are 100f and 165f.

Map 4F

LE BEC HELLOUIN (Eure) 70 km from Le Havre

Follow the river Risle, on the D 130, 23 km from Pont Audemer, through the Montfort Forest, to Bec Helalouin, whose great ruined abbey gives the hamlet a cathedral-close atmosphere. Founded in 1034, the abbey has strong links with England through Duke William's friend and counsellor, Lanfranc, who was instructor at Le Bec and subsequently Archbishop of Canterbury. His secretary, Gundulf, became Bishop of Rochester and architect of the Tower of London. A profitable way to work up an appetite for lunch at the Auberge is to climb the 210 steps up St Nicholas' Tower for a fine view over the Bec valley.

Auberge de L'Abbaye

Auberge de l'Abbaye
HR(L).
(32) 44.86.02.
Closed
12/1–26/2;
Mon. p.m.; Tue.

Given such a perfect setting – on the green in the pretty Norman village above the popular tourist attraction of the abbey – and its appearance – black and white out and beamy, flagged, coppered inside – plus the publicity bonus of a Michelin rosette, I suppose it is not surprising that the owners of the auberge should feel it unnecessary to make too much extra effort, and this was in fact the impression I got on my last recent visit there.

As the simple country inn it once was, with good Norman cooking and a few cheap bedrooms, it was almost too good to be true, but now with prices of 200f for a charmingly rustic but modest room, and a dinner unlikely to cost less than 150f, it falls into an altogether different category. I still love it but can hardly recommend it as value for money.

Map 6C

BELLEFONTAINE (Manche). 141 km from Cherbourg

One reader recommended a visit to *Le Village Enchanté* in *French Entrée 1* and I subsequently followed his directions: 'Go north from Mortain and turn left towards Villedieu' 'Up a bumpy track for a quarter of a mile.' Perhaps I was not in a mood to be enchanted, because I thought the children's attractions there – Norman village, plastic castle, ponies' track and lake – all a little uninspired; although the menus in the 'auberge paysanne' looked surprisingly interesting, I could not believe that this was the kind of environment in which to find good food, and so it was omitted from *F.E.2*. Wrong again. A French gourmet/gourmand friend tells me that he took a party there for a business lunch (imagine that happening in England!) and it was as excellent as its reputation locally had led him to believe. There are gîtes there too, year-round but the restaurant is not always open, so best telephone (33) 59.01.93). It would certainly make a good excursion, since it is all very rustically pretty, including the young, long-skirted waitresses.

Map 4D

BÉNOUVILLE (Calvados) 108 km from Le Havre; 128 km from Cherbourg

---

10 km north of Caen on the D 515

▶**Le Manoir d'Hastings**
(R)L.
(31) 93.30.89.
Closed Sun 14/2–1/3;
1/10–15/10;
Sun. p.m.; Mon.
AE, DC

I suppose the gastronomic star of the region and of this book. Loth though I am to follow meekly the dictates of Gault-Millau and Michelin, in this case I have to agree wholeheartedly that it merits three red toques and two stars. I thought that perhaps when Claude Scavinger lost his sous-chef, Michel Bruneau, to La Bourride in Caen, the standard might begin to deteriorate, but no, I find it still unfaultable.

The Manoir is a 17th-century priory, set casually in an apple orchard. The Scavingers have made it a place of gastronomic pilgrimage, which ensures that their tables are always full, but never for one moment allow their success to lure them into complacency.

The sheer professionalism of it all – the welcome, the seating, the service – I admire enormously. Aline Scavinger is always a very efficient, but smiling, hostess. Nowadays she has for sale home-made conserves, local Calvados and cookery books in a new boutique.

Her husband has named a particularly delectable dessert after her –

'Pêches Aline' are gently poached peaches, topped with caramel and served with a raspberry coulis. It's one of my favourite dishes at home, and never fails to please.

Claude is always aiming to perfect new dishes, but with a strong Norman influence; he uses cider in many of his skilful, succulent sauces. His irreproachably fresh fish comes from the nearby fishing port of Port-en-Bessin and there is usually lobster and crayfish on the menu.

The 100f menu is a bargain, especially with its attendant complimentary bouchées each end, but whatever you spend here, including the 245f *menu dégustation*, it is money well invested. Go without lunch, live on berries for a week, but treat yourself to this experience.

And here is an excellent complement:

A La Glycine (HR)S. (31) 93.30.02. Closed Mon.

Just across the road from the Manoir, a nice young couple have done up this little bar/hotel, all covered in wisteria. Their attractive rooms are bargains and you could save on bed, Glycine-style, what you had lavished on dinner, Chez Scavinger.

April Chevron, from Le Chalet at Ouistreham, recommends it:
—'Round a lawn and patio at the back are "garden rooms" which would be super for young families.'

She's right, and the cost? 88f for a double or 110f with shower.

Also at the nether end of the financial scale one reader, Mrs Crook, recommends **Le Mycène**, hard by Pegasus Bridge: *'A full car park attracted us and the customers were all French.'* She recommends the middle menu, of three, as being extremely good value.

Map 4E **BEUVRON-en-AUGE** (Calvados) 84 km from Le Havre

A picture book village, in the Auge region, south of the autoroute. La Route du Cidre is well-marked round here, and a very well-spent hour or two can be passed following it; call in at some of the farms that have the sign up and sample their (sometimes very powerful) brew. It is most attractive countryside, sometimes hilly, as at Clermont-en-Auge and sometimes flat and pastural, as around Hôtot-en-Auge, where I got hopelessly lost trying to find a restaurant called *La Lapin Qui Pêche*. It turned out to be between Hôtot and Le Ham and I *think* it looked quite promising, but as I was suffering from lack of discrimination just then, owing to the cider sampling, I don't remember enough about it to be sure.

But Beuvron is a must, centred round the wonderful old wooden *halles*, in which is to be found:

Le Pavé d'Auge
(R)M.
(31) 79.26.71.
Closed
10/12–20/12;
15/1–15/2;
Mon.; Tue.;
Wed. p.m. o.o.s.
AE.

Ravishingly pretty restaurant, commendably making full use of local ingredients. Chef is a woman, Odile Engel. Try her saumon cru, magret landais, wonderful fish dishes. Excellent 74f menu, or 97f even better.

Popular destination in the area for a delightful gastronomic excursion at weekends (vide opening days), so best book to be sure not to be disappointed.

Arrowed for traditional local food, well presented, good value, in a particularly charming setting.

Auberge Boule d'Or
(R)M.
(31) 79.25.26.
Closed 7/1–7/2;
Tue. p.m.; Wed.

If it happens to be a Monday when you wish to eat in Beuvron, the Boule d'Or's opening times are slightly more accommodating, and you could do far worse. Another attractive restaurant in this particularly attractive village. Simpler than the Pavé d'Auge, and not so well-known, but very good too. Menus from 65f. Small, so again booking advisable.

Map 3F   **BEUZEVILLE** (Eure) 48 km from Le Havre

An ideal staging post, on the N 175 south of Honfleur and just off the autoroute. We regularly use the Cochon d'Or for a breakfast stop. From then on, everything looks distinctly brighter, especially if it happens to be a Tuesday and legs can be stretched strolling round the market in the square, for that magical first sight and smell of France.

Auberge du Cochon d'Or
(HR)S.
Closed
15/12–15/1;
Mon.

Such a steady history of good unpretentious value that I think an arrow is now well deserved. Recently redecorated and subdivided, so that the erstwhile bar is now a cheerful dining-room. The food is excellent, simple, substantial Norman fare, reliably consistent, like the praise that is lavished on it by so many readers. Menus are 41f (not Sun.), 63, 80 and 112f, giving plenty of variety for all tastes. Rooms are simple, clean, perfectly adequate, costing 72–90f. Only one has a bath, so if this is a high priority, best cross the road to another, slightly more upmarket hotel, under the same management.

Le Petit Castel
(H)M.
(32) 57.76.08.
Closed
15/12–15/1.

Smarter altogether, with a little garden; all rooms have baths, loo and TV. Doubles 130–190f. It shares the Cochon d'Or's arrow, on the assumption that meals will be taken there.

One word of warning. Although these two make an ideal first or last stop, the ladies who run them (a leetle unsmiling, perhaps?) are not happy about accepting bookings from clients arriving very late, so, if appropriate, send a deposit to secure firm reservations. Nor can they offer early breakfasts for those making for the 9 a.m. sailing. Great pity.

Map 3F   **BOLBEC** (Seine-Maritime) 30 km from Le Havre

Since Bolbec is on the main N 15 and a useful distance from Le Havre for a last or first meal stop, I was particularly pleased to have the following recommendation:

**Restaurant de
la Piscine**
(R)M.
124 r. Gambetta
(35) 31.02.75.

'As you will be aware, there is a dearth of eating places in Bolbec, so to find this restaurant was even more appreciated. Run by André Saint-Genis, it is a brisk 10 minutes walk from the centre of the town. One receives a friendly welcome and an excellent choice of menu. Wise to book. A visit will mark the end or beginning of a holiday in style'. – Shirley Carte.

Map 7B **BOUCÉEL** (Manche) 144 km from Cherbourg

---

10 km south of Avranches, the D 308 runs between the D 40 and the D 998, and there is the hamlet of Boucéel. In pleasant countryside, conveniently situated for Mont St-Michel, this was one recommendation I particularly wanted to follow up, but ran out of time.

 **La Ferme de
l'Étang**
(HR)S.
*Boucéel,
Vergoncey, St-
James
(33) 48.34.68.*

Mrs Watts sent me a photograph of a charming old stone farmhouse, white-shuttered, creeper-covered, geranium window-boxed which she had discovered by chance. It is run by Brigitte and Jean-Paul Gavard, dairy farmers, who have just started offering b. and b. with an optional evening meal, featuring produce from their own farm.

'They speak very good English and offer a very high standard for just 80f per night per room, regardless of how many occupants. A really wonderful evening meal at 40f, three courses with home made cider, and Calvados, and wine thrown in. They are a most friendly and willing couple who give that personal touch rarely received these days. Just by the farm is a large pond and a manor house which a family with young children would find interesting to explore.' – Peggy Watts.

I can't wait.

Map 3G **LA BOUILLE** (Seine-Maritime) 75 km from Le Havre

Turn off the autoroute at La Maison Brûlée, follow the signs to La Bouille and enter another world. Tucked under the lofty white escarpment, heedless of the traffic thundering by just three kilometres away, lies this peaceful little Norman town, curving along the very banks of the river. Having just glided down the Seine myself in a Russian cargo ship (but that's another story!), I can vouch that La Bouille is the prettiest spot on the river, not only from land but from water too. It is set in a loop of the glittering river, lined with cliffs, woods, villas on one side and apple orchards on the other. Tranquillity and timelessness are only disturbed by the little red *bac* which fusses across every half-hour.

  Le St-Pierre
(H)M(R)L.
*(35) 23.80.10.
Closed Tue.
p.m. Wed. o.o.s.
2 weeks in
Feb. V.*

My last 'Hotel of the Year' and greatly appreciated by *F.E.2* readers, many of whom have become regulars.

The reasons I chose it then still stand:

1. *Site*: it lies like a great white ship moored alongside the river. Its terrace stretches along the water's edge and I can think of no better vantage-point from which to watch the progress of the great cargo ships, the barges, the pilot ships bound for Rouen or Le Havre (unless of course it is from the double bed in room no. 1!)

2. *Surroundings*: Rouen is just around the corner, accessible by river

bank, by autoroute, by ferry. What a combination of fascinating city and serene lodging! Paris is a mere 137 autoroute km one way, Le Havre an easy 45 minutes' drive the other. The whole of Normandy is explorable from this one base.

3. *The Hotel and its owners:* Bernard and Giselle Huet are in partnership with Patrice and Thérèse Kikurudz. Having just spent a longer than usual break with them (I warn you—the St-Pierre can be addictive), I am lost in admiration at their dedication. The Huets have lived in England and speak perfect English; Bernard is the business manager, Giselle (the tall, glamorous blonde) and Thérèse (the pretty young brunette) are the hostesses. Never once did I see either of them hesitate to leave whatever they were doing (eating dinner included) to leap to their feet and welcome an arriving guest. So obvious a courtesy, but so rare. How I hate shifting from foot to foot waiting to be noticed. When a supply of new mauve tablecloths arrived on Saturday, Giselle stayed up after midnight ironing so that she could have them on the tables for Sunday lunch. Thérèse may not speak much English but she still manages to make her *French Entrée* customers feel particularly welcome. Between them they see to it that the whole hotel gets a springclean every day.

Patrice is the chef and won his Michelin star in 1982. He is a member of the group of Jeunes Restaurateurs de France who meet to exchange gastronomic ideas and ideals. On his menus he uses a lot of fresh fish (try his mousseline d'écrivisses); he makes his own pasta, and a delectable strawberry gâteau.

Meals are served in the long dining-room overlooking the water, in the green-trellissed overflow room upstairs, or on the terrace, beneath smart green parasols. In the summer and at weekends all three can be very full with the Rouennais, for whom La Bouille is a favourite excursion.

This is all very well, but winter and bad weather tell another story. There is little passing trade and with the staff kicking their heels, the big restaurant is deserted. Obviously this is a time when English clients are most appreciated. Other guidebooks have noticed my enthusiasm and are now recommending the St-Pierre to their readers. In the case of small hotels I find this frustrating and self-destructive, but the St-Pierre is big enough to absorb them and professional enough not to allow standards to slide, and a new influx of Brits may well tide them over a difficult time.

With such a short season, prices are not low, but I can understand now, having seen how hard they struggle, why this is so. Menus start at 100f (they like hotel clients to eat one meal in the restaurant). The seven bedrooms are still a bargain at 180–220f for one of the most attractive, rather Japanesy, rooms, with luxury bathroom, in my book, and the service is perfect.

Bernard has again worked out for me a special out-of-season weekend rate. From 1 November to 1 April: *Friday night:* double room with bath for any two nights; two gastronomic dinners; two breakfasts—1200 per person, which represents more than a 20% saving.

▶**La Maison Blanche**

Another good reason for visiting La Bouille is this ravishingly pretty restaurant, with elegant rooms on three levels overlooking the river.

La Maison Blanche

(R)M.
(35) 23.80.53.
Closed
17/7–4/8;
18/12–6/1; Sun.
p.m.; Mon.

Decorated with Norman antique furniture and faience, smaller and more intimate than the St-Pierre, and run by a delightful and friendly family, the Rozadas, who give a special welcome to *French Entrée* readers; Philippe Rozada has been a finalist in national cookery competitions and produces interesting and delicious specialities, especially fish.

Perhaps to be avoided on fête days and Sunday lunches when it tends to be crowded and the prices shoot up, but otherwise highly recommended for a delightful meal, at prices from 80f.

'What a beautiful little place—an ideal half-way stop en route for Paris. It was super eating on the 1st floor with window overlooking Seine. Standard of service and food you would pay £20 a head for in London' – Anne Mager.

► **Hotel Poste**
(HR)M
(35) 23.83.07.
Closed
24/12–21/1;
Mon. p.m.; Tue.
V.

A delightful old coaching inn just opposite the St-Pierre, and altogether different. The rooms are old-fashioned but comfortable at 150f a double, and the menus start at 85f.

'Simple, friendly, excellent breakfast, good menu and cheap.'

Les Gastronomes
(R)M.
Closed Wed.
p.m.; Thur. AE,
DC.

Recently entirely redecorated, to celebrate its 20th anniversary. A bit plush for a little riverside restaurant, all Napoleon III, but the food on the 72.50 menu is good and the terrace is very agreeable.

See illustration on the next page.

BOULON (Calvados) 15 km south of Caen

East off the Thury–Harcourt road, D 562.

La Bonne Auberge
R(S).
(31) 79.37.60.
Closed Mon.;
Tue.; 3 weeks in
Sept.

Following up a somewhat vague if enthusiastic recommendation, I dutifully detoured from the main road to look for Boulon. I found the village all right but nothing that looked like a restaurant. All very sleepy and no one around to ask, so, weakly, I gave up. Now I am told by a local resident that I should have persevered in discovering one of the best little Norman restaurants in the district. She explained my location problems – La Bonne Auberge, though in the centre of the village, doesn't look like a restaurant. It is apparently very small, just seven tables, very French, and serves sublime tripes à la mode de Caen and other regional dishes. You must book at least three days ahead. Menus at 34.50, 52.50 and 65f. I shall certainly try again – sounds like a treasure.

Map 3G   **BOURG-ACHARD** (Eure) 55 km from Le Havre

An ordinary enough village, with a Monday market, conveniently adjacent to autoroute exit.

Les Gastronomes.

l'Auberge de l'Abbaye
(R)M.
(32) 56.37.04.
Closed Tue.

A lucky find—my husband had to a make a phone call and we stopped at the nearest bar in a village I had not marked for attention. Once inside, however, it was immediately clear that this was no ordinary village bar. Not many of those have a glass cage housing three gigantic pythons and sundry other reptiles! So far, so bad; when I want a drink or a meal I would rather more attention were paid to what was in my glass or on my plate than to the zoo in the corner. Snacks and snakes should be kept firmly in their place, I feel. However, the entertainment is not the only attraction here.

Behind the bar (and the snakes) is a sizeable and most attractive restaurant, serving really interesting dishes – moules au curry, feuilletés de poireaux, terrine de marcassin, – all on very reasonably priced menus. I would have been very happy with the 45f version, but there were others at 64, 95 and 120 for the gourmands. It was not lunch time, unfortunately, on this occasion, but I shall certainly return one day when it is.

Map 5B **BRÉHAL** (Manche) 94 km from Cherbourg

---

10 km north of Granville. I have never personally explored the strange spit of land leading up to *Les Salines*, but here is someone who has:
'Come here when the Grande Marée is due and see it boil through the pipes under the road, which it later completely covers. Eat at La Passerelle – good food, reasonably priced. You can dine modestly for 30f. At Bréhal eat at L'Ambassade de l'Auvergne (dinner only). 'You go through an unprepossessing women's Prêt-a-Porter, find yourself in a most elegant dining-room and are served by the equally elegant wife of the patron. A memorable meal, with aperitif, four courses, coffee, wine included for 100f.' – B. A. Brewer.

A more modest alternative is:

Gare
(HR)S.
(33) 61.61.11.
Closed
19/12–1/2;
25/9–10/10;
Sun. p.m.; Mon.

Good value, well-served food, and 9 rooms which I have not inspected. Menus from 41f, rooms 67–75f.

Map 6G **BRETEUIL-SUR-ITON** (Eure) 128 km from Le Havre

A nice little town between Conches and Verneuil, encircled by the river Iton and surrounded by woodland rich in game.

Le Mail
(HR) M–L.
r. Neuve-de-
Bemecourt.
(32) 32.81.54.

A charming 18th-century house, comfortable and elegant, in a quiet side street. Good food, immaculate *couverts* – porcelain and linen – in the beamed dining-room, with a winter log fire, garden, terrace, pool. All splendid, especially the guaranteed calm (Relais du Silence) but the prices are on the high side – 230f for a nice but not luxurious room with bath, or 180f for one with shower. Menus at 90f.

Map 2A **BRICQUEBEC** (Manche) 22 km from Cherbourg

An obvious and ideal stopping place, with an obvious and potentially ideal hotel, set into the ramparts of the nice old town, next to the castle keep. The Monday market takes over the whole town.

Le Vieux Château
(HR)M.
(33) 52.24.49.
Closed 1/1–5/2;
Rest. Closed
1/10–1/4; Sun.
p.m.

My experiences here have been happy ones; I like M. et Mme Hardy, who always made me feel a welcome guest (even before they discovered I was writing a guidebook), I liked the character of the old building, I liked the food, on the more expensive menus at any rate. I noted that some bedrooms, notably the one that Queen Victoria slept in, were infinitely better value than others, which in some cases were decidedly poky, and regretted that long association with English guidebooks had resulted almost as inevitably as night follows day, in the clientèle being mostly fellow-countrymen, but all in all I felt that the Vieux Château was still one of the best bets in the area. Now I'm not sure. Here are two recent experiences:

'No hot water, dinner in understaffed restaurant, the worst meal ever had in France.' 'No welcome, no "little touches", no reply to booking letter' 'The most uncomfortable hotel bedrooms ever, flooded bathrooms.'

Or, alternatively:

'What a tonic, I can't thank you enough. Warm welcome from M. et Mme Hardy; the food was excellent and everyone made us feel we were honoured guests.' 'The bed was the most comfortable we have ever occupied in France. We hope her Majesty had similar comfort.' 'Mme Hardy phoned for rooms outside, since she was fully booked, and we stayed in a private house owned by the café in the square, so we had a lovely dinner and a cheap room. Exceptionally helpful staff.'

I'm flummoxed as to what advice to give here. No good saying 'Make sure you see the room before you book,' because it is usually fully booked in advance. The best I can do is to advise asking for Room No. 2, avoiding the cheapest menu, and telling Mme Hardy that French Entrée sent you.

Rooms 90–212f. Menus from 42f.

Map 4F   **BRIONNE** (Eure) 76 km from Le Havre

A delightful 28 km drive from Pont Audemer, following the river Risle and skirting the Montfort forest, leads to Brionne, where the river's streams divide to form the islets on which the pleasant little town, crowned with its imposing Norman keep, is built.

The D 137 leads to two châteaux owned by the Harcourts, one of the oldest families in the French aristocracy. When the town of Thury-Harcourt was devastated in 1944, the 17th-century **Champ du Bataille** was returned to them in part compensation for their loss. Now it is open to the public from March to September (not Tuesday and Wednesday) and its glorious paintings, furniture and architecture make it a very worthwhile excursion. The gardens of the château bearing the family name, a few km away, are equally rewarding (open mid-Mar. to mid-Oct.), being planted with rare and mightily impressive trees. Back to the town for refreshment:

Auberge Vieux Donjon
(R)S.
pl. Frémont des Esserts
(32) 44.80.62.
Closed 15/10–31/10.;
15/2–24/3; Sun. p.m.o.o.s.; Mon.

Two editions of *French Entrée* with never a cross word for this little timbered restaurant in the main street earns it an arrow for *F.E.3.* Eat by the log fire in winter, admire the flowery courtyard in summer, be cheered by Serge Chavigny's warm welcome, relish the value of the good and imaginative food, and count the change in your pockets. So good is the cheapest menu at 45f that there is really no need to pay more, unless for a special occasion. I have no reports on the rooms as yet. *Please*!

Le Logis de Brionne
(HR)M.
pl. St-Denis.
(32) 44.81.73.
Closed 24/12–26/1;
Sun p.m.; Mon. (except evenings in season); Fri. p.m. o.o.s.

A rather uninteresting-looking building on the outskirts of the town, but, always provided you can master the opening times, a no-nonsense, good-value bet. One reader, who had a frustrating doorstep wait for the hotel to open at 6.15 wrote: *'The dinner was excellent and we were glad we hadn't looked elsewhere. It started with a pâté of skate, which I had never met before. The chef, husband of Madame, was very happy to explain how it was made. We were happy to revisit on return journey.'* – T. L. Haynes.

Rooms 66–145f. Dinner 45f.

Manoir de Calleville
(HR)M.
(32) 44.94.11.
Closed Tue. o.o.s. AE, DC.

4 km on the D 26 – I warn you – when the Manoir de Calleville is shut, it is more shut than anywhere else I know. On two occasions now I have tried to investigate and found it closed (and not on a Tuesday). Last time it all looked so shuttered and desolate that I decided it was abandoned altogether. It seems I was wrong:

'Don't be put off by the faded menu in the glass case as all is very well within. I started with two vast crêpes, ham and mushroom swimming in creme fraîche, then trout and almonds, followed by veal cauchoise, plus cheese and dessert – all absolutely first-class.' – Elizabeth Armstrong.

If you have better luck than me, this might well prove a treasure. Michelin gives it a red rocking chair for tranquillity and that I can certainly confirm. Rooms (uninspected) are 165 to 245f and you can expect to pay around 120f for a meal.

Map 3H   **BUCHY** (Seine-Maritime) 127 km from Le Havre

28 km NE of Rouen on the crossing of the D 919 and D 41.

I set out in search of the **Hôtel du Nord** rather than the village of Buchy, but in the event it was the latter that proved more interesting. The hotel lies desolately some kilometres away from anything of more interest than the railway sidings, and I can't think of many reasons for staying there; however, the menus, starting at 36f, looked excellent, especially the 86f *gastronomique* which included half a lobster. Locals like it and Michelin gives it a red 'R', so I am pretty confident it would be worth a lunchtime détour. Monday it was closed, very perversely, since that is the day for the best market I have discovered in the whole area, meriting a special journey. Its focus is the ancient beamed market hall, but it spills out to cover the whole centre of the town.

Do make a point of buying some of the wonderful cheeses brought there by the farmers' wives, moulded into hearts, barrels and cubes, laid tenderly on straw. This is the core of the cream cheese area, supplying the whole of France.

I can never resist buying far more than I can possibly eat, just for the sheer pleasure, but if homeward bound, the packages make highly desirable presents for gourmet friends, since some varieties are rarely seen in England.

No more can I pass by the bundles of herbs, strings of red shallots, or slender beans picked that morning, but I go to great pains to avoid catching the hopeless eyes of the doomed geese, heads protruding from paper sacks, the rabbits stupefied in their crates, and the helpless trussed-up ducks. The squeamish had better pass on to all the lively clamour and squawk of the baby goslings, all fluff and nonsense.

Map 4D	**CAEN** (Calvados) 108 km from Le Havre, 120 km from Cherbourg

A good centre at most times of the year, with all the beaches near at hand to the north, and pleasant countryside all round. Plenty of gorgeous châteaux and manorhouses to drive to. Try the elegant *Lantheuil* to the north-west; open year-round, this would make a pleasant excursion on a hot day, when the 300-years-old plane trees surrounding it provide pleasant cool, and plenty to see inside, in less good weather as it is furnished and still inhabited by descendants of the Turgo family who built it in the 17th century.

Four kilometres away is another splendid château – *Fontaine-Henry*, built by the Harcourt family in the Renaissance style. I believe there is a good restaurant nearby at Thaon, the **Auberge de la Mue**, but I have not tried it yet; there is certainly a rather lonely little Romanesque church standing deserted and now deconsecrated in the valley.

I think this is a city that also makes an ideal base for a winter break, being blessed with so much to see, do and eat.

The guidebooks all note that Caen was three-quarters destroyed in 1944. What they don't stress enough is that the quarter that is left alone merits the journey and that the modern three-quarters is unique in any rebuilt city of my experience in combining convenience with charm. I know of no other town with so many green spaces, flower borders, trees, picnic benches, paved squares and pedestrianised areas. You can stand back and admire it.

There is plenty to admire; the feeling of the old town lingers in the ancient houses, alongside the new ones, so carefully rebuilt not in dead grey concrete but in living creamy Caen stone. Below the castle in the paved r. Vaugueux there is more atmosphere of the 15th century than of the devastating 20th. Sit there by the fountain at one of the many pavement cafés and study the crazy angle of La Poterne's gables, like a Disneyland pastiche. Lots of antiques shops.

The area round the castle was cleared after the war and made into a series of colourful gardens. Walk through the castle grounds to the ramparts, from which you can get bearings. From the terrace above the drawbridge can be seen to the left the **Abbaye Aux Dames**, to the right

Caen - Abbaye aux Hommes

the **Abbaye aux Hommes** and, splendidly dominating the foreground,
the richly ornamented St-Pierre, all top priority visits (see below).

Inside the ramparts are the **Musée des Beaux Arts**; open 10–12,
2–6 in summer, or until 5 p.m. from 1/10 to 15/3. Closed Tue. and *fêtes*.

Don't miss the Perugini Virgin or the Monet water-lilies.

Here too is the **Normandy Museum**, illustrating aspects of Normandy life.

You cannot be in Caen for long without being aware of two particular influences on the town's history and character. First and foremost it is William the Conqueror's town, with references to that great duke of Normandy and to his Queen, Matilda, in street names, shops, and of course in the abbey churches. Secondly, the part that the town played in the last war is not easily overlooked and similar references – Rue 6 Juin, Ave. de la Libération, Bvd des Allies, etc – and in the war memorials bring both aspects of its history into focus.

The castle was William's. Built by him in 1060, partly destroyed and restored after 1944, it is now a pleasant, sunny enclave in which to stroll and picnic.

The **Abbaye aux Hommes** was William's outward sign of repentance at having married a blood relation against the Pope's wishes. Matilda was his cousin and she took some persuading that the marriage to a bastard was a good idea. To convince her, William had to drag her round her *chambre* by her hair; convincing the Pope he left to his Secretary, Lanfranc (see Bec Hellouin), who talked the Pontiff into rescinding his prohibition of the match. It was a nice touch for the happy pair to build their spiritual memorials at opposite sides of the city, with the great fortified castle protecting them from their worldly enemies in the centre.

The Abbaye aux Hommes protected the citizens of Caen during the bombardment of 1944; many thousands of them took refuge inside it, and the abbey and the church of St-Étienne within it were miraculously saved, (as indeed was Matilda's Abbey, though somewhat battered.)

William was buried there, but now only a slab before the high altar marks the spot, since the tomb was ravaged once when the Huguenots sacked the church in the 16th century and again during the Revolution, when his remains were thrown into the river. No doubt about priorities: 'Duke of Normandy, King of England' reads the dedication. The abbey started off in 1077, Romanesque, and was finished two centuries later, Gothic. Marvellous contrast of styles within and without. Recently cleaned, the glowing Caen stone, illumined by lots of light flooding through the three layers of windows, framed in graceful Norman arches, makes the abbey a warm, not solemn, place in which to linger.

Outside too all is bright and cheerful. The former abbey buildings that flank St-Étienne are now part of the Town Hall and are approached through a blaze of well-groomed gardens.

Matilda's church is less colourful, but impressive, as is her mausoleum inside. Don't do as I did, though, and puff the considerable distance between the two abbeys, to arrive on the threshold at 11.55, when the adamant curator was locking up for lunch.

As though some inspired history master had arranged Caen, St-Pierre provides the perfect contrast to the austere simplicity of the two abbeys. The rich merchants of Caen vied with each other to contribute decoration upon decoration. Its famous 12th-century belfry was destroyed during the battle of Caen, when a shell from HMS *Rodney* hit the spire, but it has since been restored exactly as it was and the king of all Norman belfries rules once more.

Round about St-Pierre are the main shopping areas, and Caen has the best shops in the North of France. All the main department stores are here – Le Printemps, Nouvelle Galleries, C & A, Bon Marché – but also the chic boutiques supplying real French elegance to real French women, and not easy-money tourist trade. The streets have been pedestrianised, and their flower beds, trees and cafés make shopping a pleasure. Send your husband to look at the yachts and fishing boats in the *bassin* while you make decisions.

Best of all, its main market of the week takes place on Sunday mornings, so that period, sometimes difficult to fill on a bleak winter's day, passes profitably, joining the French families' keen-eyed purchasing, and thinking how agreeable it would be if we could do the same back home.

It was almost snowing last February, but the weather couldn't spoil the spectacle of the whole quayside and square brimming with colourful stalls. The cascades of tangerines and oranges looked freshly polished, leeks were arranged in bouquets, decorative Belgian chicory and endive were being sold at giveaway prices, unfamiliar fungi begged to be brought and tasted, and over all the frosty air was aromatised by wafts from the pizza huts and biscuit stalls.

There's a wonderful cutlery stall there, where the young girl, who likes to practise her English, insists on knowing exactly how you intend to use each purchase – 'Non, non, this one not for vegetables – for cutting up ox'. Her father lovingly demonstrated some hand-forged poultry shears, showing off their craftsmanship, and now I wonder how I ever managed without them.

Time for a warm-up with a hot chocolate in one of the many cafés open thereabouts and a visit to stock up in the extra-good pâtissier, chocolatier and boulanger that sells 21 different kinds of bread. The charcutiers are open on Sundays too, and one of the best in the area is in the r. St-Jean, where last-minute perishables will be beautifully packaged for transport on the return boat. There's still time to walk to castle or abbey, have a leisurely lunch or drive to the coast for some fish, and there's a winter morning well-spent if you like.

To get full benefit from all these urban attractions, and to avoid the hassle of the one-way system, it makes sense to find a central hotel, park the car and walk around the city. Ideally situated is:

La Moderne
(HR)M.
116 Bd Mar-
Leclerc
(31) 86.04.23.
Restaurant
Closed Sun. p.m.
o.o.s. AE, DC, E.

An exception to my usual distaste for modern chain hotels (this one is Mapotel). Here the management are all exceptionally friendly and helpful and the hotel is well-run and efficient. Like most Caen hotels, it is custom-built; bedrooms are not large but comfortable and warm, and, for such a central position in a quiet pedestrianised precinct, with a garage, 165 to 250f a room represents excellent value. It also has a very good restaurant, Les Quatre Vents; it is elegant and highly regarded locally, with menus from 75f for four interesting courses.

La Bourride
(R)L.
15–17 r. du
Vaugueux
(31) 93.50.76
Closed
10/1–25/1;
15/8–31/8;
Sun.; Mon. AE,
DC.

In the ancient, traffic-free, utterly delightful r. du Vaugueux there are several restaurants, but the new star in its cobbled, peaceful firmament is undoubtedly La Bourride. I wrote about Michel Bruneau's talents when he ran the Bourride at Évrecy. He was good then, learnt even more during a stint under Claude Scavinger at the Manoir d'Hastings, and now seems set to confirm Gault-Millau's appraisal: 'the best cook in Caen and one of the foremost in Normandy'.

Certainly the restaurant is among the prettiest I have found. Small, tall, galleried, stone walls, log fire, flowery, with the most elegant of china settings and the most comfortable of velvet chairs. Such refinements do not come cheap and a meal here has to be an occasion, but a comparison with prices for a similar standard in England should help.

The menu at 140f was what had lured us there, but when this did not look inspired, we decided rape was inevitable and laid back to enjoy the carte. The salad of 'blond' chicken livers served warm, nouvelle-cuisine style, with a sharpening of raspberry vinegar, were good; the natural oysters were superb (six giants for 35f was about the best value on the menu) but the hot stuffed oysters were a disappointment – an excess of sautéed onion in their rich sauce unbalanced the dish completely. The famous 'bourride' lived up to expectations – sole, brill, bass, monkfish and scallops, delicately poached and served with a potent aioli—and the couronne of lamb was perfect – pink and melting. But the distinction here goes to the desserts. So often these are disappointing job-lots thrown in as an afterthought, but at La Bourride it is quite obvious that they are prepared with love. I would never have chosen my 'delices de chocolat' had I realised that I would get a portion each of mousse, gâteau, marquise, truffle, and three ices, in a tulipe case. The mocha mint liqueur served with them complemented the flavouring perfectly and I ate every sinful mouthful. Companions' choices all equally spectacular and delicious.

Ah – the bill. It worked out, with wine and coffee, at around £20 a head. So we did picnic next day.

Les Échevins
(R)L.
36 r. Ecuyere.
(31) 86.37.44
Closed Sun.;
Mon. lunch. AE,
DC, E.

An attractive little restaurant in one of the oldest streets in the city, leading to the Abbaye aux Hommes. Only fourteen places in two charmingly decorated rooms, ~~NEW MANAGEMENT~~. The food is rich Norman ~~NEW MANAGEMENT~~ a tarte . The sauces swim with butter ~~NEW MANAGEMENT~~ the fish is fresh and very good indeed, and the chef, Patrick Regnier, is not afraid to experiment within the traditional cuisine. The 110f menu is excellent value in this luxury bracket, but the wines are too expensive.

La Pomme
d'Api
(R)S.
127 r. Saint-
Jean
(31) 85.46.75.
Closed Sun.
p.m.; Mon.

Change of proprietor but still as good value as ever in this modest little restaurant near the church of St-Jean. For ~~CLOSED SINCE LAST EDITION~~ town centre ~~CLOSED SINCE LAST EDITION~~ 3 ~~CLOSED SINCE LAST EDITION~~ here, ~~CLOSED SINCE LAST EDITION~~ like guineafowl cooked with apples and cream.

La Poêle d'Or
(R)S.
7 pl. Laplace.
(31) 85.39.86.
Closed Sat.;
Sun.

Another change of proprietor is the reason for last edition's arrow disappearing until I have a chance to eat here again, but from all accounts it is still well merited. It was awarded last time for good value and that is still evident, with a substantial menu at 33f. Off the r. St-Jean.

Alcide
(R)S.
1 pl. Courtonne
(31) 93.45.52.
Closed
30/6–1/8; Sat.

'Run by two French ladies. Popular with locals and good value.' – M. C. Wilson.
    Menus from 45f.

Two others which local friends praise for their good value but which I have yet to try are the **P'tit Grilladin**, 3 Place Leteller, which apparently has an attractive, intimate atmosphere and menus from 41f, and **Le Zodiaque**, 15 quai Meslin, lunch only, the best meat in Caen, charcoal-grilled steaks, awful décor, about 70f à la carte.

Stégosaure
17 pl. de la
Republique
(31) 85.23.64.

Another recommendation from the invaluable April Chevron of Ouistreham's Le Chalet. She told me that she takes her small son here for a treat and it certainly would seem to be the answer for a ~~CLOSED SINCE LAST EDITION~~ quick, inexpensive, fun meal on any day of the week and she said I can't do better than quote her.
    'Very attractive modern décor, with plants and witty bits and friendly service which one orders by button pressing (with cancellation button if you get carried away). Salads, quiches, grills etc. all good and cheap and this fabulous do-it-yourself dessert trolley (13f for as much as you can stagger away with, and some people grab an apple in the other hand)'.

Le Chantegrill
(31) 85.23.52.

This one I did know about. They offer an excellent buffet for 66f. You help yourself from two lavish spreads, one of hors d'oeuvres ~~CLOSED SINCE LAST EDITION~~ and the other the amazing desserts again.
    'A wee bit posher and slightly more expensive. Sometimes you have to queue at peak times (so go before 12) and they suggest you go upstairs if you're in a hurry as there's usually room there. All great fun.'

Le Dauphin
(HR)M.
29 r. Gémare
(31) 86.22.26.
Rest. Closed
16/7–8/8; Sat.
AE, DC, E.

Much more attractive viewed from the rear courtyard than it would first appear; once an old priory, in fact, but heavily restored. Near the castle, and recommended primarily for its excellent food (the rooms are perfectly adequate and well-maintained but small and rather expensive at 215f). No criticisms of the restaurant, however, and sometimes it's very pleasant to know bed and table are not far apart.
    On the 95f menu. M. Chabredier offers Norman cooking with many personal refinements. His specialities range from honest peasant food like delicious tripe (and here in Caen is the place to try it if you dare) to recherché hot oysters, and a memorable charlotte aux pommes, served with a coulis of red fruits.

Relais des Gourmets
(HR)L.
15 r. Geole.
AE, DC, E.

I wondered whether to include the Relais this time, since it is well documented in just about every other guidebook and correspondingly expensive, but I have to admit that the restaurant (with Michelin star) is not only most attractive, airy and light, but serves excellent food, of the 'serious' variety, provided you don't mind the bill. The rooms are smaller than is warranted by the price – 182-250f – but well furnished and elegant. A bit pompous, maybe.

Quatrans
(H)S.
17 r. Gemare.
(31) 86.25.57.

I have tried hard to find an interesting and good cheap hotel in Caen, but have not yet succeeded. Quatrans is modern, clean, central and not too expensive at around 120f a double. No restaurant, but in this city that is no problem.

Hotel Malherbe
(H)M.
pl. Foch.
(31) 84.06.01.
AE, DC, E, V.

'Slightly faded elegance at 256f. Good central position, yet quiet. Very polite management.' – Ken Bell.

If you really are allergic to any city and a quiet cheap overnight stop just a few km out of Caen seems a good idea, try:

Hôtel de l'Esperance
(HR)S.
Herouville-Bourg.
(31) 93.20.33.
Closed Mon.

The best way to find this modest little hotel on the banks of the Caen Canal is to take the Ouistreham road out of Caen, turn right towards Colombelles and right again before the Pont de la Saviem on the r. Basse. The position of the l'Esperance on the water's edge sounds more attractive than proves to be the case, since the view is of wharves and bunkers rather than willows and banks, but it is always agreeable to be near boats, and here huge ships can and do edge their way past the very hotel terrace. I know, because I was on board Townsend's *Viking Valiant* when she sailed up to Caen for an Open Day in May 1983.

The welcome from Mme Paire is warm and the hotel is obviously efficiently run. The rooms are simple, clean and cheap at 70f and 75f, and the food is well-thought of locally, with a menu at 43f. Specialities are choucroute, couscous and fish.

Map 4F   **CAMPIGNY** (Eure) 54 km from Le Havre

Take the D 29 out of Pont Audemer and after 6 km arrive at a square of pollarded willows and an onion-domed church, where the signposts to Le Petit Coq lead through what seem like endless back gardens.

Le Petit Coq au Champs
(HR)L.
(32) 41.04.19.
Closed Thur.
o.o.s.; rest.
closed mid-nov.–mid-Dec.

For the last two editions, Le Petit Coq has had an arrow, awarded for its exceptional charm and excellent food. These remain, as does the welcome and expertise of the Pommiers; the thatched roofs are just as pretty, the gardens just as colourfully lupinned and hollyhocked, the calm as serene, the efficiency irreproachable. So why no arrow this time? Because, I feel, enough is enough. This book is about value for money in any category, and at 500–720f a night I can no longer accept that this is to be found here. That price should come with at least one

Michelin rosette and with more space and luxury than Le Petit Coq can supply. Nor do I approve of the compulsion to eat dinner in (the Pommiers have cleverly got round the law which gives guests the freedom to eat wherever they wish by bracketting the price of dinner and breakfast with the room price) which means well over 1,000f.

So . . . if money is no object and comfortable luxury is, do still patronise this 'simple' Relais et Châteaux member, but then perhaps you should be reading another guidebook!

Map 5B   **CANISY** (Manche) 86 km from Cherbourg

On the D38 8 km south-west of St-Lô.

Au Cheval Blanc
(HR)S.
(33) 56.61.31.
Closed Sun. p.m.

Several readers have praised this modest little Logis.

'We arrived late but there was no problem about getting a meal, even though they normally finished serving at 8.30 – convenient for the 6.30 docking. Room was 60f and a very adequate meal for 30f.' – Wilfred Bartlett.

'The room was, as last year, simple but clean and cheap, but it struck us the food was more varied and better presented. Madame Hardel is lively and eager to help.' – Rex Hamer.

Rooms are 49–70f and the menu is 36f, so this would make an extremely cheap stop.

Map 3B   **CARENTAN** (Manche) 50 km from Cherbourg

The dairy farming centre of the region, with an important Monday market.

Hôtel du Commerce et de la Gare
(H)S(R)M.
28 r. Dr-Caillard.
(33) 42.02.00.
Closed
22/12–51/1; Fri.
G. AE, DC, E.

An old-fashioned inexpensive hotel, with a local reputation for copious and original meals. M. Lamouroux puts up a good show against the Michelin-starred Normande just opposite with specialities like coquilles St-Jacques aux trois mignonnettes. Menus start at 49f but on the 90f version you could fill up for the day. Excellent value and almost arrow-worthy.

Twice we've had a look at l'Auberge Normande, only to find that we didn't fancy the menus or that it was too expensive, and twice we've finished up at the Commerce, and we certainly didn't come off second best. Certainly a lot of French people agree, because the dining-rooms were full.

'It would seem that it is a fisherman's hotel – everywhere upstairs are exhortations not to take wet boots upstairs please!' – Commander A. J. W. Wilson, R.N.

Rooms (as yet uninspected) are 85f.

► **L'Auberge Normande**
(R)M.
17 bvd de Verdun
(33) 42.02.99
Closed
1/10–10/10;
22/12–22/1;
Sun. p.m.; Mon.

I can't resist a pat on the back here. I spotted the Auberge as a winner several years back and it has been arrowed in *F.E.1* and *2*, though ignored by both Gault-Millau and Michelin. Now belatedly both august bodies have woken up to a late appreciation of M. Bonnefoy's talents as a chef of unusual ability, and in 1984 awarded him the rare (for the Cotentin) toque and rosette. That's the good news. What could be the bad is the odd report that gastronomic recognition seems to have made the welcome – never enthusiastic – even cooler, so go for the food, not the ambience. So far the prices are still very reasonable for such quality, but I have no doubt that this cannot last. The 80f menu currently is worth a considerable détour (others at 60f and a whopper at 105f).

The inn is old and creeper-covered, on the N 13 skirting the town. Inside is beamed and well-tended, very Norman indeed. There are bedrooms but reports on these are dismal.

Specialities include wonderful scallops wrapped in cabbage leaves (all the fish is excellent), a very unusual omelette terroir stuffed with camembert, cream and mushrooms, and a 'gâteau' of lobster with saffron sauce. Leave room for unusually good desserts.

Map 6A **CAROLLES** (Manche) 115 km from Cherbourg

A little old-fashioned family holiday resort, 10 km south of Granville.

Le Relais de la Diligence
(HR)S.
(33) 61.86.42
Closed
1/3–10/3; Oct.;
Sun. p.m.; Mon.
o.o.s.

Well, who would have thought it? The très-snob Gault-Millau have not only recognised the existence of this humble little family hotel but actually given the owner, Claude Duval, a toque for his outstanding cooking. That restores my faith considerably, because they've picked a winner. The Relais is my idea of what a quintessentially French holiday hotel should be; it is faded, somewhat shabby, without being self-consciously antique, very cheap, ~~with the kind of food found everywhere in Fran~~ ~~the reign of the fre~~ and microwave, but ~~cooked by a~~

It st~~ on the main road~~ particularly restful place and Ca~~rolles is not the~~ ~~resort~~. In fact it has much in common with Jullou~~p~~

NEW MANAGEMENT NOT RECOMMENDED

The r~~are~~ large, shabby, clean, cheap at 45–90f. The menus are a bargain, at 45f and 90f. I ate from the cheaper one in the busy dining-room, full of chattering French, and as I had suspected from one look at the range of the menu, here is something exceptional. You don't get a feuilleté d'asperges, with buttery flaky pastry, generous asparagus, limpid sauce au beurre, on many 45f menus. And especially not followed by a superb thick pink slice of gigôt, surrounded by garlic bulbs and served with a perfect gratin dauphinois. And a range of desserts that would not have disgraced a price tag of five times that amount. Don't miss this one.

Map 3A **CARTERET** (Manche) 37 km from Cherbourg

If the wilder coast further north hints of Cornwall, this stretch is pure

Carteret

South Devon, green, rolling, impressive without harshness.

From the lighthouse above the little town there are particularly magnificent walks and the extent of the sandy beaches below can be best appreciated. Don't fail to make this short excursion, preferably with a picnic.

The kids could hardly ask for more than all the activity on the river estuary, fishing boats landing their catch on the quay, the fine clean sand of the bay and rocks to scramble over in search of rock-pool treasures. Throw in an outing to Jersey twenty minutes away on one of the little packets that tie up in the harbour, and you're giving them a good deal. If this is France, they'll like it.

Unfortunately there is a hotel problem here. The Angleterre has now abandoned its restaurant and reports on the Plage et du Cap are deplorable. This leaves the Marine, admirable but alone. It has long been an English favourite and families book up from one year to the next, so it is not always easy to find a room here.

Hôtel Marine
(HR)L .
(33) 53.83.31.
Closed
30/11—5/3. Rest
Closed Sun.
p.m.; Mon. o.o.s.

A large, shapeless hotel dominating the centre of the little town. The rooms are good, some with balconies especially so, and I can vouch for room no. 21 on the third floor as being undeniably pretty. The waterside terrace is a most agreeable place to sit and watch the sun go down. Management and service are invariably smoothly efficient, if impersonal, and a preponderance of English clients means no language problems here.

But the main reason for choosing the Marine is still the consistently high standard of its food. The tables in the dining-room overlooking the water are elegantly laid and although one reader criticised the service as being 'disinterested' (I think he could be right at times), it's a marvel to me that standards are still so high after so many years as a favourite family hotel. The cheapest menu at 65f is a treat. I ate coquille de poisson aux deux mayonnaises, a rich and juicy côte de porc dijonnais, a perfect cheeseboard and several fresh peaches. Their plâteaux de fruits de mer take some beating and if your stomach can countenance ordering a peach melba after that you'll get it swathed in yellow Norman cream. Rooms are from 85f to 210f.

Arrowed for comfort, site, cooking.

Hermitage – Maison Duhamel I had a terrible tourist-trap meal at this newish, pine-clad restaurant on the port, but that was when it first opened and maybe they've got their act together by now. There are some indications that things have improved, but as I can't face another meal like that until I am more confident, reports here would be welcome.

For an alternative hotel, see Barneville, p.43.

Map 3F

CAUDEBEC-EN-CAUX (Seine-Maritime) 51 km from Le Havre

Only three medieval houses and the Church of Our Lady survived the fire that destroyed the old town in 1940. The hint they pass on of the character that has gone is a sad one, since now, in its concrete reincarnation, the town has little to recommend it apart from its happy situation on the banks of the Seine and of course the very fine 15th-century Flamboyant Gothic church, which Henry IV described as 'the most beautiful chapel in the kingdom'.

That is not to say that Caudebec is not a good stopping place, because it makes an excellent base to explore the Caux area and especially the bosky banks of the Seine. It also has a good market in the *Place* on Saturdays.

La Marine
(HR)L.
quai Guilbad
(35) 96.20.11.

I think it's time I reassessed La Marine. It's taken a few years to get over the disappearance of the old hotel, unpretentious, personally supervised by M. Lalonde, good value for its superb position overlooking the river, and to accept that the new version is something altogether else.

Nowadays the Marine has to be considered as a luxury hotel. By French standards it is expensive, at 200f a double, but not more than many other establishments less comfortable and without that situation. (*And* now you get much needed sound-proofing for your money.) All very glossy, with dark brown suede bar and lights so dim you can only just see your drinks bill. I thought the 3-course 130f dinner menu good value for interesting content and elegant presentation. Expect mostly British fellow-guests.

Hôtel
Normandie
(HR)S.
(35) 96.25.11.

An old favourite, good value, with the same marvellous view over the river as its more upmarket neighbour. Midweek menu 38f, rooms 60–120f.

'Friendly hotel, as you say in your guide, with very good food. We thoroughly enjoyed our stay and found it a good centre. Not at all noisy, as we had feared from your description of the hotel next door. A pity it's quite so full of other English!' – Josephine M. Oakley.

However, I understand there is a change of management here, so further reports particularly welcome.

Manoir de Rétival
(H)L.
2 r. St-Clair.
(35) 96.11.22.
Closed
2/11–30/3. AE,
DC.

This is the place to stay if you want more peace and seclusion than the Marine or Normandie can offer. The Manoir is a creeper-covered mansion in a lovely garden high above the river, but it has no restaurant and no lounge. 10 rooms, 150f–320f.

Map 7B | **CÉAUX** (Manche) 143 km from Cherbourg

Le P'tit Quinquin
(HR)S.
(33) 58.13.46.
Closed
30/9–1/4; Tue.
o.o.s.

On the main D 75 to Mont St-Michel, this little modern Logis could be noisy if you tried to sleep in a front bedroom in peak periods, but the food is excellent and merits its Michelin red 'R' for value.

'Very good Sunday lunch with lots of big family parties of French who knew when they were on to a good thing.' Rooms 85–130f. and menus from 44f. Friendly management ensure faithful regulars.

Map 3F | **LA CERLANGUE** (Seine-Maritime) 29 km from Le Havre

La Forge
(R)S.
(35) 20.50.54.
Closed Sun
p.m.; Mon.

On the D 39 just a few kilometres north of the Tancarville bridge. A useful and comfortable stop for a pleasant and inexpensive meal. The 45f menu had some interesting items like terrine de chevreuil.

Map 5H | **CHAMBRAY** (Eure) 140 km from Le Havre

If you are following the river Eure south from Louviers, the most attractive village to make for along its course is Acquigny, with its château and picturesque old houses, but as its only good restaurant, l'Hostellerie, is on a noisy corner of the nationale and ruled over by a dragon of a *patronne*, it is wise to drive on to the village of Chambray for a really good meal at:

Le Vol-au-Vent
(R)L.
(32) 36.70.05.
Closed
24/10–31/10;
Sun. p.m.; Mon.;
Tue. lunch. DC,
E, V.

But you have to be in the mood and income bracket. This is serious eating. It's all a bit surprising to find a sophisticated restaurant in such a rustic setting, but that's France for you. Nothing rustic about the interior of the Vol-au-Vent, which goes in for tapestried chairs, porcelain, crystal and head waiters in black jackets. Not the place for a light lunch – specialities are substantial in quantity and price. Feuilleté de ris de veau aux morilles is one delicious extravagance, but if you go in summer, do leave room for pastry at dessert stage – the strawberry millefeuille is not to be ignored. Allow 150–200f.

A walk down to the little bridge over the river here is a pleasant thing to do, either appetite-whetting or excess-settling.

A good autoroute stop-off, between the Vernon and Gaillon exits.

Map 6A

CHAMPEAUX St-Jean-le-Thomas (Manche) 120 km from Cherbourg

Between Carolles and St-Jean-le-Thomas, on what is claimed to be 'le plus beau kilomètre de France'. I wouldn't know about that, but the coast road is certainly spectacular, with its unique view of Mont St-Michel rising out of the watery mists; even in high season it never seems to get over-run with tourists – probably because there's a much faster inland road from Granville to Avranches. On the cliff-edge is:

Au Marquis de Tombelaine (HR)S. *(33) 61.85.94.*

 food

 hotel

A nice old building with low beamed ceilings, flagstones, flowers, where the *patron-chef*, M. Giard, cooks interesting dishes like terrines of avocados or of oysters, or sole soufflées or brill in red wine sauce, or calves' sweetbreads 'aux petits légumes'. All excellent value, as are his menus, which start at 31.50f. He also has some rooms available which I have not seen, at 62f a double, so what with very reasonably priced wines (try his St Nicolas de Bourgeuil at 38f) a stop here would not be financially painful. Friendly, pretty, cheap – what more can one ask?

Map 3B

CHEF-DU-PONT (Manche) 36 km from Cherbourg

4 km SW of Ste-Mère-Église on the D 67.

Hôtel Normandie (HR)S. *pl. Gare (33) 41.32.06.* Closed 15/12–15/1; Sun.

A small hotel/restaurant opposite the railway crossing. It does have nine rooms at around 100f, but these are uninspected. It is the food that draws customers from miles around; no wonder when a four-course meal costs 31f.

The premises may look small but the choice on the menu is enormous and would satisfy all but the most fastidious. But you must be prepared to devote at least $2\frac{1}{2}$ hours for a five course meal. Dishes are obviously cooked to order and helpings are more than generous. And the fish . . .! The chef has a wonderful way with sauces. Madame Bisson was most attentive and most helpful with choice of wines from the comprehensive wine list.' – Roy Dunn.

Map 2A

CHERBOURG (Manche)

Most changes here have been for the better, though it used to be very agreeable to sail right into the heart of the town; nowadays the yacht population has grown too numerous for that and they are herded into their own *port de plaisance*, but the working fishing fleet is still very much in evidence and vistas down many streets end in views of brightly painted hulls, masts and seagulls. You can stroll along the quays and watch them unloading on to the harbourside, where the fish is sold direct to sharp-eyed housewives.

Pedestrianisation of several central streets has been a great success. Turn up by the Tourist Bureau into the main square, the Place General

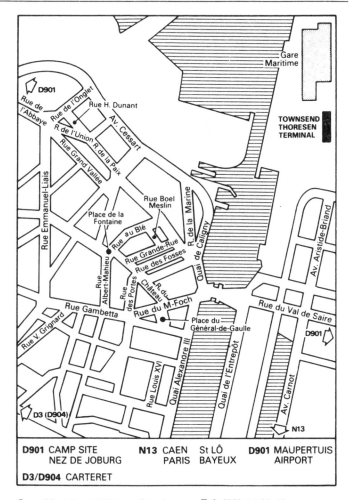

| **D901** CAMP SITE NEZ DE JOBURG | **N13** CAEN PARIS | St LÔ BAYEUX | **D901** MAUPERTUIS AIRPORT |

D3/D904 CARTERET

Gare Maritime 50101 — Cherbourg Tel: (33) 44 20 13

de Gaulle, with its splashing fountain and voluptuous theatre, and on the right, by the re-vamped *Printemps*, is a network of precincts where strolling, shopping, sitting, is a pleasure. Several pavement cafés here for refreshment.

Old buildings round the fish market in the *Rue au Blé* have had a facelift, scraped and re-shaped with local stone, and new boutiques and restaurants have moved in. Easily missed at No. 41 is **Les Baladins**, a 'Pub–Grill' in a pleasant peaceful courtyard, useful for killing an hour with an ice, drink or snack.

Old family names remain over most of the shops in the oddly-named rue Grande Rue, which boasts the best food shops. Three charcuteries: **Le Poittevin** for delicious prize-winning smoked country ham, prepared salads for picnics; **Collette** next door has sacks of nuts and pulses outside and good cheeses inside; **À la Rénommé** opposite specialises in pâtés, terrines and prepared dishes. **L'Huilley** is an elegant salon de thé with gorgeous pastries. **Cafféa** is one of a chain of shops where you can always rely on top quality coffee (and that's a good buy currently), and **Ryst** is a good old-fashioned bookshop for maps and guides. Opposite the fishmarket is **Lesdos**, where fresh oysters from St-Vaast cost from £1 a dozen, and in the r. au Fourdray you can see fresh croissants being baked at the **Croissant Doré**. For clothes in this area, there is the colourful **Benetton** and an upmarket boutique with top labels, **Yolande.**

Laulier, on the Place, is the charcutier I use most often, since it is nearest the harbour. I stock up on fresh olives from the barrels outside (covered in oil, they keep for weeks back home), but it also has a good range of meats, salads and prepared dishes and there is always a queue, so don't, like me, leave it till the last minute. Other good charcuteries are **La Boutique du Charcuterie** in the r. de l'Union and **Boschet**, pl. de la Fontaine, which has a better range of wine than most.

I found a new wine supplier recently, which I can recommend, **Les Caves du Roy** in the r. Tour Carée; they have a distinguished selection and you can taste before you buy. Wander further up the r. Gambetta and you come to the pl. Henry Gréville and there is a splendid emporium, **J. J. Fillatre**, selling all manner of breads and pizza baked in their wood-fired oven right there in the shop. Good for wines, groceries and pâtisseries too. Fruit, veg and flowers are more fun to buy in the splendid market which overflows the Place on Tuesdays and Saturdays (another in the pl. Divette on Thursdays); on other days I use **Bébert**, on the Place and usually find produce cheaper and fresher than I can buy back home, particularly when there's a seasonal glut, say of those marvellous ugly fat tomatoes. At the back of the shop they sell the luxurious *Fauchon* delicacies which make splendid presents.

Good presents too from **Le Miroir**, which has two branches well stocked with perfumes and cosmetics, gift-wrapped on request. The one on the r. Mal. Foch doesn't seem to mind more sniffing than buying.

Continent Hypermarket, open Mon.–Sat. until 10 p.m., with better-than-average restaurants, the **Cafeteria Presto** and **La Flambée** on the first floor, which are open every day, including Sundays. Bang in the centre of the town, with easy parking, the Continent has the usual amazing selection of cheeses, wine, kitchen equipment, charcuterie, garden accessories and fish still alive and kicking (though they won't clean it for you). Good too for glasses and electricals. Look out for special offers.

Parking: Don't get involved with the town centre if you can help it; either leave the car in the Continent park or along the quay on the same side and walk across the bridge. If you need to penetrate far into the town, it's best to drive round the harbour to the area round the Hôtel de Ville, where there's usually space to manoeuvre.

Bureau de Change: useful if banks are closed, open Mon.–Sat. 9–7, and Sun 10–12.30, on 55 r. François Lavieille.

Petrol: Continent is easiest and usually cheapest.

HOTELS

Cherbourg has no three-star hotel, but the **Mercure** (née Sofitel) caters for the needs of the traveller who wants guaranteed standards. It sticks out at the end of the Gare Maritime, meaning that all its rooms have seaviews. It is very comfortable and efficient and has an imposing restaurant. A room costs 261 to 470f.

Best news this year on the hotel front is the re-vamping of:

Hôtel du Louvre
(H)M
r. de la Paix
(33) 53.02.28.

M. and Madame Segonds are the youthful and enthusiastic proprietors. Complaints about the old Louvre centred on the traffic noise; now they have installed a triple glazing system, which has far less to contend with than previously, since the road outside has been semi-pedestrianised. So now we have, in the heart of Cherbourg, near the yacht harbour, a well-run, comfortable, quiet and not too expensive hotel.

The rooms, some with twin beds, are all different but well-furnished and spacious, and the bathrooms gleam with new tiles; from 87.50 to 174.70f. Pleasant downstairs reception area and breakfast room, lift and garage.

La Renaissance
(H)M
(33) 53.23.06.

Praised particularly for its friendly *patronne*, Madame Esterlingot, who takes a personal interest in her clients' comfort, keeps a file of their thank-you letters and welcomes regulars like long-lost friends. Her little hotel overlooking the harbour is bright as a new pin, hectically-patterned wallpapers, carpets, curtains, bedspreads, and fluffy toys sitting on the beds (you don't get that at a Hilton). No baths, but all rooms have showers and WCs and a view of the harbour. Doubles run from 112 to 168f.

Beauséjour
(H)M
25 r. Grande
Valee
(33) 53.10.30.

When I looked round it last, all the rooms were being redecorated, so it should be a good bet now. It is in a very quiet section of Cherbourg, yet not too far from the harbour. 53 to 220f.

It seems I did my readers an injustice in fearing they would not appreciate the character of a very unconventional hotel, the **Divette**. Or perhaps my qualified praise was clearly understood and only those likely to enjoy it actually went and reported back to me, favourably to a man.

Hôtel Divette
(H)S
15 r. Louis XVI
(33) 43.21.04

I warned that no one whose priority is an immaculate conventional hotel should go there. Do go if you like to meet charming, hard-working young proprietors and are prepared to accept that they cannot offer four-star standards at one-star prices.

M. and Mme Vicoulet-Besson go out of their way to make *French Entrée* readers feel welcome. guarantee which of their widely differing rooms you will get, but they are all spacious, and furnished with real furniture, not plastic. Some have three double beds crowded in, to make a very cheap family base; they all have cabinets de toilette, with a shower on each landing. The hotel is in a quiet square, the Place Divette, conveniently central. Here is one typical assessment:
'What a delightful, friendly, quintessentially French establishment!

The Grand Hotel has proved a disappointment. Last time I wrote about it, it looked promising, with a new young couple systematically renovating the old hotel and upgrading it from one-star status. I had thought that two years later it would prove a winner, but I find that very little has changed and the rooms, though spacious, are still badly in need of a lick of paint. Readers have withheld judgment, so there is still a question mark over this one.

RESTAURANTS

Le Plouc
(R)M
59 r. au Blé
(33) 53.67.64.
Closed
15/9–30/9;
Sun; Sat. lunch.
E.

Gone from strength to strength since I first spotted it in its old premises and it could well be Michelin's only entry in the town when it has proved its worth for the statutory period. Nowadays you'll find it much more upmarket in the smartened-up 'quartier central', an easy stroll from the ferry. It's rustic, cool, stone-walled, log-fired. M. Pain still cooks, but with several assistants now. Mme Pain still greets, less shyly, more smoothly, and takes orders. Local businessmen use it for lunch and it is prudent to book or sit down by midday. Maddeningly, it has changed its closing day, and is now useless all day Sunday and for Saturday lunch, just when we weekenders need it most.

The menus at 55f and 90f don't seem to have changed much – still a range of (recommended) house terrines and rillettes, an interesting salade gourmande, featuring pears in vinaigrette and some mercifully disguised *abat*, along with house versions of Norman specialities, like escalope de veau. Good cheeseboard and pâtisserie. Everything freshly cooked to order, so don't go in a hurry.

Le Doyen
R(S)
Passage Digard

'*Super little restaurant – not smart but very French. Excellent simple meal at 35f.*' *– Judy Wright.*

It certainly looks good value – moules, carbonnade, and pud for 35f or a five courser for 50f, service not included. A potential arrow after a personal sampling which I look forward to very much.

'*Must be the best deal in town; patron-chef, cooking from a minuscule kitchen off the bar. Dining-room is tiny with gigantic fireplace, which must be wonderful in winter. To prove the lie to Cherbourg restaurants closing early, we sat down at 9.30 p.m. and another group came in even later. We ate small clams, stuffed, sole meunière with plenty of vegs and frites, washed down by an excellent 'sur lie' Muscadet. Finished with cheese, a glass of wine on the house, and staggered out at midnight, to fond farewells.*' *– Lance Berelowitz.*

Cherbourg has been notoriously badly off for restaurants. There can't be many towns of its size and possibilities without a single entry in Michelin, but now there's accumulating a little huddle of newish restaurants in the r. de l'Abbaye, offering a choice of prices and characters. Newest of all is:

La Pêcherie
(R)M
27 r. de
l'Abbaye

Which is a smartish fish restaurant, à la carte only, e.g. moules plus raie à la crème would cost 70f. Locals praise.

Almost next door is:

Le Grandgousier
(R)M
21 r. de l'Abbaye
(33) 53.19.43.

Said to be more like the Plouc in style, i.e. a reliable bistro with imaginative specialities. Inside is vaguely art-deco—very pink, with black lacquer furniture. Menus are 57, 82 and 100f.

La Bigottière
(R)S
27 r. de l'Abbaye
(33) 53.05.23.
Closed Sun. p.m.; Mon.

Very popular with locals, especially at lunch-time. Specialises in grills over open log fires. Good value menus, with large help~~~~~~ 64f. On the cheaper one I ate moules ma~~~~~~~ an~~~~~~~h of the day, which was an excellent rai~~~~~~~~~~~~~~~ed by a particularly good cheeseboard~~~~~~~~~~~~~~~on had terrine forestière, a gigantic pork ~~~~~~~~~~~~th herbs and served with perfect frites and beans, ~~~~ped up by a Calvados sorbet.

CLOSED SINCE LAST EDITION

L'Ancre Dorée
(R)M
3 r. Bonhomme
(33) 93.98.38.

Don't do as I did and confuse a recommendation for this one with the l'Ancre d'Or on the front. Find it by turning left off the r. de l'Abbaye. Pretty, cosy; interesting menus at 75 and 109f. Potential arrow here, after a few more reports.

Across the road is:

Les Routiers
(R)S
10 r. de l'Onglet
(33) 53.08.15.

Open on Mondays, which is rare in Cherbourg. Recommended locally and by several readers for its no-frills, quick and cheerful good value. Menus from 39f. For 56f you get five courses.

L'Assommoir
(R)M
r. Victor Hugo
(33) 20.10.78.
Closed Tue.

In a quiet square on the site of the old Plouc, in a part of Cherbourg rarely discovered by tourists but still not more than ~~CLOSED SINCE LAST EDITION~~ from the port (up the r. Gambetta ~~restaurant~~ le~~ft~~ pretty little restaurant run by the s~~ister~~ of M. Brisset of the Château de Br~~icquebe~~(3~~3)~~. I haven't tried it yet but am told the food is simple b~~ut good.~~ Menu at 60f.

Le Vauban
(R)M
quai de Caligny
(33) 53.13.29.
Closed Feb.; Fri.

Overlooking the harbour, with a popular downstairs brasserie, where the 47f menu continues to be excellent value. For starters you help yourself from the circular table loaded with cold meats, terrines, fish, crudités (but get there early – it tends to look a bit d~~epleted~~ ~~after~~ p.m.); then comes a choice between two ~~main courses~~, one of them fish. I had a meltingly fresh little plai~~ce~~ ~~on the~~ bone, running with Normandy butter. Sweets are ~~nothing~~ special. A good idea if you're in a hurry, and it stays open latish. The alternative restaurant bit is much more grand. Allow 170f for the carte.

Map 5D

CLÉCY (Calvados) 108 km from Le Havre; 120 km from Cherbourg

At Vey, 1 km east on the D 133A, an imposing old bridge crosses the wide, fast-flowing river, and a scattering of restaurants and cafés make the most of the setting. Walk past them to the viaduct, with plenty to admire from the river bank.

Their balconies overhang the water and here one can sit and sip or sup, or, more energetically, hire a pedalo or canoe to explore the river up to the Viaduc de Landes or down beyond the mellow old bridge beyond the mill.

▶ **Le Moulin du Vey**
(H)M(R)L
(31) 69.71.08.
Closed Fri.
o.o.s.; by
reservation only
in Dec., Jan. and
Feb. AE, DC, V.

The hotel with the most perfect setting I know. The river cascades through its grounds and all is pure Monet – waterlilies, willows, dappled sunshine on shallow ripples. I wished I had parasol, muslin dress and picture hat.

Contrive a visit, even if only for a drink in the large flowery garden, where lots of tables, chairs and terraces take full advantage of the idyllic scene.

The hotel is a charming old watermill, and the bedrooms quite delightful. A double overlooking the river costs 145 to 240f, money well spent for such charm and tranquillity.

Meals are served in the pavilion annexe. When I was there the cheaper menu, at 90f, was uninspiring compared with the well-cooked 150f version, but my spies tell me that matters have now improved somewhat.

Moulin du Vey

Le Chalet.
Auberge de
Cantépie
(R)M *(31) 44.62.00.*

Over the river from Le Moulin du Vey.
    'The 33f menu was a bargain, the dining-room attractive, log fire,
long tables, staff cordial and attentive.' – Rupert Prior.

The Moulin Du Vey has an 'annexe', about 3 km away:

Relais de
Surosne
(HR)M.
(31) 69.71.05.
Closed
15/11–15/3;
Mon. o.o.s.

Gothicised, creeper-covered, set in extensive peaceful grounds. Demi-
pension only at 139 to 203f, or meals from 70f.

Map 5G   **CONCHES-EN-OUCHE** (Eure) 120 km from Le Havre

A smashing little town, set on a spur encircled by the little river Rouloir.
It forms the hub of three forests, Conche, Breteuil and Evreux, which
radiate from its crossroads, and is therefore a centre for 'la chasse', an
obsession with the French, who cannot see anything flying, creeping,
running, swimming, without visualising it on the table. Every little town
hereabouts has at least one huntin' shootin' fishin' shop prominently in
the main street and in the autumn the butchers are draped with gamey
loot. The most impressive of these corpses is the marcassin or wild boar,
bristly fierce and still looking very angry at the indignity of being
suspended upside down.

    The good townsfolk of Conche had such respect for their game that
they decided to honour it in the form of a statue. There in the gardens
behind the lovely old church of Ste-Foy (famed for its stained glass
windows) on a plinth commanding the best view of the whole valley,
they erected a (very bad) statue of the boar. I long to know what
Clochemerle-like deliberations, arguments, claims and counter-claims
must have been put forward to result in the glorification of the swine.
Did the town band parade in his honour? Was the mayor inspired to
recite his virtues? Was he a special boar with a story I have yet to hear?

    There is more to Conches than church, boar and gardens. The main
street is wide and pleasant, the market is held on Thursday, there is a
pleasant lake, and overlooking it the attractive black and white Logis:

Hotel Grand
'Mare
(HR)S
av. Croix de Fer
(32) 30.23.30.
Closed Mon.
p.m.; Tue.

I have used this little inn in the past as a staging post between Calais
and the Loire; the site is perfect, guaranteeing a good night's rest,
the building is old, pretty, beamy, rustique, and the bedrooms are simple,
clean and cheap (100f double). ... *NEW MANAGEMENT* ... was
disappointing ... it ... fellow-countrymen, not French and I feel it
is now suffering from over-exposure.

Le Donjon
(HR)S
55 r. Sainte Foy
(32) 30.04.75.
Closed Wed.;
Tue. p.m. o.o.s.

A cheerful timbered little restaurant in the main street, with three charming countrified bedrooms, all good-sized doubles with wash-basins, one overlooking the courtyard/garden where tables are set in summer, all a bargain at 80f.

The dining-room is beamy, low-ceilinged, with a big fire in winter, and full of locals enjoying M. Guille's excellent and enthusiastic cooking. He is a *patron/chef par excellence* – always attentive to his guests' needs, out to please and delighted to chat. His menus restored my faith in good-value French meals.

His 38f version was so good that we looked no further. Four interesting, substantial courses included nice chunky game terrines of pheasant and venison, escalopes Normandes, an excellent local cheeseboard and home-made pâtisserie. The 68f menu was better than many at twice the price, including piperade, langoustines, canard aux cerises.

A weekend spent under M. Guille's hospitable roof might ruin the waistline but not the bank balance; it would certainly give a taste of honest provincial French cooking fast disappearing.

The restaurants in Conche are an interesting example of guidebook dissension. Gault-Millau ignores the Donjon, perhaps as being too unsophisticated; Michelin gives Le Donjon two forks but fails to mention Gault-Millau's choice:

La Toque
Blanche
(R)M.
18 pl. Carnot
(32) 30.61.54.
Closed Mon.

A nice little restaurant in an old house in the main square, run by Mme Bachet. Nowadays her menus include some very un-Norman Nouvelle Cuisine ideas, which is perhaps why G-M. like her, but there are still some more solid traditional dishes, like mouclade and tripes maisons, and a feature is made of the house Calvados. Interesting menus at 70f; would be a good contrast in styles if one were staying more than a day or the more popular Donjon were full.

Map 3F **CONTEVILLE** (Eure) 42 km from Le Havre

To find the village of Conteville, head east from Honfleur on the coast road, D 312; all very rural with glimpses of the Seine along the way. From here to Le Havre is only about 45 minutes, so a last fling before catching the night boat might well be at:

Auberge du
Vieux Logis
(R)L
(32) 57.60.16.
Closed
10/1–25/2;
Wed. p.m.; Thur.
AE, DC, E.

Here in a tiny Norman inn of great antiquity and charm, Yves Louet follows the seasons and the market in preparing the delicious specialities that earned him a Michelin star. The welcome is good, and the setting, among old copper pans and a collection of antique plates, quite delightful. I remember his terrine striped with three fish purées and served with a chive-flecked sauce, with great affection. No menus nowadays and prices continue to creep skywards. Count on 200f.

Map 3F **CORNEVILLE-SUR-RISLE** (Eure) 45 km from Le Havre

At the junction of the N 175 and D 130, 6 km south of Pont Audemer.

Auberge du Vieux Logis

**Les Cloches de
Corneville**
(HR)M
*(32) 57.01.04.
Rest. closed
2/10–18/10;
20/1–15/2;
Wed. AE, E, V.*

There really is a carillon above this little eccentric Gothicky hotel, placed there by the innkeeper at the turn of the century, when the local grandee offered them to the church and then failed to pay up. You can hear the bells ring for a fee.

When I last wrote about it, the clientèle was entirely French, but it has been popular with *F.E.* readers and other guidebooks have cottoned on, so I cannot vouch for such exclusivity now. It would certainly make a useful alternative to the Pont Audemer hotels.

I ate on the covered terrace, all white wrought-iron, and the food was imaginative, well-presented, and copious. No-choice 85f menu. Good cider. The rooms are tiny but perfectly adequate at 110 to 220f.

Map 1R   **COSQUEVILLE** (Manche) 15 km from Cherbourg

The north-east corner of the Contentin peninsula is not very interesting between Cap Levy and Gatteville, unless utter seclusion is of prime consideration. The sandy beaches are deserted for ten months of the year and most of them have a sad and desolate air. Cosqueville is the most attractive of the villages in this area.

Hôtel de la Plage
(HR)S
(33) 54.32.81.
Closed
15/11–15/12;
Wed.

Not on the plage at all but five minutes' walk down the lane to the Plage du Vicq, with fine sand and a dozen fishing boats in a little natural harbour.

First impressions are not glamorous, but don't be put off. The bedrooms, mostly with a splendid view of the sea, are well-furnished, colourful, comfortable and extremely good value: 75f for a really large twin-bedded room! A bar at the entrance and basic but fresh food served on the menus, starting at 46f.

'Our tastes are for simple places and so we tried this unpretentious establishment for Sunday lunch. Our 55f meal was excellent and very good value. We so liked the atmosphere that we had to see if there was a room available for our last night in France.' – Mike Butler.

'The food is very basic, but the grilled prawns were probably the best I have ever had.' – A. G. Crisp.

When all other hotels around Cherbourg are full, La Plage usually has rooms available, except in French school holidays when Mme Cornicard's regular families arrive. This would make an extremely cheap base, when nothing but utter peace and simple food were required.

Map 7B   **COURTILS** (Manche) 145 km from Cherbourg

On the D 75 from Pontaubault to Mont St-Michel.

Hotel de la Roche Torin
(HR)M
(33) 58.41.61.
Closed
1/10–1/5; Mon.
o.o.s.

The hotel is well signposted, down a lane off the main road. It is a Gothic-style country house, offering exactly what its brochure claims: *calme, confort, espace.* In the height of the season, when hotels are full and the Mont St-Michel tourists come fast and furious, those are highly desirable virtues. New youthful proprietors have furnished it most attractively and it is a hotel with considerable character.

The restaurant is for grills only—prime meat cooked over a wood fire and served in the raftered dining-room with log fire. There is a pleasant terrace in the garden and a bar.

Perhaps at 220f for a double room with bath, 120f for one with *cabinet de toilette* or 300f for a suite for four, the rooms are a little over-priced, and the meal is likely to add up to 100f more, but I think it would probably be money well spent in this area for a guaranteed night's rest, pleasant company and an agreeable meal. I liked it very much. So far not in other guidebooks, so booking should not be too difficult.

Map 5A   **COUTAINVILLE** (Manche) 75 km from Cherbourg

The Hotel Hardy here used to be a favourite for holidays for English and French families; nowadays its popularity steadily declines, as do its standards. The season is short, admittedly, and easy profits have to be taken where they can be found, but not from my readers, I trust.

However, Coutainville is still one of the most appealing resorts along this stretch of coast and the one I make for on a hot day if I happen to be staying inland and find myself longing for a swim. Just a few unsophisticated shops there, selling mostly seasonal needs for the M. et Mme Hulots who patronise the place, and the bar at the Hardy for refreshment. The food in the atractive restaurant there is not bad, if over-priced, and the fish undoubtedly fresh.

Map 5B   **COUTANCES** (Manche) 70 km from Cherbourg

Miraculously having survived the battering of the 1944 bombardment, the largest cathedral in the Contentin, Notre Dame de Coutances, still dominates the city, as it has done for over seven centuries. The towers of its façade have stood there, in the market-place on the hill, for even longer – they were salvaged from the Romanesque original when it was burned in 1218. In complete contrast, just a step down the r. Geoffroy de Montbray, is the Renaissance St-Pierre, with its striking lantern tower.

The public gardens here are particularly pleasant, with Son et Lumière in summer on Thursdays, Saturdays and Sundays.

One reader, Commander Wilson, suggests that I should recommend some salons de thé. He's quite right – the opportunity to sit on those elegant spindly chairs, choose a pastry, rest the feet and observe the locals should not be neglected, especially as such places are becoming rarer at home. He commends two in Coutances, one at 5 r. de Geoffroy de Montbray and the other at 7 r. St-Nicholas, both good for *le five o'clock* restorative.

For hotels and restaurants, it is a disappointing town; the best I can suggest is:

Le Relais du Viaduc
(HR)S
25 av. du Verdun
(33) 45.02.68
Closed 10/9–10/10.

Hard to miss this very superior Relais Routier on the junction of the D 971 and D 7. A real bargain – rooms 60 to 110f and menus, which include lobster and duck in the more expensive range, 30 to 120f, but you might need earplugs.

'One of the very best Relais Routiers in France, in spite of its rather unattractive site. A wide range of menus all good value, spotless and good fast service. If only our transport cafés and motorway restaurants were the same.' – Air Commodore R. Sorel-Cameron.
Or see Gratôt, p.106.

Map 3D   **CRÉPON** (Calvados) 105 km from Cherbourg

A hamlet in the middle of farming country, 7 km SE of Arromanches on the D 65.

Ferme de la Rançonnière
(H)S
(31) 22.21.73.

A friend of mine, Judy Wright, came upon the farm by chance; here is what she wrote: *'This place is a treat; beautiful old farm house with a huge courtyard; all lovingly restored – antique furniture, good ambiance. It has been in the same family for years and the present young patronne was born there.'*

She's right, it is a lovely place and would make a peaceful, inexpensive base for a Norman holiday. Ideal for young children, with plenty of farm animals, chickens and cats around. Fresh produce from the farm would come in useful if you took over one of the three gîtes

St. Pierre

85

attached to the farm, which cost 900f a week and sleep four. Inside the farm house itself are another 12 rooms, some with showers, for 60–80f a night. They are all very different, but all spacious, well furnished with a mixture of antiques and practicalities.

Breakfast is extra, served in the lovely old stone dining-room on a long polished table.

Because it's a working farm, the accommodation is open year round, which is unusual in these parts. I think it would be an excellent choice for an Easter break, especially as the rooms are well heated.

Map 3E   **DEAUVILLE** (Calvados) 74 km from Le Havre

Deauville has two faces. For a few brief summer weeks it glitters like a courtesan, for the rest of the year it subsides, passée and querulous, into a fantasy, not enticing enough to please the Top People, not cheap enough for the hoi-polloi. That's not to say I don't like it, because I do. I admire its eccentricity, without wishing to become too involved in anything quite so artificial, and I always enjoy an excursion into its elegant never-never-land knowing that the real world of Trouville is (incredibly) just across the bridge.

In high season a stroll along les Planches, the wooden walkway between the cafés, boutiques, restaurants, and the 'cabines' bizarrely facing inland towards the sun, not the sea, might well reveal a famous face or two. The glitterati, here for the Grand Prix and its attendant fuss, still like to be seen at Ciro's, the ultimate in beach cafés, and the least one can do is to gawp obligingly.

Out of season I find the place depressingly shuttered, unless the weather happens to be fine, when at weekends there are usually to be seen those prosperous, well-wrapped, stout French couples, arm in arm, walking their well-groomed poodles along the well-groomed prom. The most exclusive shops are closed then, owners migrated with their summer flock, but a few chic boutiques sell out of season bargains, and the market still functions on Tuesdays.

Hotels and restaurants aren't easy to recommend in a town with such an unusually limited calendar. Sadly my *F.E.2* choice, the Pavillon de la Poste, has changed hands and is now rather seedy. I didn't find anything else as cheap, but in the av. de la République are two possibilities:

La Fresnaye
(H)L
81 av. de la
République
(31) 88.09.71.

A reader wrote to tell me how comfortable his stay here had been and certainly it is a charming hotel, lavishly furnished in *fin-de-siècle* style. Prices for a double room with bath start at 200f and one particularly pleasant one I saw, spacious and balconied, was 330f.

Hôtel la
Résidence
(H)M
55 av. de la
République
(31) 88.07.50.

A good choice. Comfortable, freshly decorated, stylish. A double room with bath and loo costs 178f; with shower 142f, which in Deauville is not at all bad.

La Joyeuse
(HR)M
172 av. de la
République
(31) 88.24.51.
Closed Jan. and
Feb.; Wed. o.o.s.

A pleasant little restaurant, with a garden, where M. Rochelle, an ex-chef of the Rothschild family, no less, serves traditional Norman dishes. There are seven rooms, but I have not inspected. Menus at 74f.
    'A very pleasant, bright, quiet restaurant. On both our visits it was full of French family groups. Delicious 3-course menu.' – Juliet Keel.

Nothing else special in the restaurant line unless you're a millionaire and then you don't need my help. **Chez Miocque**, a brasserie in the r. Eugene Colas, is usually the liveliest and you can eat just one dish here if you wish, but not cheap. **Désirez–Deauville** in r. Desiré-le-Hoc looks expensive, with its fun 'decor Kitsch', but in fact offers a very reasonable 55f menu. **La Sorbetière** in the same road has a magnificent range of ices, all made from fresh fruit and other wholesome ingredients, in thirty different varieties, and you can eat a snack salad here too.
    The biggest surprise is a Relais Routier bang in the town centre, **Aux Rois Canards** in r. Victor Hugo. Even this is more expensive than any other R.R. on my beat – 55f for the not-too-exciting menu. I tried to be encouraging about this one modest find in *F.E.2*, but there's been absolutely no feed-back from readers, and I can't say I'm surprised. To be honest, I don't think I'd go to Deauville to eat with the lorry-drivers. Trouville is a far better bet for good-value straightforward nosh.

Map 2A

DIÉLETTE (Manche) 20 km from Cherbourg

There are few hotels and restaurants on the NW coast of the peninsula, which is surprising because the beaches are good and the villages attractive. It remains an area of small farmers, who let out rooms in their grey stone homes and sites for tents in their green, unspoiled fields. The coast road around Cap de Flamanville offers spectacular views of beach, rollers and rocks; Diélette is a small, pretty port, set in a beautiful bay, but the only hotel here is:

Hôtel de la
Falaise
(HR)M
(33) 52.43.66.
Closed Fri. o.o.s.

A large modern building overlooking the water, which would make a splendid base for children's holidays. Smartening up was in process when I was there in June and it was not possible to see the rooms in process of decoration, but they cost 170 to 200f. More important, though, is that in this somewhat unlikely spot is a chef of unusual talent; M. Guy Culot is out to spoil his holiday guests with specialities rarely seen in these unsophisticated parts, like a soup made from mussels, almonds and seaweed, and a nest of fish cooked in all kinds of imaginative ways and, most unusual of all, a superb dessert trolley. (He won a national pâtisserie competition.) His 95f menu is worth a considerable detour, and the 60f one is not at all bad either.
    I predict a big future for the Falaise; watch this space!

Otherwise there is just the **Restaurant Commerce** which is better in than out (not difficult), has a pleasant view across the bay and could certainly serve a simple lunch after a morning's excursion along the coast.

Map 1G   **DIEPPE** (Seine-Maritime) 11 km from Le Havre

Dieppe gets on with its business of being a real French port, with real French fishermen and real French housewives going about their really French lives.

Into the very heart of the town probes the deep water, so that ships are part of the urban scenery, to be walked round and remarked upon, with all their evocative accessories of screeching gulls snatching at fish, engine thud, constant animation, a sense of the importance of the sea's moods.

No surprise to find many fishy restaurants lining the quays, no surprise to find them good value — when the tourists have gone, they must stake their claim for stalwart local appetites. Not so with hotels — the Dieppois don't use 'em and don't seem concerned that they are generally a sorry lot, spoiled with too easy custom, but eating . . . that's another story.

So Dieppe is first a port — and a lively, colourful, absorbing first it is — but then a market town. As easy to shop well here as to eat. And,

Dieppe.

logically enough, the Grand' Rue leads straight from one focal point, the harbour, to another, the Place de Puits Salé, the obvious conclusion to a gentle stroll through the pedestrianised shopping area being the **Café des Tribunaux.** Always lively, best in the evening when the pavement tables catch the last slant of sun; a hundred years ago it was the meeting place of revolutionary young artists, fascinated by the clarity of the coastal light – Pissarro, Renoir, Monet, Sickert, Whistler, all gathered here. The Café still attracts youthful customers, hot in debate over a 'pression'. The ghost of Oscar Wilde, exiled, disgraced, the imbiber of many a sad drink at the Tribunaux, troubles them not at all.

Opposite the Café, in the r. de la Barre, is probably the best pâtisserie in Dieppe, though it is hard to be definitive because there is an exceptionally high standard here. This one is named after the dashing Duchess of Berry who 'invented' sea-bathing. Thirty different flavours of ice-cream on offer too, so not a bad idea to sit in the Tribunaux to contemplate and decide between, say, a fraise du bois, or guava, or caramel. Not easy.

A little further up the r. de la Barre is the kitchen shop which is not only my favourite but that of most local chefs – **La Magdalene.** For serious cooking **Tout Pour La Maison** in the Grand' Rue has a good range too.

Zigzag back to the harbour between other Grand' Rue temptations, gastronomic (good charcuteries—**La Rôtisserie Parisienne** is easy to spot by the boar's head over the door—boulangeries, épiceries), sartorial (upmarket labels at B.D.T. and Le Roy-Délépouille, lots of shoe and jeans outlets) and two good teashops (Divernet/Grisch and Aux Fins Gourmets), and finish with a quick nip round the department stores, Le Printemps and Prisunic. If you're homeward bound the final fruitier, 'Royal Fruit' sells good-value fruit and veg; if there's a seasonal glut of, say, peaches, strawberries or tomatoes, this is the place to pick up a cheap kilo from the brimming stalls outside.

That is, of course, unless it's Saturday, when it would be a crime to miss the market. Hard to miss it in fact, since it takes up the whole of the pl. Nationale and spills over into the adjoining streets. It's one of the best in Normandy, exploiting to the full the regional products. If you think all butter and cream taste the same, just try some from one of the farmers' stalls there and relish the difference.

Dieppe's fishing fleet unloads its catch on the quayside. If you get up early enough you'll catch the auction, but it's always a pleasure to buy fish anywhere in Dieppe. All kinds of shellfish, including oysters, are wonderful value and there is a huge range of prime white fish, alive and kicking; on the stalls by the harbour, in the market, from shops like 'À la Marée du Jour' in the Grand Rue, or from the fish restaurant, L'Armorique, on the quay.

What's in a name? Quite a lot, apparently, if it's Olivier. In Boulogne the fromagier Phillippe is a phenomenon; here in the r. St-Jacques, his father, Claude, provides another essential shopping experience. This is where I always stock up on cheeses in guaranteed prime condition – just tell him on which day you wish to eat them – and cheap wines. You can trust his special offers or play safe with Nicolas. Usefully open on Sunday a.m.

If you're hell-bent on a hypermarket, the nearest is **Mammouth** on the

Rouen road. Allow plenty of time, though – the checkout queues can be diabolical. So is the parking in the town during July and August; because it is one of the nearest beaches to Paris, you can expect more crowds here than in other ports.

Dominating the promenade, with its wide stretches of grass dotted with picnickers, is the 15th-century castle, complete with maritime museum, displaying not only all things nautical but a fine array of ivory (closed Tuesday o.o.s.). In the castle's shadow is a plaque commemorating the controversial Operation Jubilee, the costly Anglo–Canadian raid on Dieppe in 1942.

You can't stay in Dieppe for long without being reminded, by road and café names, of one of her most famous sons, Jean Ango. He was the maritime counsellor to Francis 1. In the 16th century he took on the Portuguese fleet off the coast of Africa, with notable success, and became Governor of Dieppe. He is buried in the chapel he built in the church of St-Jacques, especially worth a visit when the evening sun floods its rose window. (See also Varengeville.)

The hotels in Dieppe are a disappointment; perhaps they've got it too easy. It used to be our delight to stay at the **Univers**, but on my last visit, after a particularly exhausting and hot day, we were made to wait an hour in the late afternoon for beds to be made. No apologies and then cigarette stubs still in the ashtrays. Casting aside nostalgia, we had to face up to the fact that the bathrooms are exceedingly poor and the high prices unjustified. Since I had a little 'encounter' with the management (we weren't keen on the atmosphere – armchairs full of snorers, dusty elephants on dusty mantelpiece – and so decided to eat out, unwittingly incurring impressive wrath from Madame on our return), I shan't be going back until I hear that matters have improved, so all reports here particularly welcome. Such a pity, because the hotel has great character and a prime position, and the food used to be outstanding.

The **Windsor** next door is probably a better bet, but my file is not enthusiastic. The **Plage** is smaller and cheaper but a bit dull, and then there's the **Aiguado**, a characterless, noisy, efficient, expensive battery. The Univers, Windsor and Rhin et Newhaven run four-day cookery courses with built-in accommodation.

To find better value it is probably best to leave the seafront.

Select Hôtel
(H)M
pl. de la Barre
(35) 84.14.66.

Stylish and elegant but with a noise problem. Insist on a room 'au calme'. Recently renovated in Directoire style, a double with private bath costs 150f, and at least one can eat out.

Le Moderne
(R)M
21 arcades de la Poissonnerie
(35) 84.12.33.
Closed Dec.;
Tue. p.m.; Wed.

From outside this looks like all the other fishy quayside restaurants, but a note of seriousness is obvious once inside the door. The tables are well-laid, the clientèle Dippoise rather than Newhavenish and the menu leaves no doubt that this one is in a class apart and deserves an arrow.

On the 73f menu I chose a perfect terrine of salmon, made piquant by a sauce of fresh anchovies, then a darne de barbue au cidre, the brill poached, garnished with baby mushrooms and onions, and surrounded by a delicate buttery sauce. After a wonderful cheeseboard, followed one of the best lemon mousses I have tasted anywhere, sharpened by a redcurrant sauce. They serve good meat here too and my husband followed his vast plâteau de fruits de mer with an excellent 'steack de gigôt à l'ail et fonds d'artichaut'. Even better would be to save up an appetite for the 100f 'gastronomique' which offered even more refined dishes like a ris de veau aux girolles.

Ideal for a wet Sunday's greediness and indeed only suitable if time is no object, since the cooking is done to order and service is distinctly harassed in busy periods.

There are three dining-rooms – the ground floor is smartest but the top has the best view of the harbour. (On a Sunday you must book.)

La Petite Auberge
(HR)S
10 r. de la Rade
(35) 84.27.20.
Closed
15/12–1/2;
Wed.

A good general rule in finding tourist-free restaurants is to divert from the obvious, and La Petite Auberge confirms this. Turn off the Quai Henri IV, after having walked almost to the point, to find it. All very basic but full of locals tucking into large portions at around 50f. I have not seen the rooms personally, but:

'Very pleasant patron who also does the cooking. Our room was very ordinary, but comfortable enough and very cheap indeed.'

Belle Époque
and **La Criée**
(R)M
3 r. G. Ternen Île
du Pollet.
(35) 82.16.17.

Between the two bridges, two restaurants under the same management, the former (cadre 1930s) open only in the evening. ~~CLOSED SINCE LAST EDITION~~ fishiness around the ~~...~~ La Criée for 75 or 90f ~~...~~ La Belle Époque at 90f or 130f. Much praised locally.

La Marmite Dieppoise
(R)M
9 r. St-Jean.
(35) 84.24.26.
Closed Sun.
p.m.; Mon. 🔳

A shame to visit Dieppe without tasting one of its specialities – Marmite Dieppoise – and this is the place to choose. Chef Jean-Pierre Toussat makes it from a variety of local fish and shellfish, enriches it with cream, and serves it up in his no-nonsense little restaurant, tucked away in a side street between the Arcades and St-Jacques. All the fish here is very good. I like the atmosphere of straightforward dedication to the food and not to the tourists. Menus are 42f, 68f (except weekends) and 120f, and house red is a remarkable 18f.

Normandy (R)S and **Le Jupiler** (R)S are almost next door to one another in the r. Dequesne, and offer very similar attractions. Both enormously popular with locals, who queue up for their Sunday lunch. The Normandy is the more sophisticated but both are hustling, very French, good value, with menus starting at around 45f.

Le Marine
(R)S
1 arcades de la
Poissonnerie
(35) 84.17.54.
Closed Tue.
p.m.; Wed.

The obvious place to go for straightforward fish, just opposite the fish market. Busy with tourists and young French. Menus start at 40f.

Le Port
(R)M
99 quai Henri IV
(35) 84.36.64.
Closed Thur.

I didn't include Le Port, the cheapest of Michelin's recommendations in the town, last time, because I thought it still looked comparatively expensive, but now I find they are trying to be more competitive, and the menu at 53f is strong on good fish. A plateful of moules, if that's all you wanted, would cost 20f, served in a bustling and lively atmosphere.

Le Sully
(R)M
97 quai Henri IV
(35) 84.23.13.
Closed
15/11–15/12;
Tue. p.m.; Wed.
V.

Well known for many years to British visitors, partly because of its mynah bird, I suspect. Had an indifferent patch, but must still rate as one of the better bets in Dieppe. Menus from 60f.

ENVIRONS

See Pourville, p.160, Quiberville, p.161, Martin Eglise, p.139, St Marguerite-sur-Mer, Varengeville, p.193, Arques la Bataille, p.35.

Map 7D   **DOMFRONT** (Orne) 100 km from Cherbourg

Although personally I find this stretch of Normandy rather dull, Domfront makes quite a useful stopping place, being an easy drive from Cherbourg well on the way south or west. An old cobbled pedestrianised street leads picturesquely up and away from the through-traffic blare to a square with what must surely qualify as the most hideous modern church in France (and that's some qualification). I think it must be a joke.

Unfortunately, there are no hotels up here in the lofty calm and the best on offer is on the busy main road:

Hôtel de la Poste
(HR)M
r. Foch
(33) 38.51.00.
Closed (except fêtes) 5/1–24/2;
Sun p.m.; Mon. o.o.s.

Well known, recommended in almost every other guidebook and by many of my readers, but I can't say it's my scene; I find it far too big, over-priced and ugly. If you must stay, do ask for a room 'au calme' at the rear of the building and avert your eyes from the hideous orange varnished corridors on the second floor. I had to ignore the sinister greyness creeping up my bathroom wall too. 150f a double.

But the hotel is run, as it has been for many years, by two friendly, helpful ladies, Yvette le Prise and her long-time friend Yvette Chenu. They speak good English and have made many faithful friends from their British customers.

The restaurant is so-so. It used to have a Michelin star and was well known for local Norman specialities. Now I find it necessary to go to the 128f menu to find anything interesting.

Map 7D   **DOMPIERRE** (Orne) 98 km from Cherbourg

Just a flowery crossroads on the D 21, NW of Domfront, but I can't resist giving it a mention in order to point out that France can still be very cheap indeed if you know where to look and are not going to fret about lack of mod. cons. At the **Relais de la Forêt** (33) 38.24.04 Mme

Lanther has one good room with shower for 45f (and some rather awful ones at 35f) and at the **Auberge du Bon Laboureur** (33) 38.23.32. Mme Humbert-Lafontaine has six for 35f. The latter is a well-known local cook who stresses that she runs a restaurant with 'Chambres familiales' rather than a hotel and cannot take guests at the weekend because she is too involved with 'banquets'. Her four-course meals at 35f are a bargain. Mme Lanther offers a 29f and 53f menu. Possibly useful in financial crisis? *Do* insist on inspecting rooms first, (a) so that you know what you're in for and won't blame me if the carpet's frayed, and (b) because some are much nicer than others.

Map 5H   **DOUAINS** (Eure) 148 km from Le Havre

Take the D 181 and 6 km NE of Pacy, with autoroute visible ahead, turn right on to D 75. From the autoroute take the Vernon exit to find Douains between the D 181 and the D 75 and the château is marked from both.

Château de Brécourt
(HR)L
(32) 52.40.50.
Rest. closed Wed. AE, DC, E, V.

A splendid place for an extravagant weekend. A new member of the Relais et Châteaux chain and priced accordingly, but offering true value for money in: 1. position, so near autoroute yet in deepest Norman countryside; 2. building, a magnificent 18th-century château; 3. furnishings, lavish and individual; and 4. restaurant, where the cheapest menu, at 115f, takes some beating.

The chef, Gildas Marsollier, used to work at the starred Prieuré de Chênehutte and no doubt has his eye on similar glories here, so this is a good time to try out some of his specialities like jambonette de volaille au coulis de tomates, brochet sur lit de choux, all served on covetable Limoges china.

The bedrooms are all different, very grand, very comfortable. Prices vary according to their size, from 250 to 450f but even the smallest is highly commendable. Good atmosphere, good welcome.

The kind of luxury stop-off where it would be hard to get going again, I'd find it hard to tear myself away from full money's-worth of park, tennis-court and pool. *New chef since last edition.*

Map 4E   **DOZULÉ** (Calvados) 80 km from Le Havre

Between Caen and Pont l'Eveque, on the N 175, very near the autoroute.

Hôtellerie Normand
(HR)S
(31) 79.20.18.
Closed 1/12–1/3; Mon. o.o.s.

A simple little Logis, commended by several readers; here is a report from one who has lived in France for 20 years, and should know:

'A comfortable modest hotel; spacious well-furnished bedroom and bathroom, heating as soon as its chilly, always plenty of hot water. Good cooking this year (better than last). Pleasing dining-room' – Anne Ortzen.

'The welcome was warm, the room large and comfortable, the shower-room spacious and the towels the largest we have ever been given in France – for 107f we were delighted. On the 52f menu we ate huge helpings of mussels, a superb tripes à la mode de Caen, guineafowl

and a very generous cheeseboard. The cider is excellent at 18f per bottle. Breakfast included both bread and croissants, plenty of butter and a huge dish of apricot jam; with lashings of coffee. Right on the cider route – what more could you wish for? I can unreservedly recommend it.' – L. B. Bloom.

Rooms 65 to 125f, menus from 48f. M. Chenevarin is *patron/chef.*

Map 7B   **DUCEY** (Manche) 143 km from Cherbourg

A village just off the N 176 from Pontaubault to St-Hilaire.

Auberge de la Sélune
(HR)S
(33) 48.53.62.
Closed
15/1–15/2;
Mon. o.o.s.
A. EC.

One of the most successful finds in *F.E.2.* Everyone liked this charming little hotel, and its young and hardworking owners, Jean-Pierre and Josette Girras. Compliments too for the food. Jean-Pierre offers his guests imaginative dishes, like gigôt de mer, bar aux langoustines, crab pie and terrine de Sélune. With garden, terrace, lounge, the Auberge is excellent value at 140 to 150f a double and menus from 60f.

'I want to confirm your remarks about the Auberge. A charming setting, a pleasant young couple. Quite the best value . . . and what croissants!' – Dr G. B. Hollings.

One caveat. It proved so popular last year that it is now often full and would-be guests have been offered rooms in the annexe, Hôtel Voyageurs. Unlike the newly-decorated, spotlessly clean Auberge, this is a dark and dismal alternative, not to be recommended until the Girras get to work on it, which I hope will not be too long.

One last-minute report complains sadly that now that other guidebooks are featuring the Auberge too, it's full of Brits! A finger-crossing situation.

Map 3G   **DUCLAIR** (Seine-Maritime) 71 km from Le Havre

Market Tuesday. Spoiled for me nowadays by the heavy lorries that thunder through the little town or queue up to cross on the ferry to Brotonne, but still a good place to observe the great cargo ships on their way between Rouen and the sea. The best view comes from:

Hôtel Poste
(HR)S
286 Quai
Liberation
(35) 37.50.04.
Closed
26/3–12/7.
Rest. closed
2/7–16/7; Feb.;
Mon; Sun p.m.
AE, E.

Not much to look at, but once famous for its duckling Rouennais. They still serve it but no longer in fourteen different sytles. Bag a table by the window to get the benefit of the marvellous detached view of all the quayside activity. Menus good value from 45f, and modest rooms (which could be noisy) from 92 to 130f.

Le Parc
(R)M
av. du Président
Coty
(35) 37.50.31.

Double back from Duclair on the Route de Caudebec and take the turning along the riverbank signposted 'Route des Fruits'. The drive will remind you of a stage setting for some romantic musical, not *Lilactime* but certainly 'Blossom time' in the spring. The combination of fruit trees as far as the eye can see to the right, and mighty river to the left is a heady one and slightly unreal. It's all a bit too neat and miniature for France – the houses are for dolls, the assorted livestock in the enclosures look as though they had been arranged by a child: one fat cow, two clean pigs, a mummy-sheep with three baby lambs, four brown hens, one collie dog . . . The scale is more Home Counties than Normandy, but very, very pretty.

Not very far along this route is Le Parc, an imposing turn-of-the century mansion, slightly faded, with a large garden, full of hydrangeas running down to the river. Very pleasant to eat here in fine weather, but a few criticisms are beginning to arrive concerning the variability of M. Patazour's cuisine. When he is good, he is very very good, offering the ubiquitous Rouennais duck under the name of Robert le Diable, and some interesting variations, like escargots cooked with hazelnuts, but when he is bad he is horrid, perhaps spoiled by too much publicity. However, wtih a menu at 50f, and that lovely setting, it would be wrong to expect heaven too. You should book.

Map 2E   **ÉTRETAT** (Seine-Maritime) 28 km from Le Havre

I have Mr David Stewart of Saxmundham to thank for persuading me to give Étretat just one more chance. It had not been for want of trying before that I had failed to work out a meaningful relationship with this little seaside resort of the much-photographed cliffs, but always the wind and the rain had convinced me that this was a bleak and unwelcoming town, tatty of front, peeling of paint. Mr Stewart wrote:

'Having known Étretat since I was a small boy, I love it like my home town and cannot allow anyone else to feel differently about it. When the weather is fine (and we used to say that no day at Étretat was ever bad all day long), it is a place of very great beauty and, as I am sure you know, its cliffs have been painted by several of the Impressionists. Alphonse Karr said of them: "If I had to show the sea to a friend for the first time, I would choose Étretat".'

So I saved up a fine July day, put my prejudices aside, and it was hard to believe it was the same place. Animated and colourful now, I found it delightful and could quite see the extent of Mr Stewart's grievance. The front was still an affront (sorry), with pop music blaring from the Casino, souvenir shops proliferating, but the famous beach had come to life, with vivid windsurfers and happily squealing children, and the hotels had all put out their wind-broken tables for lunch, next to the brightly painted fishing boats pulled up on the shore.

In the garden of the same tea room where I had previously taken refuge against the storm, I sat, nibbling a tarte au citron with my delicious Earl Grey tea (it cost 13f, but this is the only time I've come across a crocheted teapot handle protector to solve that metal burn) and watching the holiday makers swarm up the steep hill on either side of the beach, to the left the golf course and a sensational walk above the

Falaise d'Aval, to the right the sentinal church.

I visited the other church – the Romanesque Nôtre Dame – walking past the essentially French holiday villas, old-fashioned roses rampaging over their cobbled walls, white shutters now flung open and even a window daringly ajar here and there, to the cool interior of that wonderfully simple nine-centuries-old building, and was very thankful to have had my eyes opened.

It *is* obviously a very seasonal place and many of the hotels close for the whole winter.

Hôtel Welcôme
(HR)S
10 av. de Verdun
(35) 27.00.89.
Closed Feb. P. V.

(Note the circonflex!). Really jolly little hotel, all fresh white paint on balconies and shutters, smart new brown awnings, tables in garden, set back from road, a few minutes from the beach. Bedrooms are furnished in keeping with house's origin (late 19th century) and pedigree (mixed). Heavily-furnished dining-room relieved with pink cloths, nice pink stemmed glasses and pink curtains at long open windows. Mme Claude Moiret is the rotund young *patronne*. Doubles range from 138 to 178f with bath. Menus from 65 to 70f. Here is one seaside hotel that doesn't insist on demi-p. Excellent family choice.

Le Corsaire
(HR)M
(35) 27.00.25.
Closed 15/11–1/2.

On the seafront, with cosy corsaire-theme restaurant inside and another, for fine weather, on the prom. Good seafood. Rooms are from 76 to 182f with bath, and menus from 71 to 94f.

'Restaurant very popular, seating 100 in main building and 100 more on the terrace, with protection from parasols against the seagulls and the sun, if any. Staff very helpful and bedrooms very clean, food excellent. No house wine – cheapest 33f. They ask for one main meal – lunch or supper, but this is not a great imposition.' – Bobby Wolfson.

Hôtel des Falaises
H(M)
bd. René Coty.
(35) 27.02.77.

'Comfortable smallish bedrooms with bath, central heating, excellent and copious breakfast – good coffee and lots of it, baguette and croissant and best Normandy butter – and very reasonable price – 170f double. And the proprietors (he is Mayor, by the way) most obliging. No restaurant, so we dined at La Coquille Normande – fair and reasonable – four courses for 55f of which far the best was gigôt de pré salé; the other courses were a little quelconque (sorry!)' – David Stewart.

Le Tricorne
(R)M
5 bd René Coty
(35) 29.62.22.

This is the extraordinary looking wooden building opposite the Falaises.
'Excellent menu at 50f.' – A. L. Rowell.

(See also Le Tilleul p.186).

Map 5G   **EVREUX** (Eure) 120 km from Le Havre

For a Norman town, a situation near the provincial border has always meant a history of sack and pillage. Evreux, from its earliest days has faced hordes of destructive enemies – Romans, Goths, Vandals, Normans, English, French, and finally Germans, whose 1940 attacks left the city burning for a week. After each devastation the townsfolk have picked themselves up, dusted themselves down and started all over again.

It's truly a miracle that any part of Notre Dame, Evreux's cathedral, has survived but there it is, rising up above the rivulets of the river Iton, still the focus of the city, an assembly of every phase of Gothic architecture to Renaissance between the 12th and 17th centuries. It is currently closed for yet more restoration, so any attempt to view the astounding 15th century stained glass (moved for safety during the last war) will have to wait.

It is pleasant enough to stroll along the river walk and admire the cathedral from the outside but there are other towns in the vicinity where I would rather stay, particularly as I failed to find an outstanding hotel or restaurant here. The old Grand Cerf, with its perfect position overlooking water and cathedral, is now a second-rate quick service restaurant, the France is too expensive for what's on offer. Best bet is probably:

Normandy
(HR)M
37 r. E-Feray
(32) 33.14.41.
Rest. closed
Sun., Aug.
P. AE, DC, V.

Very olde-worlde beamy. Friendly staff, comfortable rooms at 102 to 255f and menus from 57f rooms on main road. Could be noisy.

Map 5E   **FALAISE** (Calvados) 142 km from Le Havre, 154 km from Cherbourg

---

Devasted during the war, re-built in the yellow local stone, still dominated by the keep of the castle over whose drawbridge, they say, rode the washerwoman's daughter, the proud Arlette, to meet her lover Duke Robert, a liaison more than usually eventful in that William the Bastard (Conqueror) was the result. His magnificent statue rears below the castle ruins.

One good reason for stopping here is that at least two hotels offer food of a quality rare in these parts, plus the alternative of the best restaurant for miles around. I would choose:

La Normandie
(H R)M
4 r. Amiral
-Courbet
(31) 90.18.26.
Rest. closed
Sun.

In a side street and therefore not as traffic-ridden as most (though I would still ask for a room at the back — 'au calme'). It looks big/ugly/modern/boring, but it is run by friendly staff and the rooms aren't bad. Not expensive either at 120f for a double with bath. With good menus at 42f, it offers an excellent-value stopover.

Poste
(H R)S
38 r. G.-
Clemenceau
(31) 90.13.14.
Closed
15/10–21/10;
20/12–15/1,
Sun. p.m. and
Mon. P. V.

A red R in Michelin and an excellent local reputation for its menus at 47f but it is on a very noisy site and I would not choose to stay there

La Fine
Fourchette
(R)M
52 r. G-
Clemenceau
(31) 90.08.59
Closed
1/2–15/2, Wed.
p.m. o.o.s. P. V.

Makes a considerable detour worthwhile, and were it not for two regrettable abberrations I would rate it even higher:

When David Donhue, the Thoresen M.D., first recommended it to me he wrote *'pity the chips take over'*. They still do. No reprieve – the army of frites invades every plate, overwhelming the most delicate of sauces. The other unwanted garniture is in even worse taste – so much so that I fear a mention might put off the doubters before giving the place a chance. Be warned – every single dish will sprout a miniature paper parasol. Please forgive and concentrate on the excellent food.

Six delicious snails, encased in three miniature tartelettes, all dripping in garlicky parslied butter for me, a mousse of chicken livers left in the earthenware terrine for my friend to help herself, started off the 75f menu in fine style. Then bass with sorrel, then duck à l'orange with the dread chips on a sublime filet de boeuf with green peppercorns. Salad, a monumental cheeseboard, and a bewildering choice of desserts.

There are also two excellent cheaper menus at 37f and 58f and a gastronomic ridiculousness at 140f, with half a lobster as the second of its six courses. Sans frites and parasols, a highly distinguished cuisine and excellent value.

Map 2F   **FÉCAMP** (Seine-Maritime) 40 km from Le Havre

I find Fécamp disappointing; France's fourth fishing port, but no outstanding restaurants, or hotels, and the interest generated by the harbour soon fades a few streets back. The much-vaunted Benedictine distillery is a joke. Housed in an eccentric 'Gothic/Renaissance' pile, stagily floodlit, the interior is a disappointment; the only good bit of the tour is sniffing the dozens of herbs and spices used in the distillation of the liqueur, but perhaps this is a personal prejudice, since thousands of visitors do come here every year and it might well fill in a wet afternoon. Open Easter–November, 9–11.30 and 2–5.30.

Contrarily I preferred the abbey, disapproved of by Michelin: 'the classical façade does not go well with the rest of the building'. It is certainly a hotch-potch of the centuries from 12th to 18th but I love it.

Not much else in the town, so for nourishment make for the quays and settle for fish.

L'Escalier
(R)M
(35) 28.26.79.
Closed
6/2–25/2;
15/11–30/11;
Sun. p.m.; Mon.
o.o.s. DC, E.

Good news here. M. et Mme Bodeux, who used to run a favourite restaurant at Yport until it was burned down a few years ago, are now installed in L'Escalier and it is now the most interesting place in town. They make a feature of the spiral staircase from which the little restaurant takes its name and sensibly concentrate on the produce nearest at hand – fish from the local fleet. It comes good, fresh and in generous portions on menus that start at 65f. Splendid hot Tarte Normande too.

If it's closing day here, make for:

Le Maritime
(R)M
2 pl. M. Selles
(35) 28.21.71.
Closed Tue.

'Charming dining-room upstairs, very helpful staff. Food good, reasonable wine list, when selected red wine proved unobtainable they brought a most acceptable and inexpensive alternative – Gamay du Haut Poitou.'

2 km away on the Bolbec Road is another good alternative.

Auberge de la Rouge
(R)M
(35) 28.07.59.
Closed
1/7–20/7; Thur.
p.m.; Fri.

'Recommended by my Belgian partner as his favourite restaurant in Fécamp. Excellent –' salade d'avocat with langoustines, rouget niçoise and a beautiful crème caramel. Reasonably priced, good pantry. We wished we'd found it sooner.'
Menus start at 55f.

Map 5G   **LA FERRIÈRE-SUR-RISLE** (Eure) 112 km from Le Havre

---

A most attractive little town, in highly explorable countryside. In the wide, tree-lined main street is:

Hôtel Croissant
(HR)S
(32) 30.70.13
Closed
15/12–15/1;
Sun. p.m.; Mon.

I like the Hôtel Croissant very much; the food is plentiful and cheap, and you need look no further than the 55f menu. Bedrooms across the courtyard in the pleasant annexe cost 170f with bath, but most of the others, roomy and comfortable if simply furnished, are only 90f.   Most readers agree that a stay in this old and picturesque country inn, run by the friendly Mme Hubert, is an agreeable experience: *'We were given the choice of anything on the menu for dinner, whether the 55f or 120f menu or the à la carte; such generosity to demi-pensionnaires was new to me. For us it made a perfect touring base and the food was excellent. The terms were so modest that we enjoyed some excellent if rather pricey wines.' – R. H. Jardine-Willoughby.*

However, a recent report from a trusted correspondent made me think twice about awarding a second arrow: *'Charming village, accueil very pleasant. Double room with bath at 170f too expensive for a hotel of this standard. And rooms would be very damp in winter – scarcely heated and stains on the walls. Dinner at 55f was very acceptable, but 17.50f was more than enough for petit déjeuner and 40f for the cuvée de la maison – nothing special – was far too expensive. We'll go back – but not in the winter or wet weather.'*

This is the valuable second-opinion kind of report that helps to build up the complete picture. The conclusion can only be that for a simple

village inn the Croissant is not cheap (though you don't *have* to have a
room with a bath), and that it would not be a good choice o.o.s.
However, pick a fine day, enjoy the hospitality and simple fare,
photograph the village, and you've got a good deal.

Map 7D   **LA FERTÉ MACÉ** (Orne) 175 km from Cherbourg

Having retreated from Bagnoles de l'Orne because of its deadly hush,
we guessed that nearby La Ferté Macé might be livelier, but although
we much preferred the town to Bagnoles, it too was quite dead in
August. We stayed solitarily at:

**Auberge de
Clouet**
(H R)M
*(33) 37.18.22.
Closed Jan.,
Sun. p.m. and
Mon. o.o.s. P.*

No complaints – bright, cheerful, quiet, flowery terrace, comfortable
rooms with thoughtful extras like towelling bathrobes, and not expensive
at 140f for a double with bath, but we couldn't face the empty dining
room and the dejected-looked staff and beat a shamefaced retreat into
the town, looking for some action.
    The best we could find was **Le Tire Bouchon**, art-deco, potentially
vibrant, but not that night. Unusual they said. The meal was good, and
cheap at 40f, but I can't recommend the place for a rave-up.

Map 2H   **FORGES-LES-EAUX** (Seine Maritime) 141 km from Le Havre

---

I was rather disappointed in this little spa town, from which I had
anticipated more elegance. However, worth noting might be:

**Hotel de la
Paix**
(H R)S
*17 r. Neufchatel
(35) 90.51.22.
Closed
15/12–4/1, Sun.
p.m., Mon. o.o.s.*

The rooms are basic and could be noisy, but pleasant enough and cheap.
It is the food here that is really quite exceptional, all cooked by the
patron, M. Remy Michel, who specialises in 'cuisine de terroir'. The
dining room is altogether more attractive than the entrance hall would
lead you to expect. Michelin gives it a red R. for its 48f. menu and the six
rooms cost from 46 to 90f, so its all excellent value.

Map 3G   **FRANQUEVILLE ST PIERRE** (Seine-Maritime) 97 km from
Le Havre

On the N 14, 7 km to the east of Rouen. Follow the 'Aeroport' signs out
of the city and on the left, just before Boos, is:

**Le Vert
Bocage**
(HR)S
*Route de Paris
(35) 80.14.74.
Closed Sun
p.m.; Mon. o.o.s.*

The Huets, of the St-Pierre at La Bouille, are in partnership here with the
Bonnetons, and although the Vert Bocage is an altogether more modest
establishment, their expertise shows.
    This is a modern building, conveniently if prosaically situated, near
Rouen. Inside, the décor, linen and glass have all been chosen carefully
and Michel's cooking and the general welcome have been unanimously
approved by numerous readers who took advantage of their special
opening offer last year.

Map 6F   **GACÉ** (Orne) 128 km from Le Havre

Not a very exciting little town — just a few streets radiating from the main square, with its Saturday afternoon market. On the corner is:

**Hôtel de
Normandie**
(HR)S
(35) 35.52.13.

Recommended by readers who needed a cheap family stop-over in this area. And it really is cheap — a double room costs 52f and the menu another 32f. Madame Forcinal does all the cooking and I am told that she and her husband are very helpful *patrons*, for whom nothing is too much trouble. One of those very simple, French small-town hotels, that look unappealing, to say the least, from the outside, and make you walk through the bar to get to the interior, but offer clean rooms and family cooking for very little money.

**Hostellerie des
Champs**
(HR)L
rte Alençon
(33) 35.51.45
Closed
15/1–15/2; Tue.
except by
reservation. P.
DC, E.
no longer
recommended

Very different. Decidedly upmarket since Christian Tironneau took over from his father four years ago. Since then a steady programme of improvements have changed the whole character of this 18th-century 'gentilhommerie', set back from the RN 138 Alençon road, south of Gacé.

All the reception rooms are now extremely elegant and comfortable and the 13 bedrooms have nearly all been renovated and refurbished. A smart new tennis-court is ready, the heated swimming-pool has one of those wizard predatory cleaners that seek out and devour the slightest speck, and there will soon be that male chauvinist bastion — a boules pitch.

The new chef, Patrick Colin, has a Bocuse background, so clearly the whole set-up is due to rise in the world. As have the prices. Double rooms now cost 167–280f. The 88f menu is good value, with three choices in each section, but to find anything worthy of M. Colin's talents it would be necessary to eat à la carte and that would involve a food bill of at least 150f. I have not yet done this, but if the chef's as good as his pedigree, that price should not be grudged. They like you to eat dinner in.

**Château Le
Morphée**
(H)M
(33) 35.51.01
2 r. de Lisieux
Closed
15/12–15/1. P.

I'm beginning to feel quite affectionate towards the chain known as Châteaux Hotels Independants et Hostelleries d'Atmosphere for spotlighting such an amazing range of truly individual buildings now masquerading as hotels. This one is a 19th-century French house, tall, all facade, narrow, thin, chequered brick, imposing entrance, fronted by murky pond set in ragged lawn.

The warmth of Madame Lecanu's welcome made me suppress unseemly giggles at the house's *folie de grandeur*, especially as I had arrived during her sacrosanct lunch-hour and caught her covered in paint. 'Tenu de bataille', as one of her visiting friends put it. She could not shake hands with me but she could and did show me every one of the charming bedrooms, all with bathrooms, quiet and elegant. They cost from 179 to 203f, and there are also two family rooms for four people, with bathrooms big enough to accommodate another family, for 313f. (Romantic names are thrown in — 'Reverie,' 'Crepescule', 'Aurore'.)

Le Morphée

Map 5B	**GAVRAY** (Manche) 92 km from Cherbourg

A fairly uninteresting town on the junction of several D roads, north-east of Villedieu-les-Poeles.

Hôtel de la Gare
(HR)S
(33) 61.40.55.
Closed mid-end June.

If in doubt, make for the station is not a bad general rule for finding a reliable cheap overnight stop in France. It works in Gavray where the ineptly named M. and Madame Villain run a restaurant/hotel in the main square. As basic as they come, but look at the prices: rooms 45–60f, menus 32–55f. Friendly proprietors, clean rooms (I looked at them all); bar and road could be noisy – ask for room at rear.

'The best value for money meal we had. On the 40f menu we ate large prawns, cockles in garlic butter, delicious veal in cream and mushroom sauce, cheese and fruit. The bar is very plain and full of locals but the smell was so good that we asked to eat and they showed us into a very small dining-room.' – Mary Glover.

Map 4E

GONNEVILLE-EN-AUGE (Calvados) 103 km from Le Havre

On the D 95 A, a turning to the north off the Cabourg–Caen road, the D 513, 7 km from Cabourg.

Hostellerie du Moulin du Pré
(H)M (R)L
Bavent
(31) 78.83.68.
Closed
1/3–15/3; Oct.;
Sun. p.m.; Mon.
o.o.s. AE, DC, V.

Ideally placed for the sea, the landing beaches, Caen and the autoroute, the hostellerie is well aware of its advantages and a stop there is not cheap; it should, however, prove to be most agreeable.

The site is that of an old mill, whose stream runs through the gardens, banks dotted with primroses, into a small lake, all well-kept and colourful, as is the hostellerie itself.

The bedrooms are tiny and the baths of the sit-up-and-beg variety, but at 90 to 140f, they are not expensive. It is when an evening meal gets added on that the bill leaps disproportionately. You don't have to eat in, and daughter and I had no intention of doing so, but when we saw the lovely old beamed restaurant with huge log fire, everything looking warm, cheerful and welcoming, and then considered the dark, cold night outside, we weakened. I'm very glad we did because the meal far exceeded expectations. There is only one menu, at 146f, and the à la carte dishes start at around 60f, so economy is out of the question.

We shared our first courses of game terrine and pâté de foie gras, and found them both exceptionally good, as were the salmon with sorrel and the charcoal grilled meat that followed. Norman cheeses in fair condition and medium-interesting puddings.

Breakfast confirmed the verdict. On time, freshly squeezed orange juice, hot croissants, real jam.

I like the Hostellerie very much because its formula of save-on-bed, spend-on-food is one that appeals to me, but even I felt our bill of 750f somewhat excessive.

Map 5D

GOUPILLIÈRES, HALTE DE GRIMBOSQ (Calvados)
132 km from Le Havre; 148 km from Cherbourg

One reader actually witnessed a train on the single track that crosses the D 171 here at the Halte. I don't think the noise from passing traffic, road or rail, would be too serious a problem in this case, though. The village of Goupillières is a kilometre away and the fishermen who populate the banks of the shallow river Orne here at the Pont de Brie are not given to jarring rowdiness. All is very peaceful, very serene and the wooded hills of the Forêt de Grimbosq rising from the river towards the main D 562 provide the perfect backcloth to the delightful rural scene.

▶ **Auberge du Pont de Brie**
(HR)S
(31) 79.37.84.
Closed
15/8–30/8;
1/2–15/2; Wed.
Credit cards
(unspecified)
accepted.

A highly successful arrowed recommendation from *F.E.2*. Everyone agrees with me about the good value offered by this little Logis. It is modern but with nice touches like a log fire, and the rooms are good sized and very comfortable. My double with modern bathroom was 70f, and that was the most expensive. Trout from the river features on the menus, 40f and 60f. I especially appreciated the *patron's* letter. He started off by saying how much he liked *French Entrée* clients and then won my heart completely by a most unusual hotelier's statement: 'nous sommes ouverts a toute critique'. Well, there's not a lot of criticism one can offer in this case.

1.5 km from Thury-Harcourt on the D 171.

Map 3H

GOURNAY-EN-BRAY (Seine-Maritime) 152 km from Le Havre; 220 km from Calais

---

Right on the Normandy border, 30 km west of Beauvais, on the N 31.

The heart of the soft cheese industry. It was here that in 1850 a farmer's wife discovered that adding fresh cream to the curds produced the palatable little creamy cheese we know as petit suisse, named after the Swiss cowherd who helped her.

The town's other claim to fame is the 11th-century (mostly) church of St Hildevert, whose crude and grotesque figures carved on the capitals of the massive columns are among the earliest attempts of Norman sculptors to portray human forms.

Le Cygne
(H)M
20 r. Notre Dame
(35) 90.27.80.

Recommended by several readers as being comfortable and friendly. No restaurant. Rooms are from 120f.

Map 6A

GRANVILLE (Manche) 104 km from Cherbourg

The largest Norman seaside resort, with a lot to offer for a weekend stay, a summer holiday with children or a stop on the road to Brittany.

After the boring sand dunes of the south-west coast of the Cotentin peninsula, it is a relief to come across the cragginess of Granville. It is a busy commercial port, with a lively town divided into two distinct sections.

The Lower Town encompasses shops, hotels, restaurants, in complete contrast to the Upper Town, which has a timeless, fly-in-amber atmosphere. There is a small museum up there, with nostalgic photographs of Granville's recent past as an elegant bathing resort; but through the narrow drawbridge, within the ramparts, the whole of the Upper Town is a living museum of a much earlier age.

The quiet, steep streets are lined with graceful grey houses, 18th-century hôtels and flowery window-boxes. With few signs of commercialisation, it all makes a delightful excursion, from the central square where there is a tabac selling postcards, a bar, an épicerie, to the encircling ramparts with gorgeous views of the harbour, the Brittany coast as far as Mont St-Michel, and the Îles de Chausey (there is a viewing table at the Place d'Isthme to help sort you out).

Walk back through the stage-setting streets for refreshment at an exceptionally good crêperie:

L'Ercharguette
(R)S
r. St-Jean
Closed Thur.
o.o.s.

Not only crêpes, but grills and excellent brochettes cooked over the log fire make this pretty, rustic little bar a good choice for a simple meal. The crêpes vary from simple and sugary to sophisticated and savoury. This is the only recommendation in the Haute Ville; in order to eat copiously it will be necessary to descend to the town.

Le Phare
(R)M
r. du Port
(33) 50.12.94.

This is the third arrow for Le Phare, which, for some unknown reason, Michelin continues to ignore. Philippe Vercella deserves better respect for his light and delicate sauces, crunchy vegetables and above all his treatment of the fresh-daily fish which form the backbone of his menus. Try the hot mousse of seafood, served with lobster sauce, and see if you don't agree with me that here is an exceptional seaside fish restaurant. The locals know how good it is and already, even without Michelin's seal of approval, it is not always easy to get in, let alone bag one of the window tables for a view over the harbour. If it is a fine evening book a place on the terrace where you can watch a panorama of little ferry boats bound for Jersey, the fishing fleet, private yachts and shabby cargo ships. (It is as well to have some diversion, since all the food here is freshly prepared to order, and that takes time.)

Granville

Don't be put off by the unpromising exterior, the garishness of the décor (or even the unsmiling service,) and I guarantee you'll be well satisfied. Menus from 65f, and this includes spectacular plateaux de fruits de mer.

➤ **Le Michelet**
(H)M
5 r. Jules
Michelet
(33) 50.06.55.
Closed
20/11–20/12;
Sun. o.o.s.

A change of ownership in 1982 suggested that this delightful little very-French hotel, on the hill above the town, might not retain its charm. But all is well – *very* well – and an arrow can be confirmed as well-deserved. The bedrooms are spacious and quiet, and the whole hotel has enormous character. A large double with bath costs 155f.

'M. et Mme Mercier are indeed "tres gentil". She willingly brought us tea in our room when we arrived about 17.30. There are no apparent changes, but beware of being allocated the room (No. 15) on the ground floor; it is quite spacious and comfortable but it is noisy, both from the room above and through the very thin wall from the salon, with TV.'

Normandy-
Chaumière
(HR)S
20 r. Dr Paul
Poirier
(33) 50.01.71.
Closed
5/10–28/10;
20/12–29/12;
Tue. p.m.; Wed.
o.o.s.

In the centre of the main shopping street, but with a thatched roof and a pleasant courtyard, where I was pleased to eat one hot June evening. Food not marvellous, but good value, if you stick to the menus, which incorporate vast platefuls of moules, fruits de mer, gigôt, good crudités, and rather boring desserts. They start at 48f.

There are seven rooms available at very modest prices, but I have not inspected.

Much local praise for a little family-run restaurant behind the Post Office. **La Poste**, r. de l'Abreuvoir. 'Their fruits de la mer has to be seen to be believed; it nearly covers the table with every shellfish you can imagine.' – *Fred and Judy Ward*; and for **Le Pierrot**, r. Cl. Desmaisons: 'Here are five menus under 100f and with such a selection on each course that anyone could be satisfied; the seafood dishes were particularly good and the red plonk was 18f a bottle. Closed on Wed.' – *David Dunham*.

Map 5B   **GRATÔT** (Manche) 73 km from Cherbourg

Take the D 44 out of Coutances and turn right on to the D 244 to find:

Le Tourne-
Bride
(R)S
(33) 45.11.00
Closed
22/12–5/1.

A nice old stone house set sideways on to the road, with a car park usually full of French cars; often coaches, too – a putter-offer at home but invariably a plus point in France since there the frequent 'reunions' seem to be organised (usually by some local gastronome) more to see good food than good friends.

Here, in the pleasantly rustic dining-rooms, are menus from 42f, and it all makes an agreeably calm country halt, just a mile or two outside the town.

Map 1A   **LA HAGUE** (Manche) 27 km from Cherbourg

Hidden in the valleys of the north-west tip of France are some of the prettiest villages in the whole peninsula. With their grey houses, flowery gardens and dry stone walls, they remind me of the Cotswolds.

The coach parties rumble up the main road to the Nez de Joburg to marvel at the wild rocks far below, or on to the Goury lighthouse where the tiny lifeboat station is one of the busiest in the world, thanks to the unrelenting Alderney race, but they never stop at St-Germain-des-Vaux, or La Roche, or Digulleville, or Auderville – all charmers.

On the Nez itself is a restaurant remarkable in that it should have maintained so high a standard in such a tourist-trodden spot. You can buy a coloured postcard there, with no room for writing on the back so full is it of its own description. I can hardly do better than quote: Henry-Paul Fauvel propriétaire. Bar, salon de thé, Restaurant. Cadre normand sur les plus hautes falaises d'Europe (128m) dîner aux chandelles.

➤ **Auberge des Grottes**
(R)M 👍
Le Nez de Joburg
(33) 52.71.44.
Closed mid Oct.–Easter;
Tue. except July & Aug.

Specialities – tous les fruits de mer
　　　　　　homard
　　　　　　gigôt de pré salé
　　　　　　crêpes normandes
　　　　　　dégustation à toutes heures.

I couldn't have put it better myself; all I can add is that M. Fauvel is a very friendly *propriétaire*, likes to practise his English and is quite prepared to keep his word and cook his specialities at any hour of the day.

Various combinations make up his menus, from 60f to 165f, on which you get 12 oysters, langoustines, a whole lobster and omelette Grand Marnier. Could this happen in a café at Land's End?

So unusual a restaurant in so unusual a site must, I think, deserve an arrow (and several readers agree with that).

Map 5B   **HAMBYE** (Manche) 90 km from Cherbourg

One of the prettiest roads in Normandy follows the valley of the Sienne to the village of Hambye, 17 km north of Villedieu-les-Poeles. There must be something special about the air here, since not one but three splendid hostelries, very simple, very French, share the location. From the village follow the river on the D 13 towards Sourdeval-les-Bois to the Abbey of Hambye and just by the entrance are two of my luckiest finds. The ruined Abbey itself is well worth a visit, approached through a gateway which has, alas, recently lost its thatch, thick with iris, but still glows with golden lichen. The setting, in the valley, backed with a white escarpment, river sparkling, fishermen posing, is pure picture-book. Make sure the camera is well loaded. A guided tour of the Abbey takes about an hour, but this requires a good knowledge of French.

►Auberge de l'Abbaye
(H)S(R)M
(33) 61.42.19.
Closed Tue.

How pleased I am to nominate the modest and delightful M. and Mme Allain as owners of *French Entrée 3's* **Hotel of the Year**. Not a single dissension among the dozens of letters from readers who happily followed my previous recommendations to stay there. Everyone was charmed with the welcome, the food, the peaceful site and the bill.

I returned myself to make sure I'd got it right. For new readers, here is what I found:

The Auberge is a nondescript building with a terrace overlooking the little green valley, hard by the Abbey gates. First impression is of Madame Allain who seems always alert for her clients' arrival, rushing out to carry in their suitcases (and this is not just for the writers of guidebooks!). She shows you the comfortable, simple room, perhaps No. 6, the one I had, dominated by the unlikely double wash-basin and corner bath. If you've driven from the boat, you'll be ready for a cup of tea on the terrace? Typical of the service is that almost before the thought has formulated, there is Madame Allain proffering one. The gentle unwinding begins.

Dinner will be delicious; the food is copious, honest, varied, from the 60f menu (not Sundays), which includes a fruits de mer, through the 78f, 105f to the 140f, all offering plenty of fish and sound, well-cooked meat dishes. If I recited the list of oysters, smoked ham, sole, contrefilet, brochette d'agneau, kidneys, fresh strawberries, it might sound uninspired, but I assure you it is not. Every dish, however simple, has the stamp of a loving cook. Nothing simple about the china, which is classy, nor the service, which is swift and efficient, nor the cheeseboard, which is mostly Norman and carefully chosen, nor the impressive wine list,

Restaurant de l'Abbaye

from patron's own cider to premier crus clarets. And always the little extra trouble – a tired English family arriving just as dinner was nearly over, the children asking for 'just soup'. Soup was what they got, swiftly and smilingly. Sorry, no rooms left, but Madame would fix them up in a gîte in the village. One client on a no-meat diet was given exclusively fish at no extra charge.

The six rooms cost 79f each.

I can't ever imagine the Allains and their Auberge ever being spoiled but the word is getting round. I suggest you visit it soon. Congratulations.

Restaurant de l'Abbaye
(HR)S
(33) 61.42.21.
Open all year.

Delightful little restaurant with a few simple bedrooms. All furnished in true country style – polished wood floors, lace curtains, wild flowers in pots, spotlessly clean. Nice Madame André apologised that she had to put the prices up to 55f for two people! A little terrace overlooks the little river and the scale throughout is limited, modest, but perfect, and – so far – totally unspoiled. The food does not claim to be *gastronomique*, but relies on fresh trout from the stream, smoked ham, fresh cream, farm produce. If you choose an omelette, it will be bright yellow, from its free-range origin. No menus, but omelettes will cost you 8 to 12f, trout meunière 25f. Charcoal grills are a speciality, especially the lobster, which has to be pre-ordered. Other good choices are moules à la crème, assiette de fruits de mer, a super cheeseboard, home-made pâté and cheese soufflé.

I can still remember the sheer pleasure of my first discovery of this unpretentious little place, and it is one treasure I am most sorry to see now bandied about in other guidebooks. Because it is so small and because readers of *F.E.1* and *2* have returned delighted and ready to go back, I cannot believe that it will be easy to get a booking there from now on. But I cannot see it being easily spoiled, so do persevere. A third well-deserved arrow.

Les Chevaliers
(HR)S
(33) 90.42.09.
Closed Wed.

An unremarkable building in the village, but with an exceptionally friendly owner and the kind of good value that gets readers reaching for their pens to tell me how pleased they've been. All the rooms are 69f and generous menus start at 60f.

Map 6E   **HARAS DU PIN** (Orne) 15 km east of Argentan

On the N 26. Another popular excursion. This is the National Stud, known as the Versailles of the Horse, equally impressive for those interested in architecture (Mansart-planned château with sweeping views over the pastures) and horses (over a hundred stallions at stud, English thoroughbreds, Anglo-Arabs, French hacks and hackneys, Percherons). The setting alone is worth the drive, with three great avenues converging on the cour d'honneur. If you're lucky enough to be there during the daily parade, you won't forget the sight.

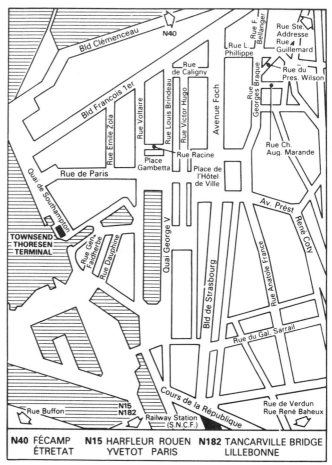

Quai de Southampton 76600 - Le Havre Tel: (35) 21 36 50

Map 8E   **LE HAVRE** (Seine-Maritime)

Old locals say that Le Havre lost its heart in 1944 and never replaced it. The new town of the architect Auguste Perret, is a strange one. For most foreigners it is merely the façade of the quai Southampton, and the bd François 1er, with perhaps a little background depth into the r. de Paris. Cardboard. The real Le Havre begins behind the Town Hall, in the most un-planned, un-coordinated way, swerving round the r. Réné Coty into the bd Réné Coty; its animation points the contrast with the leafy but lifeless ave. Foch, designed by Perret to outdo the Champs Élysées, leading to the Étoile of the pl. de l'Hôtel de Ville. What the architect forgot was that it takes people to make a living townscape and people are what the new Le Havre lacks. Who are they, those inhabitants of the coops stacked upon coops? Where do they go and what do they eat?

OK, so to know her is not necessarily to love her, but let's think positive. Accept that Le H. is not a typical French town and seemingly les Havrais are not the average Frenchmen who congregate in their Place bars and animate them and the streets in the evening promenade. On the credit side are the wide, wide avenues, and a grid road system which makes parking and street identification easy. Another bonus is the seaside, often overlooked. If you have time to kill, head for Ste-Adresse and there is the beach resort, complete with windsurfers to mock, cobbles to repose upon and a lot of water, theoretically uncontaminated.

The boring bit is the triangle between the r. Royale, av. Foch and the bvd François 1er. (François ordered the original Havre to be built in 1517, to replace the old silted-up port of Harfleur.) Sadly this is the only part that most tourists see. The scale of the town puts them off walking too far from the port. They may get as far down the r. Royale as the pl. Gambetta, where the concrete igloos of the new cultural centre effectively block off the only interesting view in the town, towards the *bassin* and the white bridge.

One modern building that is a great success is the **Musée de Beaux Arts** (10–2, 2–6 ex. Tue. and fêtes). Built entirley of glass and metal, with ingenious lighting, it looks out to sea on the point before the road swings back to Ste-Adresse. You proceed up and down ramps in this model of intelligent display to view the collection of Dufy (a native of Havre), Impressionists and Post-Impressionists, and of Boudin, born in Honfleur but attracted to Havre. Downstairs is a colourful exhibition of marine excitements – beautifully modelled boats, from fishing to steamer, and more paintings. A good bet for a wet day.

The rest of the pl. Gambetta is a pleasant enough, with the smartest shops grouped around it, a bit of green, and a bar or two. And the arcades of the r. Royale are practical in the rain.

On to the pl. de l'Hôtel de Ville – vast again, but with some attempt at a bit of bedding-out. Do you know any other French town where the central square does not have a single lively café? The Guîllaume Tell, for several generations used to provide a focus, and for me, especially in the early winter darkness, somewhere to sit and scribble in that difficult hour, with no hotel room to retreat to, before dinner and the ferry home. Now its doors are shuttered, and the pavement tables gone and another (rebuilt) Havre institution is no more. No good tea places either. There are, however, plenty of benches around on which to study the brochures and maps supplied by the *Tourist Bureau* in the square.

SHOPPING

To the right and behind the Town Hall, some of the old town survives and vivacity begins. Along the r. Réné Coty are the little heterogeneous shops, some chic, mostly very un-chic, whose juxtaposition makes a quarter like this most interesting. Here is where the Havrais shop, but again, how odd — no cafés, no restaurants.

Monoprix, the French Woolies, is here and a top department store, **Le Printemps. Les Nouvelles Galeries**, back in the pl. Gambetta, is another large store, with an excellent household department in a separate building.

I started to list best food shops, but the town is so scattered, the choice really depends on where the car is parked. However, assuming you are walking from the ferry, down what in the 18th century was a very elegant street, the r. Royale, you may be tempted to buy some oysters at 28f a dozen at the **Poissonerie Verel**, or perfume from the wide selection at **Perfumerie Univers**, which also sells interesting costume jewellery, less expensive than it looks. Good cheap vegs and seasonal fruits at **Fruits Primeurs**, the nearest tabac for p.c. stamps, and at **Antares**, those wonderful extravagant Leonidas Belgian chocs — the perfect take-home present.

Turn left into the pl. Gambetta for a very useful charcuterie — the **Rôtisserie Gaston**, which is open on Sundays and every other day except Wednesday from 11 a.m. to 10.30 p.m. Invaluable for last-minute purchases, and sells wine.

Over the other side of the Place is **Levèvre**, the biggest and best-known charcuterie in the town. Always queues here for made-up dishes, saucissons, pâtés, wines. Its own cellars are round the corner for quantity purchases, but a better selection is to be found over the other side of the *bassin*, at a splendid wine emporium called **Cann**, in the r. Faidherbe, open from 7 a.m. There's an excellent perfume shop opposite too, both oddly isolated in this area, predominantly devoted to bars.

Best shopping bet, if you're limited for time or if the weather's bad, is the **Halles Centrales**. Fine them a street or two behind the pl. Gambetta, by walking along the r. Voltaire. The best cheese shop — **Cheinisse** — is here, with a commendable assortment of cheeses, local and regional, served with pleasant advice on when to eat them. Wines too.

Cheap wine is best bought here at **Nicolas**, who always have packs of special offers available. It's all very convenient to push a trolley round the Halles, with easy parking right outside. Fruit and veg, fish and bread all on sale, and a supermarket for basics. Cheerful bar here is the **St Amour**, with tables outside for summer snacking.

Two hypermarkets serve the town. **Mammouth** is at Montivilliers, sign-posted to the right from the Tancarville road, open until 9 p.m. Monday to Friday, 10 p.m., on Saturdays; and **Auchan**, which I prefer, in the Haute Ville. Take the Cours de la République (past the station) through the tunnel and follow the signs to the Centre Commerciale. Open Monday to Saturday until 10 p.m. it's a vast complex, with an entire village of boutiques outside the main food area, selling goods as diverse as tisanes and burglar alarms.

Not far from here is the **Forest of Montgeon**, 700 acres of trees, a boating pond, a camp site, all well laid out and ideal for picnics and family outings. Here is the Southampton Tree, planted to commemorate the twinning of the two towns. Just to keep options open, the Leningrad Tree is bang opposite. M. Morgand, of the Hôtel Les Phares (see p.173) told me how he was walking up there one day with an English naval friend, who saw some workmen struggling to plant a recalcitrant tree. He took the spade and completed the job, only discovering later that he, a true British officer, had planted the Leningrad Tree!

HOTELS

The uniformity of the blocks makes many of the hotels look alike from the outside, and not much effort has been expended to individualise their rooms either. I have stayed in most of them but sometimes find it hard to remember which is which, so dull a bunch are they. However, no one is likely to spend more than the odd night in Le Havre and the following recommendations from *F.E.2* have been re-endorsed by satisfied customers this year. They all fulfil their function of supplying a clean, inexpensive night's sleep near the ferry terminal. Prices are for a double room.

Séjour Fleuri
(H)S
71 r. Émile Zola
(35) 41.33.81.
P. V.

English spoken. 70 to 102f. (Change of management.)

Hôtel Foch
(H)S
4 r. de Caligny
(35) 45.50.69.
AE, E, V.

72 to 182f.

Petit Vatel
(H)S
86 r. L-Brindeau
(35) 41.72.07.
V.

85 to 222f.

St-Louis
(H)S
18 r. Ch. Aug-
Marande
(35) 42.53.58.

70.50 to 154f.

Angleterre
(H)S
1 r. Louis-
Philippe
(35) 42.48.42.

70 to 140f.

Richelieu
(H)M
132 r. de Paris
(35) 42.38.71.

85 to 240f. New management means that complaints about sagging beds should no longer apply.

The trusted M. Morgand of the Hôtel des Phares sends his overflow to either of the following:

Hôtel Voltaire
H(S)
14 r. Voltaire
(35) 41.30.90

'On first floor of office block. Very good rooms, clean and pleasant welcome. Breakfast en famille.'

Also re-approved by readers, but in different categories are:

Hôtel Bordeaux 👍
(H)L
147 r. Louis Brindeau
(35) 22.69.44.

Havre's 'luxury' hotel. Irreproachable in its class of modern/efficient; useful for businessmen. 235 to 330f.

France et Bourgogne ✋
(HR)M
21 cours de la Republique
(35) 25.40.34.
AE, V.

In the seedy Cours de la Republique but a pleasant surprise inside. Old-fashioned but well-equipped rooms; ask for one at the back. It also has a restaurant, usefully open on Sundays, but closed July and Saturdays. 125 to 225f with bath.

Hôtel du Charolais
(H)S
134 cours de la Republique
(35) 25.29.34.

Far far better inside than out (not difficult!). Confirmed by readers that it is clean, wholesome, friendly, cheap. English spoken. 66 to 119f.

The ones to avoid, according to popular vote, are Hôtels Vikings, Celtic, Parisien, Gambetta.

See also Ste-Adresse.

RESTAURANTS

I find it totally perplexing that in a town relying heavily on ferry passengers for restaurant trade, so few of them bother to stay open when they are most needed, i.e. on Sunday evenings, when the majority of travellers are catching the evening ferry home after holidays or weekends. The town dies very early, so if you come off the evening arrival, around 9.30 p.m. local time, without having eaten, you won't find much choice.

Having now devoted a good deal of time to investigating the less obvious restaurant localities, I am happy to be able to report that the scene is not as bleak as I had thought. The secret is to get away from the few streets nearest the ferry, where the pickings are too easy. None of the restaurants listed are more than five minutes by car from the port, and I have tried to make directions explicit. The arrowed recommendations are those where the food and value are good; the others are for convenience, of locality or opening hours.

If, like me, you prefer to stroll around looking at a variety of menus before making a decision, if your budget is modest, if you like to eat with more Frenchmen than Brits, your best bet is to make for the area known as the quartier St-François. This is so near the ferry that you can keep an eye on the familiar orange. If it sails, you can relax and finish your meal.

Turn right out of the terminal, cross over the bridge and you will find a string of restaurants and bars to the left along the quai Michel-Féré which (to the right) becomes the r. Général-Faidherbe. They look a bit grim in the winter, especially in the cold morning light off the early ferry, but brighten up considerably in summer, when out come the coloured parasols. Behind them are dotted a number of newish restaurants, patronised by locals, all offering far better value than you will find in the tourist triangle. I list the best of them together for easy assessment:

Restaurant du Roy (R)S
quai Michel-Féré
(35) 42.12.39.
Closed Wed. p.m.; Sun.

Rather joyless interior, but you can always watch the fish in the aquarium. Excellent value on menus starting at 50f.

Restaurant Simon
(R)M
10 quai Michel-Féré
(35) 21.24.16.
Closed Sun.

Most popular with locals but Townsend's crew members all recommend it highly too. When I ate there recently, the entire clientêle seemed to be good friends of Mme Simon, who bustles about, blond hair puffed high, dark glasses missing not a trick, between the two small rooms, efficient but still finding time to chat to her regulars. There is a perfectly adequate four-course menu at 64f, but everyone I saw was eating à la carte because it was so cheap (and the puds are boring anyway). I had superb baby mussels steaming abundantly in a copper casserole (enough for two at 25f) and a tournedos dijonnais at 45f. Good Réservé de Simon was 18f a bottle; for aperitif the cheapest Kir I've come across at 5.50f. As I'd just been ripped off 13f for a small vermouth by the sour-faced barman at the Grignot in the pl. Gambetta (N.B!), I was particularly appreciative (*and* I got free crisps at Simons). I wished I'd had the speciality of the day – always look out for these here – which was brochette de lotte – very interesting at 45f for a well-filled skewer of monkfish, mushrooms, tomato, well-herbed and served with mountains of perfect frites.

It gets an arrow as a likeable place and a good choice for a really French meal at reasonable prices, with a lively atmosphere, and, if ferry-necessary, quick service. Book or get there early.

NEW MANAGEMENT

L'Anse du Marin
(R)S
r. du Général-Faidherbe
(35) 21.31.73.

Cupboard-sized restaurant squeezed in lengthways. Placcy cloths, noisy locals, cheerful atmosphere, absolutely basic copious nosh at 35f upwards.

La Fondue
(R)M
51 r. du Général-Faidherbe.
(35) 21.30.26.
Closed Tue.

Probably a winter place, with marvellously warming fondues – savoyarde, bourguignonne, raclette – and a log fire. Menus from 55f.

Chez Titine
(R)S
78 r. de
Bretagne
(35) 42.00.19.
Closed Tue.
p.m.; Wed.

Three streets behind the Faidherbe. This is where the docks officials take ships officers when their vessels are in dry dock. Heartily recommended by everyone I asked. Menus only, at 55f and 70f but wide choice, good atmosphere.

Le Saint-Louis
(R)M
16 r. Saint-Louis
(35) 22.56.00.
Closed Mon.;
Sat. lunch.

Clever to choose a Missisippi riverboat theme in the r. St-Louis. Little cubicles and candlelight make for an intimate atmosphere – you could be lonely on your own. Quite smart in the evenings, but still only 61f for a good three-course menu, offering specialities not at all American, like tourte de saumon, and ris de veau à l'oseille.

La Lucciola
(R)S
8 r. de la Crique
(35) 43.47.15.
Closed Sat.
lunch; Sun.

A pretty new Italian restaurant, one street behind Simons. Good for family eating, with pizza and pasta around £2.

Le Sancerre
(R)S
10 r. de
Bretagne
(35) 41.23.33.
Closed Sun. AE.

Simple décor in a restaurant specialising in the wines and dishes of Sancerre. Entirely local-patronised, some nights too quiet, others packed, but always excellent value, with highly-recommended plats du jour; fish reliable here, particularly the raie au beurre noir or an immense plateau de fruits de mer.

La Petite Auberge
(R)M
3 r. de Ste-Adresse
(35) 46.27.32.
Closed
22/2–7/3; Aug.;
Sun. p.m.; Mon.

👍

No. 1 choice in the town still. To find it most easily, drive to Town Hall, take the road behind and to the left (r. Georges Braque), follow its swing to the right (now confusingly becoming r. Président Wilson and r. d'Étretat) and **La Petite Auberge** (see p.110) is on the left. Difficult parking, unless you are staying at the Phares, where it is within walking distance.

The only two minor criticisms I have of this tiny, Norman-style restaurant are that it is always full (so booking essential) and that the service is a bit unhurried (allow plenty of time). Otherwise its honest good value is unquestionable.

Michelin gives a red R for the 69f menu (95f at weekends), and there really is no need to look further. Four copious courses include interesting dishes like mousseline de saumon, quenelles, oysters, poulet vallée d'Auge, and there is cheese *and* pud. The 110f version is five courses. No question about repeating the arrow here.

L'Athanor
(R)M
120 r.
Guillemard
(35) 42.50.27.
Closed Sat.
lunch; Sun.;
Mon. AE, DC.

See directions above. R. Guillemard is one turning on left before La Petite Auberge.

Havre's prettiest restaurant. Far more attractive inside than the exterior in sleazy street would suggest. Small, intimate, stone-walled, brick-floored, raftered, candles guttering, classy porcelain and matching green cloths. On fine days eat in little rear conservatory, covered in cool creeper and orchestrated by doves in cage. One look and I began to coo-along, too.

The 95f menu is excellent value, with some interesting possibilities like feuilléte of moules oeuf poché, or the confit d'oie maison à l'oseille. The terrine of fish was a bit pasty, but otherwise my last meal was such a pleasure (confit of duck and charlotte aux framboises followed) that I think an arrow is justified.

L'Etsoetem
(R)S–M
1 av. Foch
(35) 43.09.73.
Closed Mon.

At last! Someone (M. Arsac) has had the nous to realise what Le Havre really needs – a cheerful bar/restaurant open at times to suit customers, not *patrons*. L'Etsoetem, a name I find difficult to remember even if I could pronounce it, has taken the prominent site of the late unlamented François ler restaurant at the seaside end of the Boulevard (turn left at Town Hall or drive round prom (left from ferry) and transformed it into a bower of (plastic) greenery and pinkery, white trellissed walls and cane chairs, all very light and bright. Brightest of all are Friday and Saturday evenings, when there is live music – piano, guitar, whoever turns up.

The hours are extremely good news – open very late indeed, until 2 a.m. if called for. Last orders at 12.30 p.m. No more going to bed hungry if you omitted to eat on the late-arriving ferry. *And* Sunday what's more, again gratifying one of the town's longest-felt wants.

The menus are bargains. For 90f you get paupiettes d'anchois or Salade Irma or Oeufs hosois, then sorbet, then Truite Etsoetem or Tournedos Givry or gigot à la menthe, then salad, then cheese, then choice of dessert which I make six courses. Seven on the 110f version (fish *and* meat) there is a shorter 50f lunch menu or, joy for me, a choice of six interesting salads from 20f to 25f; e.g. Salade Lapérouse – tomato, ham, green beans, artichoke hearts, onions – for 20f. Langoustines au paprika are a mere 30f. Tournedos Givry (flamed in cognac, sauce diable) is 40f and brochettes of lamb are good for 35f. As a demi-pichet of red or rosé wine ($\frac{1}{2}$ litre) costs 18f, you could eat well for under £5 a head. An arrow for enterprise, convenience and atmosphere.

Guimbarde
(R)M
61 r. Louis
Brindeau
(35) 42.15.36.
Closed Aug.;
Sun.; Mon.
lunch. AE, V.

Best restaurant in the tourist triangle. North-west corner of pl. Gambetta, on the right of the r. Louis Brindeau. Small, so booking advisable. Menus at 65f and 96f. Recommended: avocados overflowing with patently fresh crab, crêpes stuffed with smoked salmon and drenched with vodka, sole angevin served on a bed of sorrel, scallops in champagne sauce, profiterolles stuffed with ice cream.

Le Cambridge
(R)L
90 r. Voltaire
(35) 43.50.24.
Closed Sat.
lunch; Sun.

The r. Voltaire runs first left on the pl. Gambetta. Le Cambridge is the town's smartest and best fish restaurant. Elegant atmosphere, marine photos, comfortable banquettes, knowledgeable service, highest possible standards, with irreproachable soupe de poisson, stuffed oysters, pearly turbot, tender scallops, interesting deserts. Main dishes about 70f, so expect a bill around 150f for three courses; interestingly enough, the wines are not expensive here. A Muscadet is only 36f a white Saucerre (there are red and rosé too), which is a house speciality, at rock-bottom 48f. An arrow for excellence.

La Chaumette
(R)L
17 r. Racine
(35) 43.66.80.
Closed
20/21–2/1;
26/4–2/5;
11/8–4/9; Sat.;
Sun. DC.

On the pl. Gambetta and hard to miss, since its odd thatched roof sticks out a mile on the uniformly modern pl. Gambetta. I even like the fake oak beams inside, as a relief. Still popular (so book) but getting very expensive indeed. They do have a 84f menu, but it's so dull that you might well be tempted to eat à la carte and the main dishes there are around 85f. With starters at 60f-ish and puds at 34f, that adds up to a sizeable bill, especially as the wine is pricey too. Pity, because the food is fresh and very good.

L'Huitrière
(R)M
4 r. de Paris
(35) 21.48.48.
Closed Mon.

Opposite ferry. Several original ideas here. Only smoked fish and shellfish served, all good and fresh, especially the oysters from which the restaurant takes its name. Also original is the late closing time – last orders 1 p.m. – so that oysters could be accommodated after leaving the evening. There is a menu at 85f, but you should allow 120f for the carte if you wish to eat a dessert, like chocolate mousse, too, which still makes fish fancying a good deal cheaper here than at Le Cambridge.

Other readers' recommendations, which I have not personally sampled, are:

La Bonne Hôtésse
(R)S
98 r. Président
Wilson
(35) 21.31.73.
Closed
30/7–27/8; Sun.
p.m.; Mon.

Simple food well prepared, but portions said to be on the small side. Menus 44.50 and 71.50f. Market in the square outside.

'Strongly recommended giving an excellent value for money meal. I have been there many times over the last five years.' – Wing-Commander G. K. Briggs.

(Next door is a new Italian restaurant, Biagios, which looked promising.)

La Toque Blanche
R(M)
79 r. Émile Zola
(35) 21.23.35.

Émile Zola is about the fifth road from the port crossing the r. de Paris.
Open every day, warm welcome, intimate atmosphere in tiny alcoves. Good meat but few fish dishes. Menus from 65f.

SNACK BARS AND CRÊPERIES

La Bigouden
88 r. de
Bretagne
Open 12–2 and
7–1 a.m.
Closed Wed.;
Sat.; Sun. lunch.

See Chez Titine for directions.
Breton decor, wide choice of crêpes and galettes, not expensive.

La Scaeroise
81–83 r.
Dauphine
Closed Sun.
lunch; Mon.

Next road to La Bigouden. Ginette uses her Breton grandmother's recipes for her crêpes and galettes. You can buy them to take away.

Snack bar
Deauville
11 av. Réné
Coty

'Opposite the impressive Banque de France building. Very convenient when Le Printemps and Monoprix are shut for lunch. Typical of the better sort of French café, full of life and character. Food and wine are good value.' – Derek Hallifax.

EARLY BREAKFASTS (open before 6 a.m.)

Bar de l'Esplanade, *Cours de la Republique;* **Hall Bar,** *r. de la Gare;* **Le Ninas;** *quai Casimir-Delavigne.* Follow the Rouen signs round from r. Gen. Faidherbe.

EARLY CROISSANTS

Begin, *5 r. d'Alger, Closed Tue.* Corner of r. d'Étretat. Open from 5 a.m., stays open until 9 p.m.; **Leroy,** *Cours de la Republique.* Open 5.30, 5 on Sundays.

LATE PETROL

Esso Havre–New York, *199 bvd. de Strasbourg.* Open 24 hours every day except Monday. **Station Service,** *8–10 bvd. Winston-Churchill.* Open from 7 to midnight Monday to Friday, 7 to 7 on Saturdays.

Map 3B   **LE HAYE DU PUITS** (Manche) 46 km from Cherbourg

A nice little town, totally taken over by the fascinating market on Wednesdays.

Hôtel de la
Gare
(HR)S
(33) 46.04.22.
Closed
15/12–3/1; Fri.;
Sat. lunch.

Such totally conflicting reports that I sometimes wondered if they were about the same hotel. Some are bitterly critical about the rooms 'like a YWCA hostel'), the view 'grim' the shower 'door-less' and the bath 'plug-less', with proprietor 'in a dirty apron'. Others were delighted: 'charming girl gave us a delightful welcome', husband, who cooks, 'also most friendly and helpful', 'excellent meal', 'informal and ready service, very good cooking'.

I think it boils down to price. A double room here costs less than 100f and the meal is 50f. The hotel is not a bit what one would expect from a Hôtel du Gare. In the station yard maybe, but with only three trains a week, rest is assured; in fact Michelin gives it a rocking chair for tranquillity. It's a strange chalet-type building with a hideous modern stained-glass window inside. Friends who live nearby swear by it and certainly it's often necessary to book ahead. M. Hardouin insists you eat in if you book a room.

I have also heard good reports locally of the **Hôtel du Commerce**, and one reader writes: *'excellent value lunch in simple but pleasant restaurant. Particularly recommended tripes a la mode.' – J. Mills.*

Map 3E **HENNEQUEVILLE** (Calvados) 72 km from Le Havre

On the coast road, north of Deauville.

**Restaurant
Pillon**
R(S)
Rte d'Honfleur

If the summer crowds at Trouville oppress, or the prices at Deauville horrify, if something altogether simpler is indicated, drive a few kilometres along the coast road and stop at the hamlet of Hennequeville, where Madame Pillon serves basic food (moules, chicken, salad, cheese) at basic prices (50f) in her little ginghamed dining-room, or in fine weather on her terrace.

Map 2F **HÉRICOURT-en-CAUX** (Seine-Maritime) 52 km from Le Havre

A sleepy little village on the crossing of two minor roads, the D 131 and D 149, where the river Durdent flows tranquilly through unspoiled countryside.

**Auberge de la
Durdent**
(HR)M
*(35) 96.42.44
Closed
10/12–28/2;
10/10–30/10.*

It is five years now since I first wrote about the auberge and its charming, recently-widowed *patronne*, Madame Lebarq. At that time she was wondering whether she could continue single-handed, and I admired her decision to soldier on and put everything she had into making the auberge prosper. Passers-by were rare so far off the tourist track, and few English had discovered the attractions of Madame and her inn.

I found it utterly delightful. The site, with river through both garden and (under glass) dining-room floor, the old Norman building, the cosy bar full of locals, Madame's friendliness, the simple food she served, the

Auberge de la Durdent

modest prices she charged. Readers of *F.E.1* concurred and Madame wrote to tell me how grateful she was that so many charming clients were now encouraging her auberge to flourish.

Not only under the dining-room but under many bridges has much water flowed since then. The word spread, other guidebooks caught on, a tour operator moved in. By the time *F.E.2* came out, the first red lights were beginning to flash and I decided the arrow had to go, with a stop-press caution. Nowadays the letters are roughly three to one against. Mostly they are written more in sorrow than in anger, their authors liking Madame Lebarq as much as I do. 'Water tepid', 'food rather hit and miss', 'the bed sagged badly and should have been ditched long ago' are typical comments. Worst of all are the indications that advance bookings are not always honoured or 'there was much humming and ha-ing until Madame learnt that we were willing to stay for five nights – then her problems evaporated'.

I don't think I shall go back until I hear that matters have improved. Anyone prepared for not very good food and not very comfortable accommodation served by a very charming lady in a very charming situation might like to know that rooms (in a modern annexe across the stream) cost 95f and the menus 44 to 88f. Please will someone write and tell me it's not as bad as I fear.

Map 3D

HERMANVILLE-LA-BRÊCHE (Calvados) 125 km from Le Havre, 125 km from Cherbourg

---

Between Riva Bella and Lion-sur-Mer, Hermanville is just a sandy beach and a huddle of houses, mostly firmly shuttered for all but a few months of the year.

Hôtel de la Brêche
(HR)S
(31) 97.20.40.

Chantal and Michel Boucher took over this run-down Logis in 1983 and have been slaving away ever since to get it redecorated and running smoothly as a family hotel and restaurant. They are a young French–Canadian couple (no language problems here), and most refreshingly anxious to please their customers and make a success of their investment. Already favourable reports are coming in, particularly appreciative of the friendly reception.

The rooms are all different but good-sized with balconies and sea-views. Until decorations are complete the hotel is still graded as a one-star, and prices are correspondingly low. Most double rooms now cost 70f; those with shower or extra bed a little more.

Michel cooks and again his menu prices are a bargain, at 45f.

A good choice for a family holiday or inexpensive base from which to explore the Normandy beaches and Caen.

'I am sure that this young couple will entertain many visitors from this country, who, like us, will look forward to re-visiting them as soon and as often as possible. They gave us a warm welcome, cuisine was excellent and all prices very moderate.' – D. I. Thomas.

'We booked for one week but were made so welcome we stayed for two; we made friends with a lot of French people who were there, in a very pleasant, easy-going atmosphere.' – Jim Dobie.

Map 3F	**LE HODE** (Seine-Maritime) 18 km from Le Havre

Dubuc
(R)L
*(35) 20.06.97.
Closed
5/8–27/8;
15/2–28/2; Sun.
p.m.; Mon. P.
AE, DC, V.*

On the old road, the D 982, from Le Havre to Tancarville.

This used to be the best restaurant in the ~~be~~ REMOVED ~~has now~~ lost its Michelin star and is said to ~~be~~ STAR REMOVED ~~expensive,~~ although still good. Could I ~~have~~ MICHELIN ~~some~~ reports, please!

More reports needed.

Map 3F	**HONFLEUR** (Calvados) 57 km from Le Havre

Still my No. 1 choice for a short-break destination. One or two readers don't share my affection for the place, finding it too tourist-ridden, but it would be surprising if anywhere with half the charm of Honfleur, combined with easy access to Paris and Le Havre, did not have its share of tourists. Count me among them any time.

Years of familiarity have not yet spoiled the impact of that gem of a harbour full of boats, water reflecting images of the lanky old houses surrounding it; cafés and restaurants humming, no matter what the season, picturesque and ancient Lieutenant's house guarding the entrance, fishing boats unloading catches, gulls screeching overhead. I can't think of a more pleasant exercise than to join the strollers round the cobbled quays, watching the artists at work, peering down on the boats below, watching it all happen from one of the cafés on the harbour's edge.

In some ways Honfleur reminds me of St-Tropez – that other artists' haunt – but for me it has far more genuine charm and less superficial gloss. The outer harbour is a real working port and in the Vieux Bassin the pleasure boats come in many shapes and sizes, from ocean-racer to humble dinghy.

However hard to tear oneself away from the harbour, don't omit to climb up to Honfleur's other heart, the pl. Ste-Catherine; here is the site of the market, some colourful bars and restaurants spilling out on to the cobbles in summer, and a most unusual church, which gave the square its name. L'Église Ste-Catherine is built entirely of wood, boat-hulls forming the roof of the nave. It was the local shipbuilders who constructed it from the material they knew best, to give thanks that the English had at last departed after the Hundred Years War. It's not the oldest church in the town – that honour goes to St-Étienne on the quayside, built during the time when the English actually occupied Honfleur, from 1419 to 1450.

Little snippets of historical interest keep cropping up in this fascinating town. Throughout the eight centuries of its existence it seems to have bred a particularly forceful band of men. Intrepid sons of Honfleur, mariners, explorers, men of science were for ever taking to sea in search of new experiences. One discovered Brazil, one opened up the

Mariners' Chapel
Honfleur

mouth of the St Lawrence, Newfoundland and one, Samuel de Champlain, filled his ship with pioneering Normans to sail to Canada and start a colony there.

In the 17th century, Colbert ordered the demolition of most of the town's old fortifications built to keep out the English, and constructed the Vieux Bassin. He built three salt warehouses (*gréniers de sel*) to store the salt necessary for preserving the fishermen's catch; two of these still remain behind the Mairie. There has been some clever restoration of this area recently and it is now a very pleasant place to stroll, between the stone and timbered houses, checking the menus of the numerous bistros that have opened there.

The 19th century saw the beginning of a new role for Honfleur – that of an artistic focus. Painters like Boudin and Jongkind, musicians like Erik Satie, writers like Baudelaire, were born or lived here. The town art gallery is named after Boudin; it is in the r. Albert Ier, an interesting building, half-modern, half-chapel, though I can't claim that the examples of Boudin's work there do him justice. He was the centre of the group of young artists fascinated by the effects of the crisp Northern light on the estuary waters, who attempted to capture their impressions on canvas, and later become known as the Impressionists and Post-Impressionists. Their meeting place was an inn owned by Mère Toutain, now metamorphosised into a fashionable hotel, the Ferme St-Siméon. Monet, Sisley, Cezanne, Pissarro, all knew it well; Courbet portrayed it on canvas in 'Le Jardin de la Mère Toutain'.

For a pleasant drive from the town centre take the steep and winding D 513 coast road along the picturesque Côte de Grace, to find the 17th-century chapel of Notre Dame de Grace, the Mariners' Chapel. The walls and nave inside are crammed with thanksgivings for lives saved at sea. Whit Monday is dedicated to a special pilgrimage here for all men of the sea.

Honfleur's tourist office is in the Cours des Fossés, by the bus station, and they have lists of other excursions and walks in the district.

Unrepentant though I am in continuing to favour Honfleur, I must confess I regret the way its hoteliers capitalise on the town's popularity. Time was when to stay at the Cheval Blanc was an inexpensive delight; on my last visit it was vastly overpriced and uncaring. The Dauphin was never smart but it was full of character and charm; nowadays the lack of *accueil* makes the pokiness of the bedrooms unacceptable. Some readers like the Hostellerie Lechat, and certainly it is well situated and looks most attractive, but for my taste it suffers from the same malaise of high prices and low standards as the rest.

I did manage to find one or two new possibilities but the hotel that gets the most votes from readers is:

La Tour
(H)M
3 quai Tour
(31) 89.21.22.
Closed
22/11–4/1

Rather boringly modern, but said to be clean and efficient. No restaurant, but that's no hardship in Honfleur. Rooms are 180f. The only complaint is that there are never enough pillows. *'Rooms are small and utilitarian but more than adequate and very comfortable; breakfast pleasant and nicely served.'*

Ferme St-Siméon
(HR)L
*rte A. Marais
(31) 89.23.61.
Rest. closed
3/12–1/2; Wed.
o.o.s.; hotel
closed
3/12–1/2.*

I am very pleased to have had the experience of staying here, in the days when it only cost an arm and a leg; then it was (just) an affordable treat for very special occasions, and treat indeed, for the 17th-century inn has been tastefully restored and cleverly combines apparent rusticity with subtle elegance in a way guaranteed to make you feel pampered but not vulgar. Some of the bedrooms are among the most beautiful in this book, with rose-covered chintzes and the soft aristocratic colours of sage green, lemon yellow, pearly grey, that look so right with the hard Northern light. On my last visit I wasn't happy about some of the changes, when shocking pink and startling mauves were beginning to encroach, but as the bill for a night here is likely to be around 1,000f, with demi-pension insisted on in season, adding another 1,000 or so, I need hardly worry any more if I don't like the colour of the bedroom

Le Ferme Saint Siméon

curtains. Normandy lacks luxury hotels and so it seems that the few that do exist can command virtually any price they like. The poor Impressionist coterie would have had little in common with the rich international clients of today.

In case this sounds like sour grapes, let me hasten to say that if anyone has the chance to stay and/or eat at La Ferme (me included) they would be very foolish not to do so. It is a very special place, with very special food prepared by Pierre Arnaud, and ex-Troisgros chefs don't come cheap.

Hôtel l'Ecrin
(H)L
r. Eugène
Boudin
(31) 89.32.39.

The Ferme St-Siméon has had the luxury market all to itself in Honfleur up till now, but the Ecrin is presenting a challenge. Sited in an impressive 18th-century *hôtel*, set back in its courtyard from a quiet street near the town's centre, it undoubtedly has a good start. Inside, no expense has been spared over a four-year restoration span, to impress and astonish with the lavishness of the furnishings (four-posters, drapes and swags), decoration (gilt, mirrors, crimson plush) and mod cons (filmstar bathrooms, colour TVs). The ritziest of these rooms costs 380f. On the top floor are rather simpler rooms, still extremely comfortable, at 250f. Breakfast, at 20f, is the only meal served.

The owners are trying hard to please, so this should be a good time to visit. Honeymoon-worthy: Those cherubs! That fourposter!

Ferme de la Grande Cour
(HR)S

When I first came across the Ferme de la Grande Cour, a kilometre or two from the centre of Honfleur, up the steep and winding road along the picturesque Côte de Grace, past the Mariners' Chapel, down a long picketed drive to a nice old manor house, with late-lunchers happily somnolent under the apple trees in the garden, I thought I had found my perfect hotel. It was well run by a pleasant young couple, simple but very cheap, with delicious food and a happy atmosphere. An arrow meant that many readers were directed there. Imagine my horror, shortly after publication of *F.E.2*, to re-visit and find the place unrecognisable. Slovenly, uncaring, and running pêle-mêle downhill, with a change of proprietorship. The same letters started coming, some sorrowful, some angry, all telling the same sad story of a disappointment. All I could do was write and explain and accept that here was another favourite biting the dust.

But now there is a glimmer. The youthful Madame Salamon has replied to my reproachful letters, telling me of her problems. Being strangers to the region, she and her husband had terrible staff problems initially (that would account for the glum zombie we encountered). *And* she was pregnant. Bit by bit they are redecorating the entire hotel, installing new bathrooms, refurbishing the dreary annexe, building a new reception area and dining-room. A new chef has brought new dishes to the repertoire.

I think it all augurs well. Being dropped by Michelin must have given them a nasty jolt, but now they have been accepted as a Logis de France and that is always a good recommendation. The site is pure delight, the pleasure of lunch al fresco there has never been in doubt, and the new young management is out to redeem past mistakes. It could all be very good news again for this hotel-starved region, and certainly the letters have stopped blackening my morning's post. But I do apologise to those who hit the bad patch. STOP PRESS. Wrong – latest reports say stay away.

Le Belvédère
(HR)M
36 rte Émile
Renouf
(31) 89.00.73/
89.08.13.
Closed Mon.
o.o.s.

Disenchanted with La Ferme de la Grande Cour, I set about finding a substitute in the medium-price bracket, and I think Le Belvédère will do nicely.

High above the town, just off the N 180 Paris road, its situation is peaceful, its garden green, its management friendly. M. Collet, the proprietor, is also chef and offers specialities like huitres farcies, ris de veau façon perigourdine and soufflé Rothschild, among his humbler menus (from 46f), in a dining-room altogether more elegant than outward appearances might suggest. It was packed with a *réunion* when I was there – always a good sign. The bedrooms are fine, at 93, 107 and 142.50f, some of them in a little pavilion at the end of the garden, in which summer refreshments are served.

For a really cheap stop in this generally over-priced town here are two ideas. Make no mistake – these are small, simple, family-run establishments, providing good value bed, breakfast and evening meal, with no frills. Since the rooms are so cheap, demi-pension is insisted on. Both are central, both have some rooms quieter than others, so ask to see several. In each case I have personal recommendations from satisfied clients:

Hôtel Hamelin
(HR)S
(31) 89.16.25.
16 pl. Hamelin.
Rest. closed
Wed.; Tue. p.m.
o.o.s.

230f for two, demi-pension. If you want a family room, No. 3 has two double beds.

Hôtel des Cascades
(HR)S
19 cours des Fossés
(31) 89.05.83.
Closed Tue.
o.o.s.

245f for demi-pension for two.

Restaurants there are a-plenty, but these too have to be chosen with care. The steady supply of visitors makes for easy pickings. Even in winter we have been turned away from our first, second and third choices for Sunday lunch and had to settle in desperation for disappointing overpriced meals. Mercifully, though, there are some shining exceptions to this rule, which alone make a visit to Honfleur worthwhile (but do book).

Now that my old favourite, Le Vieux Clocher, has changed hands (and is no longer to be recommended) my first choice is undoubtedly:

Restaurant Carlin
R(M)
32 pl. Pierre-Berthelet
(31) 89.39.69.
Closed
13/11–20/12;
Thur. o.o.s.; Fri.
lunch.

Approached from ground level just off the Place Ste-Catherine, the little Restaurant Carlin is already five stories high from its other aspect overlooking the harbour. Tables at its windows therefore have a perfect view of all the goings-on down below in the harbour.

But more – much more – appeals. Carlin is pretty but polished, intimate but comfortable, unpretentious but efficient and the food is super. Artichoke hearts stuffed with pâté de foie gras were good and original; so was my cassolette de moules aux poireaux – substantial little dish of juicy mussels and tiny leeks in a winey sauce, creamy but sharpened. Between us we sampled salmon with sorrel, a feuilleté of sweetbreads, and a gigôt of lamb, all excellent, all served with some individual touch. Interesting puddings too and good service, adding up to an arrow.

l'Absinthe
(R)M
10 quai de la Quarantaine
(31) 89.39.00
Closed
15/11–15/12;
Tue. o.o.s.

New management here in this most attractive little restaurant overlooking the bassin de l'Est. Very friendly, good service, elegant, but I was disappointed in the food. I could be wrong since local opinion is in favour. Menus from 71f, but the bill will be considerably higher.

Le Tilbury
(R)M
8 pl. Sainte-Catherine.

Attractively sited on the Place, this grill/restaurant has merited nothing but praise from readers:

'Set menu at 50f fantastic value; the kitchen and restaurant are open plan so that you sit and watch your meal being prepared.' – June Parvin.

'We tried the 72f and 83f menus which were excellent. All meat dishes cooked by the chef in full view. The restaurant was fully booked and lots of people were turned away. Turn up before 7.30 to be sure of a place.' – Vivianne Pratt.

Au Vieux Honfleur
(R)M
13 quai St-Etienne
(31) 89.15.31.
Closed
2/1–31/1; Wed.
o.o.s.

Right on the quayside of the inner harbour, with tables outside in fine weather. Pretty, smartish, upmarket but not overpriced for quality.

'We all judged the menus at 95f to be excellent. My chicken with tarragon was very good and the service above normal. We would certainly re-visit.'

► **Château de Prêtreville**
(H)M
Gonneville-sur-Honfleur
(31) 89.37.06.

The charming Didier Romy, from my favourite Auberge du Vieux Clocher, suggested I should look at the Château; I'm very glad he did because it does seem to offer something quite out of the ordinary and most interesting in certain circumstances.

A delightful young couple, Rémi and Mina Bodet, opened up the 19th-century château three years ago into a series of ten 'studios', which they let by the day, week or month. These are all spacious, elegant, lavishly furnished, with well-equipped bathroom, kitchenette, dining area. They sleep from two to four. The château's stunning salon is at their guests' disposal, as are the grounds, patios, heated swimming pool, and, for a small charge, sauna, clubhouse, tennis court, so there is an exclusive clubby feeling about the place – privacy but not isolation.

Both Bodets speak perfect English (Mina used to teach in Wales) and have young children of their own, so I think a family stay here would be ideal. It would be no bad thing for a couple either; preparing one's own breakfast and picnic lunch, pouring out one's own drinks, can save a lot of money, and driving 3 km into Honfleur for dinner sometimes would be no hardship.

Gonneville is just a hamlet but there is a supermarket nearby. To find the Château follow the sign to the left off the Pont l'Evêque road from Honfleur.

Prices start at 275f for two people for one night and get proportionately cheaper the longer you stay; i.e. a weekend starts at 450f for two.

Chez Laurette
(R)S
29 quai Ste-
Catherine.
(31) 89.05.34.
Closed Thur.

There are several bars and crêperies round the quay, and as long as you stick to simple dishes you can't really go wrong, but Laurette is the one that gets most plaudits for food and smiles. The place to go if you feel like a plateful of moules and not much else, sitting outside on the pavement by the harbour's edge with any luck.

Le Bistrot du Port
(R(M
quai de la
Quarantine
Closed Nov;
Dec.

One of the newer bistros opened on the quay. Trendily folksy, fun and bustle with good-humoured service. Good for a seafood tuck-in.

Map 3C **ISIGNY-SUR-MER** (Calvados) 61 km from Cherbourg

Not really *sur-mer*, but near the mouth of the Vire, which means oysters and all manner of other shellfish. There is a little quay, with green and red fishing boats tied up, and sheds full of baskets of assorted crustaceans. Not only the heart of the dairy industry but *pré salé* country, the salt marshes where the tastiest sheep come from.

Hôtel de France
(HR)M
17 r. E
Damagny.
(31) 22.00.33.
Closed
15/11–1/2; Fri.
p.m., Sat. lunch
o.o.s.

Popular as an overnight stop since it is slap on the main route from Caen to Cherbourg, in the middle of the little town. The traffic noise is abated by the fact that the rooms are set back round a courtyard, motel style (easy parking). They are plastic and ordinary but very clean and cost 90–160 f.

The food served in the severe little dining-room is generally excellent and interesting. Stuffed oysters and terrine de poisson figure on the 58f menu, followed by filet de daurade à l'oseille or poissons gratinés au four. I chose a very good truite flambée au Noilly, but found it hard to resist the brochette de coquilles St-Jacques, translated as 'insecure scallops', or the moules farcies – 'mussels with aillolic'!

Horrible puds; otherwise to be recommended as good value.

'We are full of praise for the hospitality offered and the excellent restaurant.' – Rae Mitchell.

La Flambée
(R)S

Right on the quay. Go through the crowded smoky bar to an unexpectedly attractive dining-room, with raised log fire, beams, saddle leathers. M. Philippe's speciality is brochettes – kidneys, scallops, sausages, all mixed with peppers, onions and mushrooms and charred to order over the fire, for about 25f. Delicious and just right for a quick, cheap meal.

Map 5D

LA JALOUSIE (Calvados) 121 km from Le Havre; 133 km from Cherbourg

---

On the N 158, 13 km south of Caen.

Auberge de la Jalousie
(HR)S
Closed 23/8–1/9; Feb.; Mon.

'Modern hotel with four rooms (one WC and one bathroom), poorly finished but inexpensive – 66f for a double. Excellent restaurant with good choice of dishes at very reasonable prices. Easy parking. – Lt-Col. J. F. Bassett.
    Useful for an overnight stop.

Map 6A

JULLOUVILLE (Manche) 110 km from Cherbourg

---

6 km south of Granville on a rather boring coastal strip.

► **Le Village**
(R)M
*(33) 61.94.99.
Closed Mon.;
Tue. lunch o.o.s.*

And about time too. This year Michelin has at last acknowledged the existence of a chef of rare talents. Guy Vivier's little restaurant has been awarded two forks in that cautious guide, but is still not smart enough for Gault-Millau to recognise it.
    I find it hard to understand why it has taken so long – four years in residence here and following an apprenticeship in a famous Mégève restaurant – for anyone with half a taste to acknowledge that here is an unusual talent, worthy of a cross. Perhaps the fact that he is extremely self-effacing and certainly not interested in the gastronomic rat-race has something to do with it.
    For anyone prepared to credit that behind the wine-coloured façade of M. Vivier's little restaurant, in the unlikely situation of the main road in a nondescript seaside resort there are surprises in store, a journey expressly to get here would be well justified.
    His menus start at 55f (3 courses; there are 4 courses on each of the 80 and 100f (highly-recommended) menus, and if you wish to leave the selection to Guy Vivier, there is the menu gourmand, a snip at 135f. His specialities change according to the season and market, as well they should, but for some idea of his style, here is a recent gourmand menu:

> Flan de poireau au foie gras
> Huitres chaudes aux bigorneaux
> Gâteau de St-Pierre au persil
> Magret de canard à l'aigre doux
> Plâteau de fromages
> Les desserts du Village.

Clearly M. Vivier is interested in nouvelle cuisine but for those with lusty appetites I should add that the plâteau de fromages is one of the best I have found and the desserts du Village would indeed feed a whole village. He offers a *dégustation* of them all if so required.

The Village's past neglect has been our good fortune since I first spotted this, my favourite Manche restaurant, four years ago. Clients have been discerning French, not tourist zombies and prices have been rock-bottom for this quality. Interesting to see what happens now.

Map 3G   **JUMIÈGES** (Seine-Maritime) 61 km from Le Havre

Michelin gives the ruins of the Abbey at Jumièges a rare three-star rating and states definitively that it is 'one of the greatest ruins in France'; I would agree with that. Founded about the same time as St-Wandrille, its neighbour, i.e. in the 7th century, this Benedictine Abbey was razed by the Vikings, then rebuilt and consecrated in 1067, with William the Conqueror in attendance.

The monks dispersed after the Revolution and a public auction was held to dispose of the building. A timber merchant made the successful bid and used his new acquisition as a stone quarry. It was rescued 130 years ago and now belongs to the state.

You get a lot of ruin for your money. The entire nave, though roofless, still soars 90 feet high and some of the chancel and transept remains. The twin towers either side of the main door will be instantly familiar from popular posters and photographs; the reality is every bit as impressive as the records. A most rewarding hour could be spent wondering and wandering – there are more treasures in the complex of St-Pierre church, the chapter house, cloisters and storeroom.

The Abbey is open 9–12 and 2–6 May–September and 10–12, 1.30–4 in the winter.

Hôtel des Ruines
(HR)S
(35) 91.84.05.

Useful to know that refreshment is near at hand after a clamber round the ruins. Here you can take a breather ~~in the~~ NEW MANAGEMENT more seriously inside ~~~~, or a charcoal grill; fuller menus ~~~~ of:

'Superb dinners on both menus.' – Lyn Wilson.
There are four simple bedrooms at 90f.

►**M. Regis Chatel**
pl. de la Mairie
(35) 92.51.93.

Hard by the Abbey walls I have admired in past years the attractive little black and white house in the square, shining with fresh paint and bright with windowboxes. When the 'Gîte de France' sign went up I knew I should investigate.

I found the house as appealing inside as out, with two bedrooms (double beds, washbasins), well-furnished, warm and comfortable, to let. They cost 100f for two people, including breakfast, and the thought of staying here and eating at the Bac (see below) is an unusually attractive one. I suspect that, as soon as I have done so, this will be a sure-fire arrow.

From Jumièges and several other spots along the river you can take a ferry boat – a *bac* – across to the Forêt de Brotonne. It costs 9f to take a car on one of these efficient little boats, and the driver gets the bonus of being able to view the scenery from mid-stream.

Abbaye de Jumièges

Restaurant du Bac
(R)S
(35) 91.84.16.
and
37.24.16.
Closed Tue.
p.m.; Wed.;
Mon. p.m.
o.o.s. Aug.

When I first started making enquiries about little Norman restaurants in this area, better known to locals than English guidebooks, 'the café by the bac, of course' was a phrase that kept recurring. Stupidly, I got the wrong bac and the wrong café and dismissed the idea. I am doubly grateful therefore for a more precise direction from Alan Clarke. He pinned the location down to Jumièges and wrote thus: *'About 1 km down the road opposite the Abbey entrance. A picturesque stone and half-timbered building, with a terrace. Beautiful peaceful setting by the river. Attractive interior with atmosphere – three smallish rooms with beams and panelling, polished copper and pistols etc. for decoration. Monsieur cooks and Madame serves delightfully and efficiently. The place soon filled up with French people – always a good sign. A sunny day, lunch at the restaurant and a visit to the Abbey gave me much pleasure and contentment.'*

Usually the quantity and quality of the food are in inverse relation to the attraction of the site. Not so here. I would eat at the Bac if it were in a slum; situated where it is, I would make it the focus for a weekend visit. If it's winter, you will find log fires, and candles on the dinner tables.

It was lunchtime when we ate there in December last and we were saving our big guns for dinner, so we chose the 45f menu. How wise we were. Four delicious courses all showed evidence of individuality from the *patron* cooking by M. Alain Morisse; from the chunky terrine of marcassin to the steak au poivre, the Norman cheeseboard left on the table, to the coconut tarte. As it was, dinner was a struggle; had we chosen the 65f five-courser Bac menu, it would have been out of the question. Popular with locals, so do book.

Map 4E

LÉAUPARTIE (Calvados) 87 km from Le Havre

The Auge region either side of the autoroute from Pont l'Evêque to Caen is full of fascination and well worth a diversion. Immediately deeply rural, as if no main road were within miles, it is a countryside of rich pasture and small farms. Many of the farmers' wives have taken to catering for visitors and a complete list of these 'chambres d'hôte' where meals can be provided, or 'gîtes rurales', which are rented cottages or flats, can be obtained from the French Government Tourist Bureau in Piccadilly. Because each one is only likely to be offering two or three rooms at a time, it would be futile for me to describe more than one example, but fairly typical is:

Le Bois Huret
Cambremer,
Léaupartie.
(31) 63.01.99.

Léaupartie lies south of the autoroute, NE of Lisieux on the D 16. To find the Guérins' pretty stone farmhouse, look for the bridge over the Dorette or ask in the village. Madame Guérin was preparing a family lunch party for twenty on the 1 May *fête* when I called, but chatted cheerfully between chopping beetroot and shredding carrot for the crudités and putting some plump farm chickens in the oven. Lunch was laid in what is usually the dining-room of the gîte, across the courtyard. A crackling log fire brightened up the damp spring day and it all looked very cosy and encouraging. The gîte, which sleeps four, costs 550f for a weekend.

Otherwise there are three double rooms, for which she charges 120f, including bath and two breakfasts, or 150f for a family room. Dinner, of three courses, is 45f including wine.

The Guérins also own another three-bedroomed gîte in the village, so there is a fair chance here of accommodation being available.

Map 4G   **LÉRY** (Eure) 111 km from Le Havre

South of Rouen the countryside deteriorates into an unpleasant industrial sprawl around Louviers and Le Vaudreuil. It comes as a pleasant surprise to find, near the banks of the Eure, a picturesque little square with a charming old inn nestling peacefully beside the church.

Beauséjour
(R)L
(32) 59.05.28.
Closed Nov.;
Sun. p.m.; Mon.

I hesitated whether to include this one, partly since its fortunes have been so precarious but mainly because of its prices. It's the kind of rustic place near *agglomerations* where well-heeled businessmen take their clients or secretaries for a 'simple' lunch. Losing a Michelin star, as the Beauséjour did in 1982, can be a traumatic experience for a French restaurant and I think in this case the lesson has been learned that clients have to be wooed, not chastened. Annie Nauwelaerts, the daughter-in-law of Franz, who first made the restaurant famous and died not long ago, now welcomes warmly, and the staff seem particularly anxious to please.

The traditional Norman dishes are still prepared in time-honoured style and served with elegance in the flowery dining-room in winter and in the garden in fine weather. The tarte aux moules, civet de langouste à la crême, escallope vallée d'Auge and the hot tarts made with seasonal fruits and accompanied naturally by Norman cream are all rewarding experiences for an indulgent and cossetted frame of mind. Expect to pay around 250f for the pleasure of sampling these specialities à la carte. A cheaper way is to accept the limited choice on the carefully chosen menus. Three courses will then cost 120f.

Map 4B   **LESSAY** (Manche) 54 km from Cherbourg

It seems I am not alone in being strangely moved by Lessay's stunningly beautiful abbey. Several readers have written to say that they too have sensed an extraordinary uplifting when they walked between the massive stone pillars of the wide nave. It has something to do with the proportions, so perfect that pleasure is instinctive, something to do with the light, flooding through the plain glass and illuminating the ochre stone, and something else besides that I for one can't define.

Anyway, do make the détour along the deep inlet of the windswept and sandy west coast and see for yourselves. The Romanesque abbey was badly damaged in 1944 but the restoration has been unusually skilfully achieved, using the original material — the golden stone that makes the whole vast building glow.

Another claim to fame for Lessay is the St-Cross Fair for cattle and horses, said to be the biggest and best in Normandy, which takes place on 11, 12 and 13 September.

Sadly the popular Hostellerie de l'Abbaye has been converted into

L'Abbaye de Lessay

flats and the Normandie opposite, even with a recent change of management, draws only brickbats.

| Map 3F | **LILLEBONNE** (Seine-Maritime) 37 km from Le Havre |

Until it silted up, Juliobona, now Lillebonne, was the Romans' main port, from which they controlled this part of Gaul from 65 BC until the end of the 4th century. Its 2nd-century theatre ruins are one of the few remaining Roman remains in Normandy. It was in Lillebonne that William the Conqueror assembled his nobles and persuaded them that Harold should get his come-uppance for breaking his promise to support William's claim to the English throne. Ruins of the keep remain. Nowadays there is not much else to delay the traveller in Lillebonne, but it is conveniently near Le Havre and might make a suitable overnight stop.

Hôtel de France
(HR)M
1 bis r.
République
(35)57.51.05.
Closed Sun. P.
AE, V.

An old-fashioned hotel in the town centre, recently refurbished under new management; the rooms are comfortable rather than lavish, keeping the price down to the level where this would make a cheap last-night/first-night stopover, i.e. from 90 to 145 f. Menus start at 71f. I think the cheeseboard is the most notable item on them.

'M. and Mme Darcy were very helpful and concerned about visitors' comfort and the hotel was well heated throughout. We all had an excellent meal from the 85f menu and the Reserve wine at 28f.' – Heather Rowland.

| Map 4E | **LISIEUX** (Calvados) 79 km from Le Havre, 171 km from Cherbourg |

I know little about Lisieux. I did try once to investigate, but hit the town in a rush hour, failed to park, and retreated frustrated and not at all attracted by what I had seen – domination of modern buildings and an awful lot of traffic. Unfair, because the only way to discover the heart of a town is on foot and that I will certainly do one day, finding time for what I am sure is the magnificent interior to the erstwhile cathedral of St-Pierre.

The town is best known as the place of pilgrimage to the birthplace of St Teresa of Lisieux. I did catch a glimpse of the hideous basilica built in her honour. Because of the pilgrims who make the voyage here in September every year, the town has more hotels and restaurants than usual, and provided one checked the sound-proofing – 'chambres insonorisées' – it would make a good winter base from which to explore the Pays d'Auge.

It is surrounded by fascinating manor houses, abbeys, old villages. Look for **St Germain de Livet** to the south, moated, glowing with the pinks, blues and greens of mosaic tiles. To the north-west, an attractive drive through country lanes, to Pré d'Auge would find the 16th-century **Victot**, another mosaic-tiled house in a particularly lovely setting, and not far away is the former abbey of **Val-Richer.**

Here are some ideas for Lisieux stops:

Hôtel de la Place
(H)M
67 r. Henry-
Cheron
(31) 31.17.44.
G. AE, DC, E.

'Clean, comfortable, run by young husband and wife. Very friendly.' – A. J. Mitchell.

Right in front of the cathedral, apparently lacking exterior charm, but with spacious rooms and a summer terrace. Rooms are from 190f, so it *should* be good.

La Coupe d'Or
(HR)M
49 r. Pont-
Mortain
(31) 31.16.84.
Rest. closed
20/12–20/1;
Sat. p.m. o.o.s.
G.

I like the sound of this one. 16 rooms, all said to be comfortable and sound-proofed, from 112f and splendid cooking from M. Lion, the *patron*, who changes his menus every day, offering for 65f four interesting courses and three specially selected wines *en promotion*.

La France
(R)M
5 r. au Char.

'We have visited this restaurant seven times in the last twelve months, run by a very friendly couple. Typical Normandy cooking – excellent.' – A. J. Mitchell.

Recommendations from local gastronomes always include the restaurant Le Parc in the bd Herbert Fournet, but mysteriously both Michelin and Gault-Millau suddenly omit it from their current guides, so there must be something significant going on here. Reports particularly welcome.

Map 5E

LIVAROT (Calvados) 100 km from Le Havre, 189 km from Cherbourg

---

Best-known as the home of one of Normandy's great cheeses – the golden-rinded, creamy, strong-smelling Livarot, made in these parts for 600 years. A good place to try it is:

Hôtel Vivier
(HR)S
pl. G. Bisson
(31) 63.50.29.
Closed
20/12–25/1;
rest. closed
Mon.

An unpretentious little hotel, well-known for its honest cooking. Rooms 90–120f, menus start at 50f.

'We based ourselves for four nights here in this pleasant small one-star hotel with a twin bed double room at 84f with shower. Evening meal is very good.' – P. Logan.

Map 4D

LOUVIGNY (Calvados) 112 km from Le Havre, 124 km from Cherbourg

---

A hamlet on the banks of the peaceful, willow-fringed river Orne, just 4 km south of Caen. Take the Venoix exit from the ring road, and Louvigny is on the D 212.

Auberge de l'Hermitage (R)M
(31) 73.38.66.
Closed Sun. p.m.; Mon.

I discovered the auberge in August last year and thought how delightful it looked, old and creeper-covered, so near the coolness of the river, but it was closed and as I had no other reports to go on, I could not include it in *F.E.2*. Now April Chevron writes: *'Owned by an Anglo-French couple, the Beauregards, she being the Anglo bit. Gorgeous cooking to order, quite expensive but well worth every penny.' 'Quite expensive'* in this case means around 120f.

Map 3H

LYONS-LA-FORÊT (Eure) 121 km from Le Havre

30 km to the east of Rouen lies the old hunting ground of the Dukes of Normandy, the forest of Lyons. To drive there makes a perfectly delightful excursion, with all kinds of possible diversions: to follow the valleys of the swift-flowing rivers, Andelle or Crevon, to visit the castle of *Vascoeuil*, the abbeys of *Fontaine-Guerard* or *Mortemer*, to walk amongst the massive beeches, some of them 140 ft high, and picnic in their shade. Or of course you could go, in time-honoured fashion, and pray for a husband at the Source Ste-Catherine.

In the centre of the forest, approached by the charming D 321, is the picturebook town of Lyons-la-Forêt. Centring on the old wooden covered market hall, the crooked Norman houses, black timbers, white plaster, red geraniums, are the focus of many an American and Japanese camera, and the fact that many of the shops are *antiquaires* is no coincidence.

It is a delightful, tranquil place, but inevitably self-consciously tourist-oriented. This preoccupation is sometimes reflected in its two hotels/restaurants, which never lack for custom, **Le Grand Cerf**, and **La Licorne**. Both are very old, very Norman, very attractive, fairly expensive. Currently, under new management, I would choose:

Le Grand Cerf (HR)M–L *NEW*
pl. du Marché
(32) 49.60.44.
Closed
15/1–16/2;
Wed. E.

Spoil yourselves – the food prepared by Philippe Colignan is delicious (menu at 160f). Try his version of the local speciality, terrine chaude de canard rouennaise, washed down by the best local cider. The bedrooms are countrified and delightful, from 130f to 236f. Book, obviously.

Map 6E

MACÉ (Orne) 151 km from Le Havre, 186 km from Cherbourg

Take the Caen road (RN 158) out of Sées, and then the D 303 to the right. Clearly marked from then, down various narrow lanes, is:

L'Ile de Sées, Vandel (HR)M
(33) 27.98.65.
Closed
1/1–15/2; Wed.;
rest. closed Sun.
p.m.

Unexpectedly imposing gates lead to the little Logis. Built only a couple of years ago, but nothing stark or aggressively modern about its creeper-clad appearance. Nice garden, tables, utter quiet. Inside is quite plush, with luxurious lounge and smart dining-room. Bedrooms too are very comfortable indeed. They all have private bathrooms and cost 145 to 169f. Menus are 70 (not weekends), 95 and 125f, and several readers assure me of their palatability.

'Run by a Breton couple, with 100% silence, by day only cows

grazing nearby and yet only 5 km from the horrid N 138. Nice food and Madame very friendly.'

However another regular correspondent warned that the wines could be expensive, the house wine being inadvisable, and reported, rather surprisingly, that there was a disco on one night (not near enough to the bedrooms to disturb, however).

Map 5B **MARIGNY** (Manche) 84 km from Cherbourg

An unremarkable little market town on the road between St- Lô and Coutances, with an outwardly unremarkable little restaurant in the market square (busy on Wednesdays).

 **Restaurant de
la Poste**
(R)M
*(33) 55.11.08.
Closed
15/9–15/10;
13/1–23/1; Sun.
p.m.;*
Mon.

Joel Meslin continues to cook unusually good and interesting food in his erstwhile hotel. Menus start at 80f and extend to the 200f version, though you'd have to starve for a week to tackle this one. Lots of choice, imaginative, copious, good value. A third arrow is well merited for unpretentious value for money.

Map 1G **MARTIN ÉGLISE** (Seine-Maritime) 117 km from Le Havre

---

If you take the D 1 out of Dieppe, the suburbs come to an abrupt halt only just before Martin Église. One minute it's factories and lorries and the next rolling fields and cows.

**Auberge Clos
Normand**
(HR)M
*(35) 82.71.01.
and 84.71.01.
Closed
15/11–1/3;
Mon p.m.; Tue.
P. AE, V.*

The restaurant presents one face to the village street and another to the large leafy garden running down to the river Eaulne. Bedrooms are in a converted stable block, covered in creeper, balconied, timbered, faded. The *chef-patron* cooks on an open range at one end of the delightfully rustic, beamed and coppered dining-room, bright with red gingham cloths and lots of flowers. I ate his 'tarte aux moules' and duckling, slept peacefully in the pretty chintzy bedroom with its own bathroom (at 140f) and awoke to no more harassing sound than moos, clucks and ripples. It all looked very good news indeed to me, and bearing in mind that accommodation in Dieppe had proved disappointing, I unhesitatingly gave it an arrow for good food, pleasant surroundings, position.

But now the son-in-law of M. Lesaulmier is in charge, since when reports have been decidedly mixed. One points out the menu never changes and is extremely limited for a stop of more than one night. The welcome has been criticised as less than warm, and the efficient dark-suited waiters who so impressed me have vanished. So has the nice old wooden furniture which made a meal in the garden such a pleasant experience, 'replaced with the usual white plastic stuff'. 'The whole atmosphere is one of boredom and of a "lazy" concern – card-playing of more interest than running the place.'

It seems that the bedrooms vary tremendously. One reader had a

Auberge du Clos Normand.

horror, with poor light, cobwebs, sagging bed and flimsy partitions; the loo along the corridor had a cracked seat. I could hardly credit this was in the same hotel as the one I slept in, but reports confirm that the standard varies alarmingly.

There have been favourable comments on the food and setting, but I fear that the general conclusion must be that recommendations must now be qualified; for a one-night stop in delightful peaceful surroundings near to Dieppe I believe the auberge would still please, but they really should try harder. Rooms are 80–160f and dinner à la carte is obligatory.

Map 4E

MERVILLE-FRANCEVILLE-PLAGE (Calvados) 102 km from Le Havre, 128 km from Cherbourg

---

On the coast road, D 514, 6 km west of Cabourg.

Chez Marion
(HR)M
(31) 91.30.43.
pl. de la Plage
Closed 3 weeks
in Oct.; Jan.;
Mon. p.m.; Tue.
o.o.s. AE, DC.

From the exterior this substantial Logis de France looks like any other seaside hotel, but very few seaside hotels I know have a restaurant like Chez Marion's. Crafty locals come from miles around to eat there at weekends (so booking is essential); here is a recommendation from one of them:

'Don't eat for a fortnight if you go to Chez Marion. French country cooking at its best; enormous portions and they also let you taste a bit of everything on the dessert trolley if they see you getting in a sweat about

making a choice. Quite expensive, so only for serious knife-and-forkers. – April Chevron. The cheapest menu is 90f.

The brothers Marion have now taken over from their father, and Bertrand was previously head fish chef at the Tour d'Argent; try his cocktail de coquillages farcis or ragout de joues de raie, or mammoth assiette de fruits de mer and you will have to admit that for such expertise and quality this is a bargain.

The other brother runs the hotel part; the rooms cost around 150f.

Map 3G | **MESNIL-SUR-JUMIÈGES** (Seine-Maritime) 74 km from Le Havre

---

To follow the loop of the Seine southwards from Jumièges is a very attractive and peaceful drive. In the autumn the road is lined with stalls selling the produce of the surrounding orchards, and here is a little bar/restaurant following the apple theme:

La Pommeraie (R)S *(35) 91.94.87. Closed Mon.* | A change of management here has meant a new young couple in charge and a fresh and attractive red and white apple theme décor. It makes a good place to pause for a drink or a cuppa, but there is also a simple 68f menu.

Map 1H | **MESNIL-VAL** (Seine-Maritime) 132 km from Le Havre, 166 km from Calais

---

A hamlet with tiny beach, 5 km south of Le Tréport.

Hostellerie de la Vieille Ferme (HR)M *Criel-sur-Mer. (35) 86.72.18 Closed 3/1–31/1.*

Extremely picturesque, all black and white timbers, stone walls, geraniums and lovely cooking smells wafting from the old farmhouse dining-room. Pressed for space, I didn't include it in *F.E.2.* for several reasons: it had recently changed hands and I feared it might be resting on past laurels, and it is so well known, with rocking chair in Michelin and write-ups in just about every guidebook imaginable, that it is very difficult to get a room or even a meal without a lot of planning. Now I hear that, although the prices have gone up considerably since it was just a simple inn, and the cooking is altogether more sophisticated, it is still a good choice, and so I can recommend it wholeheartedly, for those prudent souls who get their house (and hotels) in order well ahead.

The bedrooms are pretty if not spacious, a short step across the courtyard, and cost from 90 to 220f. The meals, relying heavily on fish, would come to not less than 120f.

'Our second visit, this time for a week on a demi-pension *basis with room and bath at 162f per person per day. Good French bourgeois cooking. Not far from beach. We enjoyed ourselves.' – G. M. Semper.*

Map 3G | **MONT CAUVAIRE** (Seine-Maritime) 106 km from Le Havre

---

Château de Rombusc (HR)M *(35) 34.68.72.* | How wrong can you be? Researching for *F.E.2* and trying to find something of interest north of Rouen but within easy access of that fascinating city, I came across a stunning 17th-century château, faded perhaps but in the process of being lovingly restored by the Livieux family, who greeted me kindly and showed me their beautiful home. Clearly they were not professional hoteliers, but they had decorated and furnished the bedrooms charmingly, and seemed determined to work hard at making a success of entertaining their guests. I thought it looked very promising indeed, and said so. The menus I was not so sure about and could not recommend personally, but Madame assured me that she used only fresh produce and I hoped that what they lacked in originality they would more than make up for in honest goodness.

NEW OWNERS

I wrote 'Perhaps not a winter place, unless absolute peace and quiet were needed, but heaven in the summer and a colourful and cheap base from which to explore Rouen.'

Clearly I owe the readers who followed my recommendation an apology. Numbers of them have written to say that the food was dreadful, the service appalling, the welcome cool. The family Livieux apparently consider it right to take their meals in the dining-room with the guests (which just might be acceptable in a less grand setting) with their television set turned on throughout the meal (which is inexcusable wherever). The atmosphere generated has not been of friendly accommodation but of unwelcome intrusion. *'We were made to feel uncomfortable.'*

GOOD REPORTS

Most letters were more in sorrow than in anger. Like me, their writers could see the potential of the place and felt doubly let down. I wrote to Madame Livieux to pass on the complaints, and had a disarming letter back, 'Where am I going wrong? What can I do to get it right?' I told her, but there seems to have been no improvement to date. Since I now have little reason to commend the Château, I shan't be going back, but I wonder if I am right? Perhaps all the Livieux need is experience and a steady cash flow? The first they should be gaining by now and the second should be forthcoming now that other guidebooks have followed *F.E.2's* recommendation indiscriminately and included this nigger in their woodpiles (snigger, snigger – it's hard when they pinch the gems!). All reports particularly welcome.

Stop press: Here is the latest report:

'It rained relentlessly and was cold in the evening, so M. Livieux moved our table into the salon, lit a huge log fire and turned on the central heating. Residents had dinner in the Livieux's sitting room – a lovely room with large fireplace and walls of bare red brick.

There were numerous deficiencies: our daughter's room had a defective bidet, lacked curtains and the shutters did not cover the window. The carpet on the lovely stairway remained unvacuumed for three days – an aesthetic crime!

By contrast our bedroom was very attractive, with very comfortable bed and spotlessly clean. Although as demi-pensionnaires we had no choice at meals, Mme Livieux's cooking was excellent, using produce from their own kitchen garden. But to see it being run by the Livieux with no regular help apart from their grown-up daughter, made me fear for their future.' – Rupert Jardine Willoughby.

I think this confirms the best and the worst and hope that readers who do decide to visit the Château will now feel fully in the picture.

Map 2B   **MONTEBOURG** (Manche) 27 km from Cherbourg

A rather dull, reconstructed village, but strategically situated on the popular D 913 and therefore a useful halt.

Driving past the **Hôtel de la Place** recently I spotted a 'changement de propriétaire' notice up and I know *French Entrée* fans will be as sad as I am to learn that M.Robic died suddenly, and Madame has had to sell up. The new young *patronne* was very friendly and showed me the bedrooms (which are unchanged – clean and very good value at 65f; her husband cooks menus from 40f), but we shall have to wait for more reports, since it was the welcome above all else that pleased so many previous clients.

NEW OWNERS

Map 5B   **MONTPINCHON** (Manche) 85 km from Cherbourg

13 km SW of Coutances.

Take the D 7 out of Coutances, turn left on to the D 27, and follow signposts to:

Château de la Salle (HR)L *(33) 46.95.19. Closed 1/11–27/3. AE, DC.*

An imposing if somewhat grim, one-time prison, member of the Relais et Châteaux chain – its sole Cotentin representative. The setting more than makes up for any severity. A walk through the beech woods behind the Château, misty with bluebells in April, down to the little stream in the valley will make home cares seem more than a day away. My favourite luxurious hideout in this area, well deserving a third arrow.

Furnishings are appropriate to the nobleman's home it once was. At

Château de la Salle

one stage the Bishop of Coutances lived here; he was able to keep an eye on his cathedral from home base by ordering all the land in between to be cleared.

One caution: it took me several visits to realise how widely different all ten bedrooms are. We have enjoyed vastly being pampered in both the dignified, tapestried, four-postered version, and even more in the light Directoire room, all elegant apricot, but last time we drew a really cramped monastic-like room, with midget bathroom carved out, sit-up-and-beg bath and portable bidet. They all cost the same, 340f, so it's worth being picky.

I wrote in *F.E.2* that I found it inexplicable that the Château should not have a rosette, since the food was so patently superb; I see that this year both Michelin and Gault-Millau have come to concur and the appropriate awards have been made. From now on *French Entrée* readers may well find it (a) more difficult to book and (b) more expensive, but it's worth persevering, believe me. The 105f set menu is, a bargain still, prepared by Christian I'Haridon, a chef of undoubted talent. The range of house pâtisseries from the trolley, which are included in the menu, are worth the price alone. If you stray away from that, it gets expensive, but look out for specialities like millefeuille de saint-pierre au beurre de cresson, or his tender young pigeons lacquered in honey.

The perfect place for a stylish weekend.

Map 7A   **MONT ST-MICHEL** (Manche) 153 km from Cherbourg

'Le Merveille' they call it, which says it all. Like Venice, Mont St-Michel exceeds well-briefed expectation every time. I have known it in winter, grey with the sea and the sky, eerie and remote, in the spring when its colours change like those of nature from sullenness to sparkle, in autumn when it swims in early mists and catches fire from late sun, and in the summer – when it is best left to other tourists and admired from afar across the dazzle of fast receding water. It never fails to captivate the imagination. From a northern approach particularly it dominates every landscape, glimpsed from little seaside resorts around the bay, to Avranche's heights, to marshlands surrounding; the magnetism is undeniable.

The Archangel Michael, whom it honours, is said to have become irritated with the neglect of Aubert, Bishop of Avranches, who failed to build the customary hilltop shrine in his honour on Mont St-Tombe, as the mount rising from the forest was then called. A few preliminary dream visitations failed to spur Aubert into action, so Michael tapped him so forcibly on the forehead that he dented his skull – there for all disbelievers to see for themselves in St-Gervais in Avranches.

Left in no doubt about his boss's wishes, Aubert built the first oratory in 907, replaced by a Carolingian abbey on which successive generations piled more and more elaborate edifices in Romanesque and Gothic styles. Each one demanded formidable dedication of skill and industry, with granite blocks having to be imported from the Chausey Islands and Brittany and hauled up to the crest of the Mount.

The many sections are too complex to describe here but these of the

Merveille (14th-century) to the north of the Mount are certainly not to be missed. Allow more time than you think necessary. Ideally a circumference on foot (having first checked the tides!) is the way to get bearings and assess the scale. You may have to paddle a little.

The combination of this man-made miracle set in the natural miracle of the racing water, which leaves only a causeway for the pilgrims to make their way across the water meadows and at new and full moons surrounds the Mount completely, has always drawn admirers. Modern pilgrims come by car in the summer in their thousands and shove and jostle their way up the narrow lane to the summit between souvenir shops and crêperies. Restaurants there open only for a few short weeks and know they must extract the last shekel then. I strongly advise avoiding their rude avarice and that a picnic eaten amongst the sheep in the meadows is a better way to find space and calm to marvel at the Merveille.

The only exception might be to eat once at the famous:

Mère Poulard
(HR)L.
(33) 60.14.01.
Closed
1/10–31/3.

Michelin-starred, American-admired, a stylish haven in the midst of tat. It's come a long way since Mme Poulard tossed the first omelette there. Fluffy with extra egg-white, foaming with butter, seething in liqueur, they make the dessert choice easy – as long as you go easy on the other specialities, like lobster or lamb from the salt marshes.

Don't fail to take into account that Mère Poulard too must finance the whole year in a few feverish months, and prices correspond. Allow 200f à la carte, and if you spend a night – and it would be intriguing to share the atmosphere when ghosts take over from tourists – full pension is obligatory, so think in terms of 700f for two.

Mont Saint-Michel.

Map 7 F **MORTAGNE-AU-PERCHE** (Orne) 165 km from Le Havre

A delectable little town. What a perfect centre it would make for a peaceful rural weekend. The Perche area is hilly farming country, dotted with studs and famous for its horses, particularly *le percheron*, the heavy cart-horse. Forests, full of game, are criss-crossed with straight avenues, offering delightful rural rides and good picnicking territory.

The D 930, which approaches Mortagne from the north, is especially rewarding, cutting through the Forêt du Perche, close to some of its many lakes (*étangs*). We crunched through the frosty beech leaves one winter morning and came across one of these natural beauties shimmering with morning sunshine, surrounded by utter stillness; another at Soligny-la-Trappe, near the Trappist monastery, had a café and pedalos, all laid up at this season, but potentially, along with the bathing, a great summer attraction. I shall certainly go back to see if it's just as lovely then.

We drove into the central square of Mortagne to find the local band on parade. The tuba, the trombone, the trumpets preceded the less spectacular woodwinds, the huffing and puffing visible as well as audible in that wintry air. Presumably there is no crime nor fire hazard allowed in Mortagne on Sunday mornings, since the gendarmes and pompiers have more important roles at the end of the procession. When we stopped later at a bar to ask the way, a bevy of tipsy policemen spilled out, like the chorus of *The Pirates of Penzance*, to give friendly if conflicting advice.

Mortagne is an appealing town in many aspects. I like its Saturday morning market, bursting out of the ancient *halles* into the square, where there is the statutory bar with tables outside for watching all the activity. A Relais Routier caff serves a steaming lunchtime bowl of vegetable soup for 3f! It has more than its share of mellow old buildings in narrow streets, and quiet tree-lined backwaters. What's more, it is well off for hostelries.

In one particularly tranquil square stands:

Hôtel du Tribunal
HR(M)
4 pl. du Palais.
(33) 25.04.77.
P. E, V.

A charming old stone building, 13th and 18th-century, furnished in keeping with its origins, interior garden, pleasant dining-room. Double rooms are from 83f to 142f with bath. Menus start at 52f.

Hostellerie Genty Home
(HR)M
4 r. Notre Dame.
(33) 25.11.53.
Closed Mon.

A find. Opened in 1982, this is a elegant restaurant serving delicious and interesting food, in an old stone house, with three comfortable rooms. They all have shower/loo/basin and though not spacious are luxuriously furnished. Excellent value at 140f a double. Menus start at 60f. Friendly and anxious to please Madame. A potential arrow, I feel.

Hôtel du Grand Cerf
(HR)M
25 r. Sainte Croix.
(33) 25.04.88.
Closed Feb.;
Sun. p.m.

An old-fashioned hotel with something for everyone. The rooms vary wildly. Some are spacious and well furnished, with two beds and bath for 154f, some are plain and simple, one large bed, for 65f. Some look over the road, others over a courtyard, so specify carefully. The restaurant is equally universally accommodating, with a range of menus to suit all purses and most tastes. It was full of locals for Sunday lunch, and the smells were delicious (from the food, I mean).

 food   hotel

Map 6E

MORTRÉE (Orne) 150 km from Le Havre, 187 km from Cherbourg

On the D198 between Argentan and Sées.

Château d'O

Obligatory excursion here. I insist that anyone within striking distance of Mortrée should visit this chequered fairy-tale of a castle, rising from the waters of its lake and wide wide moat. It takes the strange name from the family of Jean I d'O. The inner courtyard is enclosed by three pavilions, one Gothic, one early Renaissance and one 18th-century, and a balustrade, and you can tour the interior every day except Tue. for 10f.

The surrounding park is spacious and green. One marvellous hot July day I had the picnic supreme there. Deserted at 1 p.m., the château and grounds were all mine. A stone bench to spread out pâté and peach, a glass of wine to ease away the hot car fatigue, and then what a banquet, in what a setting! The swans swanned, the doves cooed, the fish leapt, two beagle puppies drooped in the courtyard, dragonflies hovered purposefully like mini-helicopters over the moat, and the lime blossom plopped into my lap. When someone inside the château started playing a violin, I thought this is all too much, but the strains persisted, mingling with the birdsong and insect hum, in a very satisfactory harmony until I fell asleep in the shade of the lime. I can tell you there can't be many more agreeable visions to open eyes upon than the towers of Chateau d'O.

But if it's not picnic weather, another excellent reason for a visit to O would be for its unusually good restaurant.

Restaurant de la Ferme d'O
(R)M
(33) 35.35.27.
Closed Feb.;
Wed.

Built into what I suppose were once stables or a barn, here is a beautiful beamed room, cool, airy and elegant, with most interesting menus from 70f.

Just 4 km away is another beautiful château, **Médavy**. Far less grand than O, it was built of mellow stone in the 18th century. Dominating the grounds are two impressive towers, one now a chapel, which are all that is left of a medieval fortress, all surrounded by a moat full of the fattest, most complacent trout. The château is still inhabited by the Médavy-Grancey family and is open to the public from 10 to 12 and from 2 to 4 from 14 July to 14 September.

Map 2H	**NEUFCHATEL EN BRAY** (Seine-Maritime) 105 km from Le Havre, 160 km from Calais

An unexciting town in the heart of the cream-cheese-making Bray area. A useful stop because of its position, about halfway between Abbeville and Rouen, the hub of a wheel of Nationales.

Hôtel de Lisieux
(HR)M
*2 pl. de la Libération.
(35) 93.00.88.
Closed
22–30/11; Feb.;
Thur. o.o.s. P.
AE, V.*

'A very good impression – modern, clean and comfortable. Menu varied and well prepared, with "something extra" in every dish. Parking easy and staff co-operative.' – D. R. McDougall.

Under new management

CLOSED SINCE LAST EDITION

Hôtel Mouton d'Or
(HR)S

I have yet to check this one myself, but: *'Clean and comfortable with beautifully cooked dinner on 50f menu. Easy parking, right in town centre by church, very friendly management. A good stop.' – Anthony Warner.*

Map 3F	**NORVILLE** (Seine-Maritime) 45 km from Le Havre

A nothing-village high above the Seine, on the D 428, south of Lillebonne.

Auberge du Norville – Bon Accueil
(HR)S
*(35) 39.91.14
Closed Fri. p.m.;
Sat.*

A puzzle, this one. It seemed to me that here would be a very popular choice for an overnight stop, peaceful, within easy reach of the port, inexpensive, friendly family management, English spoken, casserole in Logis de France for good cooking by M. Tr*** *** ***ce I wrote about it in *F.E.2*, not a single *** *** *** *** has arrived. I wonder if this is because pe** *** *** *** *** re often in ire than in complacency. *NEW MANAGEMENT* Or maybe *** *** *** closing times are against it (but it is open on Sundays, which is a big plus). Anyway, until told otherwise, I continue to think it good value. It's much more attractive inside than out, with good views of the river. Food is unpretentiously good, with menus from 50f, and a double room costs 90f.

Map 1A	**OMONVILLE-LA-ROGUE** (Manche) 24 km from Cherbourg

Just a tiny harbour and a bar restaurant, **Du Port** ((R)S), where we have on occasion eaten a plateful of seafood and been well pleased. A pleasant drive out from Cherbourg and useful for yachties. *'The largest, most tender and tasty pork chops we have ever had. Very reasonable, clean and with excellent service. – R. B. Dexter.*

Map 5F   **ORBEC** (Calvados) 93 km from Le Havre

One of my favourite towns in one of the most attractive valleys of the Auge. Orbec is a lively place, full of character. Its r. Grande is particularly colourful, with ancient wooden-gabled houses and glimpses of courtyards and gardens. Debussy was inspired by one of them to write 'Jardins sous la Pluie'.

This would make an excellent base from which to explore the Auge region, surrounded as it is by *châteaux* and manor houses, some open to the public, some to be glimpsed down long avenues, mostly on minor roads, dominating tiny villages; some are well-maintained, many are shabby and lead to surmise as to who can afford, or cannot afford, to live there. **Bellou, St Germain de Livet, Grandchamp**, the moated **Compesarte** and many others are all within an easy drive. The paper shop in the r. Grande has postcards of them all, and the friendly lady selling them advised us which ones to make for.

Le Caneton
(R)L
r. Grande.
(31) 32.73.32.
Closed Oct.,
Feb., Mon. p.m.,
Tue.

Normandy's answer to the Nouvelle Cuisine. The diet-watcher's nightmare, the ultimate in gourmandise married to gourmetise. 175f may seem a lot to pay for a meal, until you take into account: (a) that after a Caneton version you would certainly not wish to eat again that day and would probably be prudent to sup lightly the night before and after; (b) that if you wish to gain an insight into what Norman table traditions have been in the past and are unlikely to be in the calorie-cholesterol-conscious future, you could find no better place for enlightenment; (c) that you can share a menu, as I shall explain.

On offer is simply one gastronomic menu at 175f, or the carte. The menu is six dishes, each one of which alone would satisfy the average appetite. Predictably duck is the speciality and, in four different guises, it appears as Course No. 3 (with alternative ham or fish). So . . . we ordered one menu, and one duck à la carte.

I ate: Course No. 1 – a beautiful terrine aux poissons, incorporating chunks of coral salmon and creamy scallops, served with a herb-flecked mayonnaise. Then I paused while my husband tackled Course No. 2. He could have chosen a gratin of langouste aux epinards or poached salmon but settled for trout. His was a sublime specimen, say $1\frac{1}{2}$ lb of fat pink freshness, surrounded by cream, mushroom and white wine sauce.

Then a duck apiece. Mine was 'St. Antoine', its lightly grilled slices of breast – eight of them – showing that chef M. Ruaux had indeed heard tell of Nouvelle Cuisine but didn't go along with serving his sauce underneath the meat, when it seemed too good in all its winey, bloody, oniony goodness to hide. I have to say that I think my husband's choice of the more traditional 'Ma Pomme' style was cleverer. His bird was meltingly tender, the cream and apple sauce perfection. He finished every last lick and professed himself out of the contest, leaving me with only three more courses to go.

No. 4 is the one that sorts out the men from the nouvelles. The choice was between fillet of lamb or home-made pâté de foie gras with salade d'hiver. I weakly chose the latter because I needed the freshness of a salad (and a very good, colourful interesting one it was – enough for four normal portions), but somehow the pâté slipped down too.

The cheeseboard was one of the best I have ever seen, anywhere, any time. And I include some of the most famous tables in France. On a trolley came about thirty choices, all in prime condition, the bottom layer all goat and ewe. Mme Ruaux patiently and knowledgeably explained them all. The Camembert fermier would put you off pasteurised 'Camemberts' for ever; husband nibbled a morceau of Rocquefort – that too was sublime.

We had been asked at the onset if we would like a hot soufflé for pudding and wisely said No. Now we saw them arriving, Calvados or chocolate, puffing above their family-size china dishes like illustrations in cookery books. Something slighter, I thought – like a 'biscuit chocolat au whiskey, sauce anglaise'? Restaurant desserts nowadays are rarely worth the guilt. This one I was ready to do penance for.

So our total bill, with a bottle of Beaujolais Nouveau kindly proposed by Madame as being excellent (also one of the cheapest items on an amazing wine list which went up to 3,600f for a '61 Haut Brion), worked out at about £16 a head. Save up, if you must, but go, I beg you.

The food is so important here that I quite forgot to mention that the Caneton is in the oldest building in Orbec, utterly delightful, beamed, polished brasses, professionally immaculate, tiny, must book.

Hôtel de France
(HR)M
(31) 32.74.02.
Closed
20/12–20/1. V.

Not far to stagger up the r. Grande after a Caneton blow-out to this elegant 18th-century post-house. M. Courbet, the young and cheerful *patron*, cooks if you prefer to eat in. Menus are 52–120f, but some readers didn't think much of them. There has been an extension built since *F.E.2* was written and the superior rooms there are 200f upwards. Those in the original building are from 76f.

Map 3E

OUISTREHAM-RIVA-BELLA (Calvados) 122 km from Le Havre, 127 km from Cherbourg

The Côte de Nacre since June 1944 is probably better known for landings than mother-of-pearl. For those with memories of the drama as it unfolded, a visit to the Calvados beaches, Utah, Omaha, Gold, Juno and Sword, will be an illuminating pilgrimage; to post-war generations, here is history brought to life. To turn a corner in a sleepy Norman hamlet and find its square dominated by a souvenir tank jolts the holidaymaker into a previously half-perceived experience.

Most of the little seaside resorts along the Côte de Nacre are obviously new. Ouistreham-Riva-Bella on the mouth of the Caen canal was one such town rebuilt on the ruins of German occupation and subsequent evacuation. The 4th Anglo-French Commando reduced the town to rubble on the morning of 6 June. A Landing Museum (open 1/6–15/9, 9.30–12 and 2–6.30; Easter to June, Sats, Suns and fêtes, 10–12 and 2.30–6) shows wartime memorabilia.

It is a lively little town, though with a short season. I would put it top of the list on this coast for a family holiday. Caen is only 12 km away, and would provide wet weather grown-up diversion. The sands are magnificent, stretching for miles in all three directions, the bathing is safe and well-supervised, there are lots of organised activities on the beach for young and not so young.

Le Châlet
(H)M
74 av. de la Mer
(31) 97.13.06.
Closed
1/12–26/2.
P. V.

It seems that the gamble taken by the Chevrons – April from Bristol, and her French husband Jacques – is beginning to pay off. They bought a little hotel in the centre of the town and ran it for a couple of years on a wing and a prayer. Before they could commit themselves further to a programme of refurbishment, they had to test the water, relying on their natural friendliness, hard work, and anxiety to please their clients more than on expensive decorations. I expressed my confidence in the hotel in *F.E.2*, and now Mme Chevron writes: *'We have continued to make improvements since your visit, including automatic telephones in each room, replaced carpets and curtains. The bar too has been perked up and we hope it looks inviting. On our rare days off we enjoy using* French Entrée *and have also had the pleasure of meeting some charming people who arrive at Le Châlet waving it triumphantly.'*

Other guidebooks have noticed my enthusiasm and are now writing about the Châlet, with the prospect of their being featured in a BBC programme too. So all looks set fair for the Chevrons, but they have a soft spot for *French Entrée clients*, who were among their first, and have agreed to make a *Special Offer* to them, using a new and most attractive little restaurant, **Les Tisons**, which is next door to supply either lunch or dinner.

Off-season: Bedroom with private bathroom, breakfast, lunch/dinner (with complimentary Kir), for two people 260f per night.

High Season ditto 368f.

If you are thinking of taking them up on this, do so soon, before everyone gets in on this most desirable act. I think it would make an especially good base for a family break, with the sea no distance down the road. The Chevrons know how to look after children, having a small son of their own. General terms are 170f for a double room with bath. An arrow for general popularity.

I am grateful to April Chevron for some very useful local tips, e.g.: *'very jolly Friday morning market in Ouistreham, and every day during the summer. Marvellous clothes bargains to be found by those prepared to rummage.'*

Hôtel
l'Univers.
Rest. La
Broche
d'Argent
(HR)M
pl. de Gaulle
(31) 97.12.16.
G. AE, DC.

Open every day year round. A most attractive hotel and restaurant, near the port, all tastefully redecorated recently. The green and white restaurant is light and airy with expensive accoutrements like cane chairs, good china and napery. Eighteen bedrooms equally comfortable, from 133 to 174f.

M. Romagne owns and cooks. On a cold winter Sunday, we found the restaurant lively and almost full; improvidently arriving without a booking at 2 o'clock, a rejection seemed likely, but no, a table was efficiently found and our modest order for a variety of single dishes accepted without a flicker of disdain. I had superb mussels in a cream and leek sauce and all the other chosen fish dishes were equally good. Menus start at 65f.

Le Normandie
(HR)M
*71 av. Michel
Cabieu.
(31) 97.19.57.
Closed
1/11–20/11,*
*1/3–15/3; Tue.
p.m.; Wed. P.
AE.*

A very popular little Logis in the town centre, recently up-graded to 2 stars. It is run by the charming M. et Mme Christian Maudouit who write to tell me that they have effected 'un transformation'. Rooms are still from only 95f and menus, which include excellent seafood, start at 45f.

Les Tisons
(R)S
av. de la Mer.

Next door to the Chalet and highly recommended by the Chevrons.

'We are delighted with a small cosy restaurant called Les Tisons; it has recently changed hands. Very clean with fresh flowers, huge log fire. Their first menu at 50f is marvellous value, e.g. terrine de poisson with aioli or moules; fresh salmon and sauce crevette or bavette done on the open fire, tarte or large home-made mousse au choc. Their wine list is worth looking at as they have some very good bottles at ancient prices. Very much an F.E. place I feel.' – April Chevron.

Madame Chevron also recommends in Ouistreham Le Channel on the port for crêpes or grills and Le Chateaubriand opposite the supermarket Banco. A little further away she suggests Le Montgomery on the beach at **Colleville** and La Ferme St-Hubert (*'the first is fishy, the second more gamey, with a very chatty Gran'*). And a particular favourite is La Chaumière at **Longues-sur-Mer**, with new young owners. I can't think of a more valuable source of information than an Englishwoman married to a Frenchman, keeping a hotel in France, and I am sure all these recommendations will prove winners.

Map 3E   **PENNEDEPIE** (Calvados) 63 km from Le Havre

Take a pleasant drive along the delightful Côte de Grace road, west of Honfleur, for 6 km to find:

**Moulin St-
Georges**
(R)M
*(31) 89.12.00.
Closed
Oct.–Easter
except
weekends.*

An old inn at the side of the road. I picked a bad time to check it out – after what had obviously been a lengthy Sunday lunchtime session. Red-faced French families were beginning to stagger out to their cars and siesta was in the air. The menus (from 60f) looked good to me so I was pleased to have some confirmation:

'Terrine of duck, half a grilled lobster, coffee and a bottle of Muscadet for 110f. Excellent country inn.'

Map 2B   **LA PERNELLE** (Manche) 32 km from Cherbourg

Inland the north-eastern Cotentin countryside swiftly reverts from stark coast to Norman lushness. The valley of the Saire is typically green and flower-studded and the D 125 from Valcanville to La Pernelle especially pretty.

Take a left turn from this road to the hamlet of La Pernelle where a patchwork panorama unfolds far below the bluff commanded by a tiny church. A viewing table indicates Gatteville lighthouse to the left, Grandcamp cliffs to the right. On a clear day you can see for ever, or at least to the Percée Point, the islands of Tatihou and St-Marcouf and the La Hougue fort.

What is more, there is **Le Panoramique** (Closed Sun. p.m.; Mon.) Gorgeous view out to sea from the surprisingly smart restaurant, Café open all day for crêpes, home-made ices, etc.

Map 2A | **LES PIEUX** (Manche) 18 km from Cherbourg

Mme Bonnissent (HR)S
rte du Rozel
(33) 52.47.38.
Closed Sun.
o.o.s

Pleasant, grey, wide-streeted town with full complement of bars, restaurants with 35f menus, Relais Routiers and a rare petrol station. As so often, it was by getting lost that I made the most promising discovery in the town. On the Le Rozel road is a carpenter's shop and alongside is Mme Bonnissent's little hotel and restaurant. She has five spotless good-sized double rooms with showers for 75f each. Downstairs is a pleasantly rustic bar and restaurant/crêperie where you can eat three courses for 35f:

Very unsophisticated but good value for a family holiday since there are few hotels in this most attractive area, with marvellous beaches nearby – Le Sciotat etc.

Map 4A | **PIROU-LE-PONT** (Manche) 60 km from Cherbourg

From Lessay to Coutainville the route touristique is not very interesting, cutting as it does through the flat countryside of the sand dunes. Just a few kilometres inland the D 72 runs parallel – still flat but more attractive in that it is greener and passes through some unspoiled villages.

Between the hamlets of Pirou-le-Pont and Pirou-le-Bourg there is a grey stone house, set at an angle to the road.

Auberge de la Guérand (HR)S
(33) 46.34.41.
Closed
12/11–5/12; Fri.
o.o.s. AE.

A very attractive dining-room, beamed and with a great fireplace, well-laid tables, leads into a tiny bar. *Madame la patronne* does the cooking. Her menus include luxuries like oysters at unluxurious prices – 48f for three courses, 65f for four and 85f for five.

There are eight spacious bedrooms attractively furnished and decorated in country style. The most expensive, with cabinet de toilette, in 82f and the cheapest is 72.50f. Good value.

Nearest markets are on Sunday and Friday. Madame will advise.

Map 7B **PONTAUBAULT** (Manche) 141 km from Cherbourg

7 km south of Avranches on the N 175.

Les 13 Assiettes (HR)M *(33) 58.14.03. Closed 15/11–15/3; Wed. o.o.s.*

Logis de France, France Accueil, motel, on the main tourist route to Mont St-Michel, it is hardly surprising that this is a popular stop. It seemed to me that they got a lot of practice in turning people away. But if you do get in, you get a bargain.

The thirteen dishes are the traditional ones served at old banquets in the region. The food nowadays maintains the tradition of being copious and good, with menus from 44f and house wine at 26f.

35 chalets offer a peaceful night, from 80 to 130f.

If the 13 Assiettes is full, one reader heartily recommends the Hotel Restaurant **Les Touristes** as being clean, comfortable, good value, *'rooms with view across country'.*

Map 3F **PONT AUDEMER** (Eure) 48 km from Le Havre

Our favourite stop for breakfast, especially if it is market day, when that marvellous first taste of France – giant cafés crèmes, buttered baguette

Auberge du Vieux Puits

and jam – can be eaten in the midst of one of the most colourful scenes I know.

The whole of the main street is closed to traffic on Monday for the general market and on Friday for the *marché maraîcher*. Gems of specialist stalls – pulses laid in patterns like mosaics – green flageolets, white haricots, orange lentils; or dried fruits – fat apricots, giant prunes, dates in great variety, and exotic figs, all to be sampled before a purchase is decided upon. Only the French would mix together the variety of unsophisticated flowers that blaze away on another stall – pink daisies and wallflowers, marigolds, narcissus and hyacinths, made into posies; outside the church in the spring are black-shawled old ladies selling delicate wild daffodils.

It's a lovely church – St-Ouen. Magnificent stained glass, some Renaissance, some modern Max Ingrand, but not intimidating. Always lively, with scarved matrons chatting at the door or resting their shopping baskets while they sit quietly enjoying the patterns of coloured light. What with the enviable pâtisseries, charcuteries and fish shops just across the road, their shopping must be a pleasure.

This old part of the town is the most attractive, with little streams from the river Risle reflecting the ancient overhanging timbered houses, but it is all lively and has an independent, self-contained character which makes it a great favourite.

Unfortunately the town is not well served with medium-priced hotels or restaurants. The choice lies between the luxury of the Vieux Puits and the simplicity of the Hôtel de la Risle.

Auberge du Vieux Puits
(R)L
6 r. Notre Dame du Pré.
(32) 41.01.48.
Closed
2/7–11/7;
17/12–16/1;
Mon. p.m.; Tue.
V.

New rooms.

One of the hazards of a restaurant-weary travel writer is to underestimate the obvious. In *F.E.2* I wrote that I was becoming disenchanted with the Vieux Puits, for several reasons. I quoted the sameness of the menu, unchanged since M. Folz's father's time as *patron* here, the sameness of the clientèle – nearly always exclusively Brits. Neither did I approve of the lack of welcome or unhelpfulness over a necessarily early morning start, nor of the complacency of the management guaranteed by a steady flow of regulars.

Since then I have had such a mockingly witty letter from M. Folz, disarming me of most of these carpings, that I am able to take a fresh look at what was once my favourite restaurant, forgive it its past failings and believe that it might well give enormous pleasure to those who have not already made the pilgrimage.

He writes that he has engaged two young chefs, who will ensure a revision of the menu (but retain the trout Bovary and the duck with cherries which I had described as 'inevitable'), and (tongue-in-cheek) that he will endeavour to offer his guests a welcome 'moins lugubre' in future. In fact, 'desolé par le desenchantement' expressed in *F.E.2*, he will generally try to do better.

Rare to find a restaurateur prepared to admit a fault, unprecedented to find one not inclined to shrug it off, especially when he knows that every other guidebook gives him undiluted praise. M. Folz, I salute you. If you see a lady in a false beard in your restaurant, 'twill be I, very much more inclined to rediscover the many virtues of the Vieux Puits and its *patron*.

For the unitiated: the auberge is 17th-century, utterly charming, authentically furnished, lots of flowers, log fires, leafy garden with the old well from which the restaurant takes its name and which Flaubert described in *Madame Bovary* (when it was in the Hôtel du Cygne in Rouen). An unexpectedly peaceful haven from the busy ring road.

The food merits a Michelin star, with a 180f menu, or the legendary duck with bitter cherries at 88f. No house wine but a good Sancerre, for example, at 75f. The rooms, in an annexe across the courtyard, are tiny but extremely pretty from 85f to 175f for one with twin beds, shower and loo.

▶**Hôtel de la Risle**
(HR)S
16 quai R. Leblanc.
(32) 41.14.57.
Closed 20/8–10/9; 20/12–14/1; Sun. p.m.
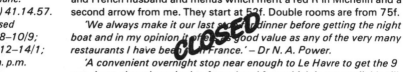

One of the most popular hotels in the book, discovered not by me, but by astute readers who penetrated beyond the unattractive modern façade and found solid value for money. Don't expect the Ritz and you will be well pleased with the spotless rooms, showers, helpful English *patronne* and French husband and menus which merit a red R in Michelin and a second arrow from me. They start at 52f. Double rooms are from 75f.

'We always make it our last stop for dinner before getting the night boat and in my opinion it offers as good value as any of the very many restaurants I have been in France.' – Dr N. A. Power.

'A convenient overnight stop near enough to Le Havre to get the 9 a.m. boat, though we had to forgo breakfast which is not available till 7.30. Much patronised by English tourists. Parking on street outside not very easy but possible. Room clean and comfortable with view across street straight into horse butcher's shop!' – Mrs P. J. Wood.

'Recommendation strongly endorsed. Seeking a simple meal after some rich Normandy cooking I found it here, perfectly presented – jambon de Bayonne, côte d'agneau with salad, Pont l'Evêque and a bowl of cherries. A good room all astonishly inexpensive.' – Alan Clarke.

Le Bras d'Or
(R)S
6 r. Aristide Briand.
(32) 41.11.03.
Closed Wed.

It's always good to have a choice of restaurants in an attractive town like Pont Audemer, and as they tend to be either expensive (Le Vieux Puits, La Frégate) or full (Risle) a newcomer is particularly welcome.

'A five course meal cost 58f and we thought the standard of cooking and service was very good indeed. There was a wide variety of dishes on offer.' – P. Hannam-Clark.

Map 4G | **PONT DE L'ARCHE** (Eure) 102 km from Le Havre

Ferme de la Borde
(R)L
(35) 23.03.90.
Closed 6/8–30/8; Sun. p.m.; Mon.

A ravishingly pretty old farmhouse converted into a luxury restaurant, south of Pont de l'Arche just off the N 15. The welcome was warm even though we weren't going to eat there and an apéritif (expensive) in the charming raftered dining-room gave me plenty of opportunity to study the menu. It looked a shade uninteresting, concentrating on straightforward grills and fish, but Roger Marie is a *maître rôtisseur*, standards are reputedly high and the setting, particularly in the summer when the garden is in use, would make a pleasant break from the autoroute. Carte – allow 115f.

If you have a little more time, a better choice would be to make for **Les Damps**, just 1.5 km from the town.

La Pomme
(R)M
44 rte de l'Eure
(35) 23.00.46.
Closed
20/7–22/8; Sun.
p.m.; Tue p.m.;
Wed. P.

Follow the road along the river to find this charming little restaurant with flowery garden. I wrote last year that I was sure this would be a new arrow, but, maddeningly, the opening days have beaten me and I haven't managed a meal here since then; no feedback from readers either, so arrow-less it will have to remain. But I am pretty sure it is a good bet. Alain Oper is an imaginative chef, who combines traditional Norman cooking with the best of Nouvelle Cuisine. Pleasant, smiling service, and good value with menus from 52f. Reports *please*.

Map 6D   **PONT D'OUILLY** (Calvados) 150 km from Cherbourg; 145 km from Le Havre

This little town on the river Orne was almost completely devastated in the war, but thanks to its surviving charming old market hall, retains a certain character.

**Hôtel du
Commerce**
(HR)S
(31) 69.80.16.
*Closed Jan.; Sun
p.m.; Mon. o.o.s.*

A modern logis in the square, whose food is highly recommended by local friends. Menus from 46f, clean and wholesome rooms 70 to 130f.

**Auberge St-
Christophe**
(HR)M
(31) 69.81.23.
*Closed Sun.
p.m.; Mon. o.o.s.*

I thought this little Logis, 2 km out of the town on the D 23, was quite charming, and I liked its young owners, Gilles and Françoise Lecoeur, who have recently decorated its seven bedrooms in pleasant country style. It is all bright and cheerful and although right on the (minor) road most of the rooms look out at the back over a pleasant garden. However, I have a recent letter from a reader who was disappointed by food and *accueil*, so my recommendation is qualified. A double room costs 170f and menus are from 75f.

Map 4E   **PONT L'EVÊQUE** (Calvados) 64 km from Le Havre

Not my favourite town, and as its best-known inn, the Lion d'Or, stands on a busy crossroads and is impossibly noisy, I have never stayed there. but:

**Auberge de la
Touques**
(R)M
(31) 64.01.69.
*Closed
15/11–1/1;
Mon. p.m.; Tue.*

We knew we were taking a risk in not booking lunch on 1 May, but it had been a last-minute decision to extend the weekend. Two other desirable restaurants had turned away our whetted appetites and it was 12.30 – late by French *fête* standards. It seemed too much to hope that we might squeeze into the Auberge, which I knew had a very high local reputation, but they pushed the last two small tables together and we could relax and anticipate. The rain was making outside look very unattractive and the prospect of spending a couple of hours inside this pleasantly beamed old inn by the river Touques a most agreeable one.

It went on being like that. The menus were 80 and 120f, and on the latter I ate a superb mousseline St-Jacques au fenouil, a tender crispy duckling, a selection of Norman cheeses and a perfect marquise au chocolate. Other dishes approved were tarte à l'oseille, steak au poivre and careé d'agneau. I don't feel so bad about Pont l'Evêque now.

Map 7A   **PONTORSON** (Manche) 156 km from Cherbourg

Right on the Brittany border.

Le Montgomery
(HR)M
r. Cousnon
(33) 60.00.09.
Closed
11/10–7/4; Tue.
in April and
May. AE, DC, E,
V.

I found this ancient home of the Counts of Montgomery most attractive, with its polished wood staircase, flowers, terrace, elegant dining-room and good food cooked by the venerable M. Jacquet. However, changes are obviously in the wind and one reader had a disastrous visit there. Another sums up the situation:

'Here's the scandal; their chef, M. Jacquet, was caught stealing from the kitchen and is now dismissed, disgraced and under arrest! But don't worry, the patron *has maintained standards and insists the food is better than ever. I have no reason to disbelieve him after dining there, on lovely local lamb, washed down by a bottle of 1967 Château la Croix, Pomerol, personally selected by the* propriétaire, *who has a very good knowledge of his excellent wine list. They too were full the day we left. So another tick in your book.' – Lance Berelowitz.*

For those brave enough to risk it, the cost of a good-sized double with bath (ask for one overlooking the garden) is 175f and the menus start at 65f. 'France Accueil' have recently added it to their organisation, so perhaps the storm in the saucepan has abated.

Bretagne
(HR)M
r. Couesnon
(33) 60.10.55.
Closed
1/11–1/2; Mon.

Not so outstandingly attractive as the Montgomery and therefore less well patronised but pretty nice all the same. 14th-century, restored, pleasant interior, menus from 55f, rooms 85 to 180f.

Map 3G   **PONT–ST–PIERRE** (Eure) 109 km from Le Havre

The scenery around Amfreville, with its great locks dividing the tidal from the fluvial Seine, is particularly attractive. Here is the **Côte des Deux Amants**, a lofty spur overlooking not only the Seine but the valleys of the Andelle and Eure. The two lovers in question were Caliste, daughter of the Baron of St-Pierre, and Raoul, a humble peasant. The baron decreed that in order to prove his determination to marry Caliste, Raoul must run to the top of the escarpment with Caliste in his arms, without pausing once for breath. The good news was that the handsome young man achieved his target, the bad that he dropped dead from exhaustion, and that Caliste had no alternative, in the best romantic tradition, but to die beside him.

Put all thoughts of tragedy aside, though, because this is a spot to contemplate all the joys of nature rather than its sadnesses. In the village of St-Pierre, a few kilometres to the north, is:

Bonne Marmite
(HR)M
(32) 49.70.24.
Closed
23/7–11/8;
25/2–15/3; Fri.;
Sat. lunch; Sun.
p.m. o.o.s.

In the main street in the centre of this small and attractive town.

'Very comfortable rooms for 190f. We all had a very good meal in the most attractive dining-room, with lobster tank and antique decor. Service excellent – a good stop.' – Peter V. Marshall.

Rooms are 160 to 215f and the menu is 70f except on Sat. p.m.

Map 3A

PORT BAIL (Manche) 45 km from Cherbourg

I love Port Bail, with its two ancient churches, wide chestnutted square for the boules players, intriguing river, sea and sand-dune combination, on which the light always seems strangely intense. Good walking and marvellous picnic sites along the river bank. There are few hotels along this stretch of coast, so useful to know is:

La Galiche
(HR)S
pl. E. Laquaine
(33) 54.84.18
Closed
15/10–30/10;
Feb.; Mon. o.o.s.

Just a simple little bar-restaurant/hotel, with rooms from 80 to 140 f. and menus starting at 50f.

Les Rendezvous des Pecheurs almost opposite has new management and the best food (38f menu) and **La Fringale** nearer the water has good atmosphere and is fine for a snack (I ate a bowl of fresh prawns and salad there recently, which made the kind of good light lunch not easy to find in France).

Map 3C

PORT EN BESSIN (Calvados) 100 km from Cherbourg

Nice little port with fishing boats pulled up alongside the quays right into the heart of the town and plenty of fresh fish to buy if you're *en route* for the afternoon Cherbourg boat home. Fishy menus everywhere, best at:

Le Vauban
(R)S
6 r. du Nord
(31) 21.74.83.

Excellent fruits de mer. Menus at 51 or 83f. Popular locally and often full.

'Superb fresh fish – raie, lotte, huge moules grilled with garlic butter as starter and good sorbets.' – Hillary Bill.

The Hôtel des Bains on the front looks grim to me, but is also well recommended for fish.

Map 1A

PORT RACINE (Manche) 29 km from Cherbourg

'The smallest port in France'

Hotel L'Erguillère
(H)M (R)L
(33) 52.75.31.
Closed 5/1–1/3;
Sun. p.m.; Mon.

The bedrooms need that remarkable view to compensate for their rather basic accoutrements; the bathrooms are spartan rather than sybaritic. I had a double room to myself and had to use all four threadbare handkerchief towels to dry with after a less than luxurious shower (none of the rooms have baths), *but* . . . one look out of the bedroom window and all – or almost all – is forgiven. The view dominates the dining-room too, and the bar and the terrace, and alone is justification for a visit to L'Erguillère. Every time I have been there the sea far below has seemed unnaturally blue, the sun unnaturally light on the sheep-dotted hills, the grass astonishingly green; perhaps on a grey, windswept day the chill of the bathroom tiles would predominate and the view over the uninviting water would not compensate, but it's definitely worth taking the risk.

I was surprised that there were no Brits there – the hotel is well-known and in every guidebook. Germans and French made up the clientèle, but perhaps fellow countrymen have been put off, as had I previously by the necessity to book so far ahead. After two years of being refused spur-of-the-moment bookings, I had to accept 'Well, what date can you have me?' I cannot even claim that the Logis's much-vaunted *accueil* was much in evidence. Lights out and front door locked at 9.30, which seemed even earlier on my first day on French time. The only glimpse of the proprietors was when I had to pursue them to their cosy, well-lit sitting room to ask for a replacement bedroom light bulb. Breakfast was awful – no fresh bread and foil-wrapped butter.

Most customers obviously came for the lobsters, prepared in various ways, but at 250f a kilo it became too difficult for my arithmetic, so I played safe and chose from the 120f menu – langoustines, and pavé de filet de boeuf, cheese and pud. All very good, but the waiting was so assiduous that barely was fork laid down than the next plate was offered. Clearly the aim was to clear the dining-room in the shortest possible time.

The double rooms cost 247f. I think a visit is still justified for the peace and beauty of the setting, but the thought that the management are so obviously cashing in loses the arrow.

Map 1G **POURVILLE** (Seine-Maritime) 110 km from Le Havre

Au Trou Normande
(R)S
(35) 85.11.45.
Closed Sun.
p.m.; Mon.

If you feel like a little excursion from Dieppe, you could do worse than wind down the green and hilly coast road, with a splendid view of cliffs and bay, to the (insignificant) beach of Pourville. Not much else here, but the little Norman-style Trou Normande serves an excellent lunch. Good fish, good value, at 49f or 79f, with a friendly atmosphere.

Map 6D **PUTANGES-PONT ÉCREPIN** (Orne) 146 km from Le Havre

Nice little twin towns of Putanges and Pont Écrepin connected by a modern bridge (replacing the mediaeval one blown up in 1944) spanning the willow-fringed river Orne. The market (Thursdays) on its banks has taken place there for over 400 years.

A few kilometres outside is the extensive Lac de Rabodanges, where you can bathe, picnic, take refreshment at a restaurant on water's edge and mock at the amateur windsurfers and water skiers.

Hôtel Lion Verd
(HR)M
(33) 35.01.86.
Closed Fri.
p.m. o.o.s.; 24/
12–31/1.

One of the most agreeable little hotels in the area, with gravelled terrace overlooking river, pleasant dining-room with above-average choice of menu (lowest is 35f). Rooms are bright and cheerful, but regrettably refurbished not in country toiles but in fierce vinyls. A good-sized double with bathroom costs 120f.

A popular and well-documented Logis, so necessary to book in advance.

Map 5B

QUETTREVILLE-SUR-SIENNE (Manche) 79 km from Cherbourg

A village on the N 971 10 km south of Coutances.

Auberge de La Tournée
(HR)M
(33) 47.62.91.
Closed
1/10–15/10;
Feb.; Mon.

A nice, old-fashioned Logis, well thought-of locally.

The chef here, Gilbert Deslandes, has became a local celebrity in winning regional competitions for his specialities like escargots en feuilletage, paupiettes de saumon à la quettrevillaise. Beautiful fresh bass with smooth sauce, and unusual home-made blackcurrant gâteau. Reasonable wine list. Menus start at 55f, and the 150f includes the freshest of lobsters.

All the bedrooms have been recently redecorated and now cost 110-170f.

Map 1G

QUIBERVILLE (Seine-Maritime) 100 km from Le Havre

Can't say I cared much for this unlovely stretch of beach, crowded in summer, with souvenir stalls, but we enjoyed watching the fish being sold from the fishing boats dragged up to the roadside and still alive and kicking. With Dieppe's hotel shortcomings, it might be practical to stay here just 16 km to the west.

l'Huitrière
(HR)S
(35) 83.02.96.
Closed Dec.;
Sun. p.m.; Tue.
p.m.; Wed. in
winter.

A spruce modern Logis, with a surprisingly elegant dining-room. Food is good value enough to merit a red 'R' in Michelin, and the menus from 61f obviously feature lots of fish. I didn't look at the bedrooms, which cost 85 to 160f a double, but most of them have balconies overlooking the sea and the general impression was of a well-run and clean hotel.

 hotel   food

Map 2B

QUINÉVILLE (Manche) 42 km from Cherbourg

King James II wept at Quinéville when he saw his last hope of regaining the English throne literally go up in smoke; his allies in the French ships were intercepted off Barfleur by the Anglo-Dutch force and annihilated, in the four-day battle of La Hougue in 1692.

Today the sight of Quinéville is not particularly cheering – ragged,

Chateau de Quinéville

seaweedy beach, better perhaps for walking on than looking at, sand dunes, a parking lot, a few deserted beach huts and a shuttered café.

The grandeur of the Château viewed from the gates comes as a pleasant surprise, but closer inspection reveals the need for a lick of paint and some weeding. King James would now hesitate to stay here, as once he is said to have done.

Château de Quinéville
(HR)M
(33) 41.21.50.

Definitely different. The bedrooms are another pleasant surprise – not at all seedy but light and bright and well-furnished. At 150f for a double with bath they are good value. Cheerfully-served food – not bad – and menus start at 55f.

Parisiens love it and it is usually fully booked in the season, when full pension is *de rigueur*. At other times of the year it is not difficult to get a room and very few Brits have discovered it. If the building were tidied up a bit it would be stunning, the surroundings utterly peaceful; there is a long lake where they fish for carp and a wide terrace from which to admire the view.

'We made straight for your *Château de Quinéville*. It is certainly a lovely, peaceful place and as you say completely different. We had Chambre No. 7, 145f plus 20f for a single bed, private bath and separate loo, but very small towels and hot water only morning and late evening. We would go again. We took the 55f menu which was rather dull, but *the house wine was good at 21f. We were the only GB.' – Air Commodore R. Sorel-Cameron.*

Map 4E

RANVILLE (Calvados) 105 km from Le Havre; 130 km from Cherbourg

Cross the historic Pegasus Bridge over the Caen Canal, heading towards Cabourg, and the D 37 will lead to Ranville. Little to show from the quiet roads, flowery cottage gardens and the church on the hill that this is anything but a typical Norman village, but its place in the history books is assured by the chance that this was the first village to be liberated, on 6 June 1944 – by the 13th Battalion, Lancashire Fusiliers, as the commemorative plaque points out.

Auberge Les Platanes
(HR)S
rte
d'Hérouvillette.
(31) 78.68.48.

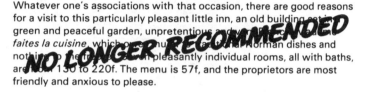

Whatever one's associations with that occasion, there are good reasons for a visit to this particularly pleasant little inn, an old building set in green and peaceful garden, unpretentious and comfortable. *faites la cuisine,* which one can nurture on Norman dishes and nothing to hectic. Its pleasantly individual rooms, all with baths, are from 130 to 220f. The menu is 57f, and the proprietors are most friendly and anxious to please.

Map 2B

RÉVILLE (Manche) 31 km from Cherbourg

A village on the D 1, between Barfleur and St-Vaast.

Au Moyne De Saire
(HR)S
(33) 50.10.06.
*Closed
11/11–31/12;
Sun. p.m; Fri.*

Strange how next-door St-Vaast should be such a Brit stronghold and Réville all but ignored by any but the French. This is a charming little Logis, run by friendly management, serving good, reasonably priced food (menus from 45f) in a charming dining-room; its bedrooms have all been recently redecorated in country style (doubles cost from 75 to 160f for a good-sized twin-bedded room with bath and loo).

Map 4F

LA RIVIÈRE-THIBOUVILLE (Eure) 137 km from Le Havre

The river Charentonne, a tributary of the Risle, winds swiftly through its damp-grassed valley; its teeming fish providing diligent French anglers with ample reward for their perseverance. Local hostelries are not slow to profit from this abundancy and fresh fish features strongly on their menus. For non-anglers the area provides plenty of opportunity for enjoyment in exploring the several Risle tributaries, in country green with beech and studded with Norman castles and churches. Unfortunately, La Rivière-Thibouville, looking so promising on the map, astraddle the streams, proves disappointing in reality. Sugarbeet mills dominate the little town. However, it would make a good centre from which to spin off in exploration, and I have very good reports of the substantial Logis de France situated there.

163

Soleil d'Or
(HR)M
(32) 45.00.08.
Closed Feb.;
Wed. o.o.s. 👍

An attractive dining-room overlooks the swing-ridden lawn. Rooms are 85 to 220f and could be noisy if you got one on the main road. Menus, with a casserole for good cooking from M. Hervieu, start at 62f.

Map 3G   **ROUEN** (Seine-Maritime) 88 km from Le Havre

I had always rated Rouen top of my list for a winter break, because of the variety of diversions there – the three wonderful churches, the Musée des Beaux Arts, the Joan of Arc memorials, the shops, the excursions and the restaurants – but my last visit was spent during the extraordinary weather of April '84, when a summer sun shone for a fortnight, the blossom on the cherry trees fell like confetti on the tables in the squares and the Rouennais came out in force to promenade along their pedestrianised precincts and take up every bench in the sunshine. I realised for the first time what a marvellous summer break could be spent in this lively and lovely city.

Every square, every alleyway has its quota of cafés, but none more so than in the old market square, the pl. Jeanne d'Arc. Always animated, with its amazing new market buildings, it was particularly colourful that weekend; as we sat in a café there and surveyed all the changes that had taken place recently I realised that almost everything I wrote about the place in *F.E.2* is now null and void.

The old Marée is a new wine bar – Le Bouchon de Rouen – a new experience for the French who, strangely, are only just beginning to copy us in the idea of offering a glass of good wine and simple food; the two most famous restaurants, La Couronne and l'Écu de France, have changed hands and characters; La Tôque d'Or is no longer to be recommended and (here is the good news) there is a splendid newcomer, Bertrand Warin (see p.168). At a lower level, but also highly recommendable, is another innovation, La Mirabelle (see p.170) and lots of new charcuteries and pâtisseries, like La Moule au Gâteau, where you can buy delicious buttery brioches, gâteaux and quiches, or Le Vieux Nice for home-made pasta and pizza.

The rest of Rouen looked enchanting too. It's always a good idea to start off at the Tourist Office for maps and guidance, but here it is worth a visit for its fascinating old building alone, just opposite the cathedral. In fact it's a city where it doesn't really matter in which direction you stroll; you cannot fail to catch glimpses of the ancient Rouen – narrow alleys where the top storeys of timbered houses almost meet, opening into sunlit squares, planted with trees and flowers, and everywhere cafés just when you need 'em most for sedentary appraisal. Its plan is compact, so that all the most interesting parts can be visited comfortably on foot.

Don't, of course, fail to walk from the Vieux Marché down the r. du Gros Horloge, where the familiar colourful clock is reinstated over the narrow passageway. I started to list some of the more interesting food shops here and in the rest of the city, but found so many excellent specimens, I gave up.

You can't go wrong. I know of no other French town with so many

Cathédrale Notre Dame

superb chocolatiers and pâtisseries, for example, in this case showing off their skill for the coming May Day celebrations. But I must single out **Périers** in the r. du Gros Horloge for special mention. Delightfully old-fashioned, with wonderful pastries to be elegantly wrapped to present or be eaten there in the salon du thé. Behind this is a more attractive restaurant with central aquarium, and walls decorated with ancient bakers' utensils, and beneath this is a visitable 13th-century crypt. A good location not only for a cuppa and indulgences but for a light lunch (open till 7.30, closed Sun.). *'A good spot for morning coffee and mid-day snacks, particularly quiches and omelettes, excellent at 8 to 10f each – and delicious cakes and chocolates.' – D. H. Upton.*

The magnificent cathedral terminates the vista along the r. du Gros Horloge. Sit quietly in the square to take in some of the details. As Monet realised, it is a building of many moods. Fascinated by its complexity, he painted twenty versions, different times of day filtering different light on the façade and offering him twenty alternative visions. One is in the Musée des Beaux Arts.

The cathedral might serve as a catalogue of architectural styles, developed over nearly eight centuries. Each age has added what it considered its finest possible contribution to the original 11th-century building. Of the two main towers flanking the 16th-century west door, the Tour St-Romain on the left is a relic of the 12th-century church, early Gothic on a Romanesque base; the right-hand Butter Tower is pure Flamboyant Gothic. It got its name in the 17th century, when those who wished to indulge in butter in Lent were prepared to buy forgiveness by a contribution to the church. The openwork spire is the tallest in France.

At least two other churches are essential viewing, on even a short visit to Rouen: the charming church of St-Maclou, built in the 15th–16th centuries, all Flamboyant Gothic, and the Abbey Church of St-Ouen, 14th–15th-century, where summer concerts are held in the beautiful chancel, making full use of one of the best organs in France.

Walk behind St-Maclou and between it and St-Ouen to discover the oldest part of Rouen. Skilful restoration is a continuous process here and a stroll along narrow lanes like the r. Diélette, full of antique shops, will be orchestrated with cheerful hammering.

Your tour of discovery is bound to lead you past the *Palais de Justice*, formerly the site of the Normandy Parliament. Severely damaged in 1944, shell holes much in evidence, the restoration of this elegant building is still going on. The Renaissance *Hotel de Bourgthéroulde*, just off the Vieux Marché, has famous bas-reliefs of the Field of Cloth of Gold, *Joan of Arc's Tower* is the keep of the castle (1204) where she faced torture. *The Musée des Beaux Arts* (closed Tue. and Wed. a.m., entry 4f) is one of the most important art galleries in France, particularly strong on post-Revolution artists, like Géricault and David, and on Impressionists and Post-Impressionists.

Winter or summer, try and find time for a visit to the Rouen Corniche. Take a picnic lunch with you, perhaps, to Ste-Catherine Hill, where an astounding panorama of the whole of the city and the loops of the Seine lies spread out below. To do this, drive along the north quays and turn left just past the last bridge. The 'Rouen Corniche' is clearly marked from here. Follow its twists and turns for about 4 km and stop at a sharp bend where a viewing table helps identification of landmarks. All the city's

Le Gros Horloge

many spires and towers rise up to the right, the industrial blocks to the left, and the bridges span the great shining river, dotted with ships and small craft. Eerie in the morning mists, spectacularly beautiful in the sunshine, exciting in the evening with the lights below beginning to sputter, not to be missed.

Few of Rouen's hotels have restaurants, but that is no hardship in a city with a good restaurant around every corner. There are now two new Michelin stars in the galaxy. Their set menus, one at 90f and one at 95f, illustrate perfectly the best bargains to be found in France. For this modest price, you get the chance to sample the cooking of potentially great chefs. These two could easily command five times this price if they worked in a better-known restaurant. Bertrand Warin, in fact, was a Guérard trainee. Their stars are fresh and so are their chefs, still anxious to work hard and prove they've earned them. Their menus will be chosen from the best produce of the daily market. Trust them. Here is a chance to try something unfamiliar and with any luck add to your gastronomic experience with a touch of inspired originality.

► Le Beffroy

(R)M–L
15 r. Beffroy
(35) 71.55.27.
Closed Aug.;
Sun.; Mon. AE,
E.

An old favourite, going from strength to strength. An extremely ancient building tucked away in a quiet street near the Beaux Arts. Small, intimate, elegant. I don't know how many starred restaurants have women chefs, but there can't be many in the whole of chauvinist France, and I suspect they have to be specially talented to be noticed. Dorothée l'Hérault has made it. Perhaps it is her lighter female touch that is responsible for such delicate sauces, such refinement of flavours. Try her scallops, with astonishingly green watercress sauce, or her pear charlotte with strawberry coulis to see what I mean. Booking wise. Menus 90 to 150f.

► Bertrand Warin

(R)M–L
9 r. Pie
(35) 89.26.69.
Closed 5/8–3/9;
Sun.; Mon.
lunch AE, V.

Two years is an unusually short time for a chef to be Michelin-accepted and starred, but the young Warin has achieved this speedy elevation. His little restaurant – just nine tables – behind the Vieux Marché is a joy. Useless to try and get in without booking for dinner, so we settled for lunch, guiltily leaving a beautiful summer's day outside. We needn't have worried that inside would be any less agreeable. Glass doors opened on to a green courtyard and wide shafts of sunshine penetrated the beamed dining-room in a very cheering style. Not that we needed much cheering. Complimentary *bouchées*, arrived very promptly, feuilletés de bigorneaux – buttery pastry encasing minute winkles (think of the shelling – with a hat pin?) – setting the scene for a meal of high standard. Two pots of butter, one salted, one fresh, lent confirmation.

The no-choice three-courses 'menu de la Pie' was exactly what I would have chosen anyway for a lunch on a hot day; each dish was superb of its kind: a terrine of chunky hare, jellied, cleverly patterned with crunchy baby beans and red peppers, flavoursome, light, perfect. Then turbot with a delicious sauce aux ciboulettes, and coulis of fresh tomatoes, then four sorbets, beautifully presented with tuiles d'amandes. Coffee came with irresistible petits fours.

These two are in a class of their own, and I strongly urge you to go there first, but they are often full. Resisting the temptation to point out only the sublime, I would suggest, as reserves, in the luxury class:

Dufour
(R)L
*67 bis r. St-
Nicolas
(35) 71.90.62.
Closed Aug.;
Sun. p.m.; Mon.*

Interesting old building, smartish, mostly grills, of high quality. Carte only – say 160f.

**Les P'tits
Parapluies** 👍
(R)L
*46 r. Bourg
(35) 88.35.26.
Closed Aug.
Sun.; Sat. lunch.*

Very pretty little restaurant in an old umbrella shop; a good exemplar of Nouvelle Cuisine. Lunch menu is 90f; otherwise allow 160f.

**La Cache
Ribaud**
(H)S(R)M
*10 r. du
Tambour
(35) 71.04.82.
Closed Sun.*

In a quieter side street near the Gros Horloge, and useful as a restaurant-with-rooms. There are only nine of them, all clean, simple, good value at 110f. There is no obligation to eat in but the restaurant has long been a Rouennais favourite; although the *patron*'s attention has been diluted somewhat by his recent acquisition of the Absinthe bar/grill, he still offers excellent value here in the medium price bracket (menus start at 49f).

Try one of the house specialities – *'ribaudie'* (which is a very good casserole of duck), or the cassoulette of snails, or the brill with mushrooms. Good traditional atmosphere in what the French call *cadre normande*. Small, so best book.

Rouen is exceptionally well provided for in that rare French facility – the good, cheap, quick eating place. All the following have been tested and not found wanting, in offering honest, unsophisticated food in comfortable surroundings:

Le Charles
(R)S
*139 r. du Gros
Horloge
(35) 98.16.03.*

I am full of admiration for the range offered by this restaurant/bar/brasserie in the centre of the city where it would be all too easy to catch the tourist's eye and chequebook. It just gets better at every visit. The building it occupies is one of the oldest in Rouen, but the inside has been modernised in *fin-de-siècle* style, with plenty of room to move, lots of plants, good place settings. Service outside too at the tables on the precinct.

Particularly useful are its hours, open every day, year round, until 11 p.m.

Food is far better than in most busy popular restaurants and the menus include half a bottle of decent wine, and service. The cheapest is 49f but fish is a house speciality and for 55f you can take the 'menu pecheur' with assiette de fruits de mer, oysters, etc. Highly recommended in its class.

Le Café des Postes
(R)S
43 r. Jeanne d'Arc

Similar in price and hours but very different in atmosphere. This is a traditional brasserie, in the Paris style of the 1900s, not as bright and cheerful as Charles and with rather grumpy, overworked waiters, but more authentic and very good of its kind, with a wonderful, affordable wine list. Stays open every day from 7 a.m. to midnight.

This is the place to fill up cheaply with a good omelette, bowl of onion soup. Three courses will cost around 60f. *'Typically French – excellent value.'* – D. G. Pinder.

Le Roi d'Ys
(R)S
92 r. de la République
(35) 70.88.86.
Closed Sun. p.m.; Mon. AE, E.

Recommended principally for a good cheap meal, perhaps on a bad day when a couple of hours over lunch seems a good idea. Atmosphere of safe respectability, so don't go here for a giggle but for excellent cheap *menu touristique* at 39.60, or a fish menu at 88f. *'Very good value for money. We found them most welcoming and helpful.'* – L. P. Blum. Gault-Millau recommends it, so best book.

La Mirabelle
(R)S
3 pl. du Vieux Marché
(35) 71.58.21.
AE, DC, E.

The best bet nowadays for everyday eating on this marvellous site. You can sit outside on the extensive terrace and watch the itinerant musicians, long of lock and sexless of jean, strumming and piping, among the Rouennais shoppers selecting shiningly fresh fish, or deux cent grams cut from the hunk of Normandy butter, or a blowsy hydrangea from the colourful display right outside the Mirabelle. After lunch this side of the square loses the sun but inside all is bright, cheerful, yellow. They pinched the chef from Dufour so the cooking is of a high standard, with specialities from Alsace, like a gargantuan choucroute. Menus from 50f, open every day until 11 p.m. *'We ate here twice – absolutely excellent but advisable to book, especially in the evenings.'* – Wilfrid R. Hazel.

Another pleasant and cheap bet to eat outdoors, popular with the locals as well as tourists is:

Café des Fleurs
(R)S
36 pl. des Carmes.

This one has the doubtful advantage of a cabaret of boules players, whose pitch is in the middle of the tables. All very serious stuff and not without hazard.

Pascaline
(R)S
5 r. de la Poterns
(35) 89.67.44.

I thought this newish bistro-bar by the flower market was a bit too chi-chi, with its 1900 décor, for inclusion in *F.E.2*, but it has actually improved with experience and the addition of a good new chef, as its popularity with locals shows. Open every day till 11 o'clock, serving a good menu at 55f or specialities like terrine de ris de veau or gratin de calamars au pistou. Lively and fun.

La Poule au Pot
(R)S
*13 r. du Père Adam
(35) 71.09.53.
Closed Sun p.m.; Mon.; Aug.*

Nothing outstanding gastronomically but chosen for its position in the oldest and most picturesque part of Rouen, between St-Maclou and St-Ouen where most other restaurants are tourist traps. This one has pleased readers and continues to offer good value on menus from 34f. There is a choice of simple brasserie or a more expensive rôtisserie in three rooms of quite different characters, so have a good look round before settling down.

La Marine
(R)S
*42 quai Cavalier de Salle
(35) 73.10.01
Closed Sun. p.m.; Sat.*

The best choice on the left bank. Small, unpretentious restaurant specialising in fish. Not a lot of character but good value, with menus from 46f. Beautifully fresh turbot and above-average desserts.

HOTELS

Hôtel de la Cathédrale
(HR)M
*12 r. St-Romain
(35) 71.57.95.*

I like this hotel because of its character (antique but charming) and its position (very quiet, between cathedral and St-Maclou). Inside there is an unexpected flowery central courtyard. Snags are that parking is difficult – you have to find the nearest slot and hump your baggage down the pedestrianised area – and that its popularity means booking well ahead.

23 rooms are all different and moderately comfortable, though they're a bit mean with their towels. 120 to 220f.

Very different are two modern hotels, safe, efficient, with easy parking. I don't normally suggest big modern hotels like this, but choice is limited in Rouen and these two have the unusual bonus of exceptionally good restaurants.

Hôtel Dieppe
(HR)L
*pl. Bernard Tissot
(35) 71.96.60.
AE, DC, E.*

Comfortable, near station. Rooms 249 to 323f. Restaurant Les Quatre Saisons has an excellent 100f menu and a grill room for cheaper quicker snacks.

Frantel
(HR)L
*r. St-Nicolas
(35) 90.06.98.
G. AE, DC, E.
Rest. closed Sun.*

Quiet, central. Vastly improved cooking by a new chef in restaurant *Le Tournebroche*. The 62f menu is a bargain. Rooms 338 to 478f, which I think is a bit much.

Grand Hôtel du Nord
(H)M
*91 r. Gros Horloge
(35) 70.41.41.*

A strange hotel tucked away in an alley off the pedestrianised r. Gros Horloge (and therefore difficult for parking). Full of surprises, the rooms are built round an ugly concrete courtyard, but in fact themselves have a lot of character. There are 64 of them, all different, none expensive. Worth asking to see several before making a choice between the different permutations of position, bath/shower, twin beds/doubles, etc.

85 to 178f. *'We stayed here over Christmas. A really good spot from which to see Rouen – slap bang in the middle. Striking clock no problem, but water pressure and temperature variable – not uncommon in France.'*

Morand
(H)M
1 r. Morand.
(35) 71.46.07
V.

I liked this little hotel in a quiet central street near the Beaux Arts park, with pleasant helpful owner. Comfortable rooms, the ones overlooking the courtyard particularly agreeable, from 135 to 220 f.

Viking
(H)S–M
21 quai au Havre
(35) 70.34.95.
AE, EC, V.

Could be noisy, overlooking a busy main thoroughfare, but good views over the river. *'Comfortable and inexpensive.'* Rooms 84 to 180f.

Hôtel de Lisieux
(H)S
4 r. de la Savonnerie.
(35) 71.87.73.

A little modern hotel between cathedral and the quai Pierre Corneille. 70 to 164f.

'Clean, comfortable and reasonable. Parking in front of hotel. Pleasant staff. Two double beds and shower 126f.' – D. G. Pinder.

Map 3F   **ROUTOT** (Eure) 54 km from Le Havre

Just north of the autoroute 18 km east of Pont Audemer. Turn off at Bourg Achard and take the D 144. It's a nice little town with a huge market square.

L'Écurie
(R)M
(32) 57.30.30.
Closed 10/1–30/1;
Tue.; Wed.

A well-groomed little restaurant in the square, rustic but comfortable, and particularly useful in that (a) it is an easy diversion off the autoroute, and (b) it is open on Sundays and Mondays when so many other restaurants don't care. It has a well-cooked 85f menu.

Map 3H   **RY** (Seine-Maritime) 106 km from Le Havre

Ry is a favourite excursion destination for the Rouennais, just 20 km away from their city, and it's not hard to see why. Flaubert designated it as the birthplace of Madame Bovary, there is a notable and wonderful carved wooden porch from the 16th century by the church, and the forest of Lyons surrounds the peaceful little town. Moreover:

**Auberge la
Crevonnière**
(HR)M
(35) 23.60.52.
Closed Aug.;
Tue. p.m.; Wed.

Suspiciously pretty. One feels nowhere could look as romantic, as ancient, as peaceful as La Crevonnière, with river Crevon cascading through its gardens, willows sheltering white tables, dovecots, roses, blackened beams, gardens – and not cash in. But, here is the honourable exception to the rule that maximum natural attraction spells minimum proprietorial effort.

When I tell you that on a busy Sunday lunchtime the *patron*, M. Laine, found time to telephone for me to another restaurant to say we would be delayed (having found it hard to tear ourselves away from La Crevonnière), you can appreciate that the management here aims to please.

I can't say the food is a great gastronomic experience. I can say it is well cooked and presented and that an hour or two spent in one of the four delightful small dining-rooms should bring great pleasure. Menus start at 60f weekdays and 90f weekends. Specialities are entrecôte marchand du vin, filet de veau à la cauchoise, tournedos périgourdine.

Four very pleasant countrified rooms (120 to 150f), with no more raucous sound than the splashing of the waterfalls to disturb a night's sleep.

Map 3E

SAINTE-ADRESSE (Seine-Maritime) 2 km from Le Havre

I have for long been singing the virtues of this leafy residential suburb of Le Havre and, judging by the letters, readers have not been slow in following my advice to turn *left* out of the ferry gates, avoid being embroiled in the town at all, follow the coast road for a bare two kilometres to find themselves in a pleasant beach resort, headquarters of the Belgian Government – no less – in the First World War.

Ste-Adresse was spared the 1944 devastation and retains its character. In one of its tall, narrow, white-shuttered, gravel-fronted, iron-gated houses is the hotel I prefer to all Havre's plastic efficiency:

► **Hotel des
Phares**
(H)S
*29 r. Gen. de
Gaulle*
(35) 46.31.86.
G.

Take the Étretat road and turn first right at statue of King Albert. The fattest file of all testifies to the pleasure *F.E.* readers have found in staying with M. and Mme Morgand. Christmas cards pour in from their client-friends, presents arrive for their grandchildren, bookings are made from one year to the next. It's certainly the only hotel in the area where I don't mind staying *toute seule*. Not really *seule* at all, because M. Morgand is a friend indeed and a very present help in trouble.

And not only for me: *'Nothing is too much trouble'; 'They made room in their garage for our two classic cars'; 'I left my shaving brush and M. Morgand had it waiting for me five days later'; 'A very affable hotel indeed. We enjoyed having our petit déjeuner with the affable French businessmen'; 'He offered without being asked to give us a call for the early ferry';* and so on.

The old hotel has rooms from 71f, but if you want a bath you must settle for the modern annexe, where the largest double, with double beds and an extra single, costs 120f. None of it is luxurious, but the Morgands' benevolent influence soon makes you forget that.

It is very pleasant to sit on the seafront, high above the stony beach, and watch all the marine activity. An equally good view can be had from any of the four restaurants on the front, and we often use the *Beau Séjour* on a summer Sunday evening before catching the ferry home. It still feels like holiday. I have to apologise to readers who recently used the Nice-Havrais on my recommendation. It is a strange restaurant, in a marvellous setting up on the cliffs; it has been up as high as a Michelin star, and down as low as a depression with all stages in between. I caught it last time swinging upwards after the first depression and hoped for continued progress, but it gave up the ghost shortly afterwards.

Le Beau Séjour
(R)M
3 pl.
Clemenceau
(35) 46.19.69./
46.19.96.
All cards.
Open year
round.

'We had a magnificent five-course menu with the accent on fish for 105f. Very good value. Mind you I chose a bottle of Pouilly Fuissé, which cost me another 105f, but it was well worth it.' – H. L. Emmett.

'Miserable wet afternoon in Le Havre. Dinner at Le Beau Séjour as soon as it opened on Sunday evening. Excellent dinner with courteous and quick service.' – Dr W. M. Edgar.

I know exactly what the Edgars felt – this is a refuge. Comfortable, warm, friendly, wonderful view over the water, and open when you need it most. I personally don't think the food's marvellous, but it's not at all bad, if you play safe, with straightforward fish, perhaps. Expect to pay at least 80f, and to meet several fellow-refugees all enjoying their meal.

Yves Page
(R)M
7 pl.
Clemenceau
(35) 46.06.09.
Closed
15/8–15/9;
Sun. p.m.; Mon.
All cards.

A tank full of lobsters announces the restaurant's fishy affiliations. Interesting food appreciated by locals, making booking essential if you want a window table, with that view. Not cheap, at about the same prices as its neighbour, Le Beau Sejour, not such convenient opening hours, and service much slower, probably better food, nice *patronne*.

La Plage
(R)S
11 pl.
Clemenceau.
(35) 46.16.25.
Closed Fri. p.m.

Recommended by several readers for its good-value menus. Much less up-market than the other two neighbours, with prices from 35f. Lots of fish on the menu.

Map 4B   **ST-AUBIN-DU-PERRON** (Manche) 60 km from Cherbourg

---

St-Aubin is a well-kept secret, lying east off the Périers road. The château is even more obscure, since it isn't in St-Aubin at all but 3 km nearer Périers on the D 52.

► Château du Perron
(H)M
St-Sauveur-Lendelin
(33) 46.63.69.

The only indication on the road that the Château exists is a faded 'chambre d'hôtel' sign on the right side heading north. The long and impressive avenue seems an unlikely introduction to a bed and breakfast arrangement, and if doubts don't arise then they well might when the full view of the chat's imposing façade comes into sight. Have courage. This is the winter home of Madame Gauthier of the Hôtel des Bains at St-Jean-le-Thomas (see p.177) and there are indeed five rooms available throughout the year.

The 19th-century château is very French, very beautiful, slightly faded but certainly not seedy like some, and the grounds and lake are gorgeous. It took me exactly one hour's drive from Cherbourg to locate it and the peace and restfulness of the place were immediately soothing.

The rooms are all newly decorated and spacious, but all very different, so priorities must be decided upon. The two most stunning are on the 1st floor, long windows overlooking lake, one of them with swagged corona over a double bed, but neither of them has a bathroom. Those on the second floor are also assorted, some with bath, some with shower, some with neither, one twin-bedded, one single, the nicest rooms in the front, those with best view at rear. All extremely comfortable and arrow-worthy.

The only meal served is breakfast in the dining-room, and this is included in the room prices of 140f for two people, with bath, or 110f without, 85f for a single. There is a elegant salon to relax in and those fabulous grounds and *allées* to explore and picnic in. Beaches are only ten miles away and there are plenty of restaurants around for evening meals.

Auberge des Bonnes Gens
(R)S
Le Mesnilbus
(33) 07.66.85.

An old inn, where M. Harvel cooks regional specialities, washed down with local cider, all for 36f.

There is an association of *gîtes ruraux* around this oddly-named hamlet, many of them in old ancestral homes which would have fallen into ruin had their owners not seized the opportunity to renovate them and let out rooms. They have combined to make a *centre de loisirs* with pony club, bicycle hire and tennis court, and with thirty gîtes to choose from, there should usually be no accommodation problem. The number to ring is (33)07.75.99. All very interesting and so far unexploited.

Map 7E   **ST-DENIS-SUR-SARTHON** (Orne) 209 km from Le Havre

11 km west of Alençon on the N 12.

La Faïencerie
(HR)M
(33) 27.30.16.
Closed 15/11–
Easter. Rest.
closed Tue.
lunch.

Another member of the Châteaux Hôtels Independants et Hostelleries d'Atmosphere chain. They certainly vary the atmosphere bit. This one is an old pottery, but who would have thought it now, elegantly converted as it is into an hotel and restaurant. The bedrooms are lovely, spacious and well furnished. 200f with bathroom, or 85f with a loo across the passage. Menus from 85f.

Map 2B

ST-GERMAIN-DE-TOURNEBUT (Manche) 25 km from Cherbourg

A hamlet in the maze of little lanes south of the D 902, 5 km north-east of Valognes. No hardship if you do get lost trying to find it, since the pleasure of discovering such totally rural unspoiled country, seemingly unchanged for centuries, outweighs any frustration. My careless map-reading took us down farm tracks, up manorhouse drives, splashing through fords, held up behind herds of unhurried cows. A total change of pace and all a mere 18 miles from the port. I was looking for:

Louis Sanson, Au Bon Acceuil (R)S
*(33) 41.13.12.
Closed Wed.*

'We had a four week holiday in a gîte here and the café-restaurant in the village is a must. We had their fixed price menu – the best meal we ate in France.' – Des Rigby.

Louis Sanson proved to be a sleepy little bar/restaurant, house dog dozing in the sun outside, undisturbed by any traffic. Inside is a log fire, over which Madame Sanson grills the meat that features on her 68f menus. Preceded by a gratinée de fruits de mer, the fish of the day, and followed by salad, cheese and dessert. It's all good wholesome country cooking. There's also a four course 55f menu including a gigôt of lamb. I suspect the choice is always the same, but no harm sticking to what you do best.

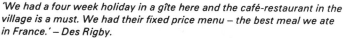

Map 7B

ST-HILAIRE DU HARCOUET département; 147 km from Cherbourg

I was somewhat disappointed with St-Hilaire, which was completely rebuilt after the war, and didn't stop long to investigate its hotels, but it appears to be a favourite overnight stop, judging by readers' letters.

Relais de la Poste
HR(S)
*r. Mortain.
(33) 49.10.31.
Closed
11/6–30/6; Fri.
o.o.s. E, V.*

'Quiet hotel in town. Good dinner, pleasant room with bath. Nice friendly atmosphere.' – S. E. Brown.

A double room is 135f. Menus from 36f.

Hotel Cygne
HR(M)
*rte Fougères
(33) 49.11.84.
Closed
24/12–3/1. DC,
E, V.*

The Cygne is in the main street and has rooms with showers only. Its annexe, La Residence, is newer; rooms with bath available. Prices vary from 130 to 190f. Restaurant has menus from 56f.

Lion d'Or
HR(M)
r. Avranches.
(33) 49.10.82.
Closed
15/10–3/11;
3/2–24/2; Sun.
p.m.; Mon. lunch
o.o.s.

This is the one I would recommend for a meal. Michelin gives it a red 'R' for good value and the locals patronise it well. Menu at 50f. It has rooms that I know nothing about from 85 to 165f.

Map 6A   **ST-JEAN-LE-THOMAS** (Manche) 128 km from Cherbourg

---

Pleasantly sleepy village, with one main street leading eventually to the vast sandy beach, where the tide recedes for miles and the cockle-gatherers gather. Mont St-Michel swims on the horizon.

**Hôtel Les
Bains**
(HR)M
(33) 48.84.20.
Closed
11/11–15/3;
Wed. o.o.s.

Half the village now seems to belong to Mme Gautier. Apart from the main Les Bains building, with pleasant dining-room full of flowers from her garden, and small heated swimming pool, she not only governs the annexe across the road but two other nice stone houses nearby and another by the sea, in all of which breakfast alone can be taken. It depends where your priorities lie as to which you might choose, so try and discuss them when booking.

And book you must, for the hotel is an old-time favourite with the British and is usually full throughout its short season from May to Oct.

The rooms are on the small side and cost 185f for a double but the food is copious and good with the Michelin red 'R' ensuring even more customers in the dining-room. Sadly, a few significant quibbles are beginning to be registered:

'Now taking coach parties; lounge gets far too full and smoke-filled. It would appear that they are attaching more importance to earning money fast than to running the nice family hotel it used to be.'

In the winter Mme Gautier retires to her beautiful château at St-Aubin du Perron and there she lets out five rooms year round. See p.175.

Map 4C   **ST-LÔ** (Manche) 78 km from Cherbourg

St-Lô has the sad title 'Capital of the Ruins', and I have dodged staying there because I find its concrete reincarnation so sad, but it is a natural centre to the area, and because the restaurants are used by people who work in the town rather than tourists, good value can be found.

Local recommendations are for Hôtels **Terminus**, **Gare et Le Marignan**, **Voyageurs**, **Grand Hôtel Univers**; and for restaurants: **Hôtel Gare et Le Marignan** and **La Cremaillère**.

Market days are Saturday in the town centre and Tuesday on the banks of the Vire.

Map 3F	**ST-MACLOU** (Eure) 44 km from Le Havre

On the N 175, just north of the autoroute on the Honfleur road, D 180, 9 km from Pont Audemer.

La Cremaillère
(H)S (R)M
(32) 41.17.75.
Closed
28/9–4/10;
16/11–7/12;
Wed. p.m.; Thur.

It was Thursday when I tried to check out this little hotel, on the crossroads in the centre of the village, conveniently placed for a breakfast stop, or cheap lodging near Honfleur, so I am particularly indebted to a reader for his report:

    'A small charming restaurant and hotel; the food was really enjoyable, and the service friendly – chef de cuisine, M. Lefebvre. We did not see the bedrooms but judging from the restaurant, toilets and kitchen, which we did see, they would be good.' – Peter V. Marshall.

    The rooms are certainly cheap, at 90f a double, and menus start at 62f.

Map 4G	**ST-PIERRE-DU-VAUVRAY** (Eure) 112 km from Le Havre

Hostellerie St-Pierre
H(L) R(L)
(32) 59.93.29.
Rest. closed
Jan.; Feb.; Mon.
p.m.; Tue.

Michelin gives the Hostellerie three red turrets for style and a rocking chair for peace and it is a Relais du Silence, so perhaps expectations were too high for a fair assessment of this odd, towered, turretted, fake-beamed, fake-old Norman hotel. Or perhaps the adrenalin involved in just finding it took the edge off the appreciation.

    I didn't have the hotel brochure at the time, which devotes a whole page to a map and instructions as to how to avoid the spaghetti junction of autoroute A 13 and Nationale 15, dodge the encroachment of Louviers and find the way to a turning off the D 313 before the bridge over the Seine.

    The dining-room is a refuge of peace and elegance after the auto-horrors, with log fire, rafters and many windows overlooking the river. This is not a specially attractive stretch of the Seine, but it is always soothing to feel the presence of water and diverting to watch the laden barges pass by.

    The food is expertly presented but of mixed quality. The sorrel sauce for my salmon was excellent but the slices of fish were thin and dry. Moules were good, as was the *terrine du canard* and the *tarte Tatin*. Menus at 90f, 130f, 220f.

    I thought the rooms, even with the river view, very expensive. The one in the tower was pretty enough, with modern fourposter, beams and bathroom, but not 380f worth.

Map 2B	**ST-PIERRE-ÉGLISE** (Manche) 15 km from Cherbourg

Never a favourite town, even on Wednesday when the morning market introduces at least a little colour into the prevailing greyness, but only 2 km away, on the D 901 Barfleur road is a find:

Château de la Brehoulle
(HR)M
Varouville
(33) 54.24.07.

M. and Mme Brisset renovated this manorhouse, well set back from the main road, and opened their doors to the public in 1983, but it is still a well-kept secret from other guidebooks, with obvious advantages.

The rooms are lovely, spacious and well-furnished, with views over the tennis court and garden to the distant sea. There are variations of shower, bath, double or twin bed, but all are most attractive, verging on the luxurious. Prices for a double run from 190 to 250f. Elegant lounges and dining-room, calm, and the pleasant M. Brisset add up to a good deal.

He does the cooking himself, on menus from 80 to 140, which I have not yet sampled, but on talking to him soon discovered that he cooks with enthusiasm and knowledge. He told me he has given up offering *magret de canard*, since it has become such a Nouvelle Cuisine cliché (how I agree) and his favourite dish now is *langoustines à l'estragon*. I should be very surprised to hear that the food is anything but delicious (but reports especially welcome please).

Not so cheap as some in the area, but altogether the most pampering spot for a weekend break.

In order to introduce French *Entrée* readers to such a treat, M. Brisset is making them a Special *Offer*. From October to Easter, for two people, he suggests: one splendid double room for one night, two breakfasts, two dinners for 600f. So, just as an idea, the 9 a.m. sailing from Portsmouth to Cherbourg would get you to the château by 3.30 French time, still allowing plenty of time for a drive out to St-Vaast, for example, for tea, or some shopping in Cherbourg, and the 6 p.m. sailing home the next day would ensure another full day enjoying the many simple pleasures of the Cotentin peninsula.

Map 2B   **ST-VAAST-LA-HOUGUE** (Manche) 30 km from Cherbourg

---

A real fishing village on the eastern coast of the Cotentin peninsula, where the far-receding tide leaves vast stretches of muddy sand and rock. You can walk to the little island of Tatihou at low water. Edward III landed his troups here on the way to Crécy.

But there have been great changes in the last year or so. An extensive marina is being constructed in the harbour, with attendant yacht club, bar, administrative offices, lock control, shrubberies, all lavishly conceived. Hard to tell what effect a fundamental addition like this will have. Local interests are thrilled at the prospect of increased trade and year-round prosperity; everyone I spoke to looked forward to more British visitors, and whether this predominance will spoil the character of a place cherished for its archetypal Frenchness is hard to say.

Meanwhile the charm remains; the colourful fishing boats, though now outnumbered by pleasure craft, go about their business impervious to the yellow wellie brigade, the seagulls screech above the clangour of the halyards, the oyster sheds sell oysters, not bed and breakfasts, and St-Vaast is still the most delightful spot to stay on the east coast.

There are several bars, cafés and fish restaurants along the harbour where a plâteau de fruits de mer and some local oysters can be enjoyed, but the star is undoubtedly:

► **Hôtel France
et Fuchsias**
(HR)M
*18r. du Mal.
Foch.
(33) 54.42.26.
Closed
10/1–20/2;
Mon. o.o.s. DC,
V.*

How often are there disappointments in returning to old haunts! Different moods, different times, different company have frequently meant different, less enthusiastic impressions. I feared it would be so with this old favourite of mine, simply because it is now also the favourite of many many other fellow-countrymen. I knew that Mme Brix is never short of customers, regulars and initiates, and that often leads to fatal complacency. What an added pleasure, therefore, to discover that in this case further acquaintance led to even deeper affection.

Other aspects of St-Vaast may change, but not the France et Fuchsias. Or, rather, if it does, it seems for the better. Five new rooms will mean more lucky customers will get reservations. They are built at the rear of the house, overlooking the garden, guaranteeing peacefulness. The old rooms retain their character – tiny, wooden floors, simple without tattiness, (fresh flowered wallpapers, obvious spit and polish), and the kind of bath that leaves me wondering whether legs should hang over the side or climb up the wall.

The fuchsias still rampage up to the roof, and drape themselves around the glass walls of the conservatory/dining-room; their colour is nicely echoed in the pink walls and table linen, and when the superb breakfast arrived, croissants in basket, real butter, real jams, the tray was laid on pink and white gingham; all small touches that add up to a huge feeling of caring.

The basic success, of course, lies in the family background to the hotel. Madame Brix no longer cooks herself but woe betide the careless

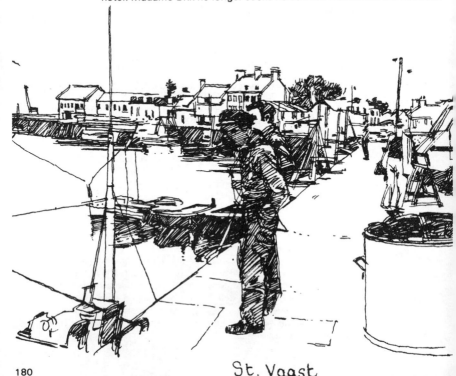

St. Vaast

cuisinier who tries to get a slovenly dish past her all-seeing eye; she tastes every sauce before it arrives at the table. Her husband presides genially in the office, emerging to embrace regular guests or make a fuss of visiting children; their son does the marketing of whatever produce does not come from the farm, where he lives with his charming wife and three children. Vegs, butter, cream, poultry, rabbits are all home-produced and most of the fish comes locally, but he was off to Ouistreham to buy the delectable fresh scallops I ate for dinner that night. Young Madame Brix welcomes, smiles, takes orders and is generally helpful.

The food was even better than I remembered it and very lavish indeed. Admittedly I was greedy enough to go for the menu gastronomique, which, at 95f, was a snip – terrine de lotte with hollandaise, six fresh scallops with purées of fennel and carrot, divine cassoulette of sweetbreads, cheese, raspberry charlotte – but my daughter Charlotte's 65f version was amazing value – soupe de poisson, flavoursome terrine maison, and rillettes, rabbit with prunes, chocolate marquise with whisky-impregnated sponge fingers and lashings of Chantilly cream. The cabaret of the evening was watching the diners' faces light up as the desserts arrived on each table, overflowing with calorific home-made ice creams and dollops of Normandy cream.

You really couldn't do better.

There is also an arrangement in summer months for accommodation in an annexe: *'large house, very near port, down an alleyway that opened up on a delightful garden. Food and accommodation superb.'* – A. G. Crisp.

Map 1F	**ST-VALÉRY-en-CAUX** (Seine-Maritime) 72 km from Le Havre

---

Considering how badly it was bombarded in 1940, the little fishing town retains a good deal of character. Several of the old buildings survived across the drawbridge, but the market-place and its surrounds are entirely post-war. A forest of masts rise up from the yachts tied up in the river mouth, and fish is sold straight from the fishing boats along the quays. The beach is stony, and seems forever windswept, but I was reproached for a too-hasty dismissal of the hotels along its sunless prom:

Terrasses
(HR)M
(35) 97.11.22.
Closed
15/12–30/1;
Fri. E.

'Don't write off the hotels along the front. We used the Hôtel des Terrasses for three nights. The hotel was of a good standard for a non-Logis but the meals were superb. "The best trout I've ever had," says my wife, and the côte de porc provençale was in a class of its own.' – Keith R. Whettam.

Apologies.

Here are the details:

Rooms 112 to 196f. Meals from 75f.

Les Bains
(HR)S
pl. Marché
(35) 97.04.32.
Closed 1/12–
15/2; Mon.;
Sun. p.m.

'Good, cheap rooms and an excellent table. Muscadet at knock-down prices. Madame speaks no English but speaks French especially slowly for the foreigner.' – G. S. Parkinson.

Le Port
(R)M
(35) 97.08.03.
Closed
20/9–10/10;
20/12–6/1;
Mon.; Thur. p.m.;
Sun. p.m. o.o.s.
V.

Always packed with locals, excellent for fish, but the menu has now gone up to 73f and the opening times are distinctly problematical. Just a little way out of the town to the right of the Veules-les-Roses road, by the old church is:

Le Pigeon
Blanc
(R)S
(35) 97.03.55.
Closed
10/1–10/2;
Fri. V.

Get there early or book, because this little chalet restaurant in a nice garden is always full of locals who know a bargain when they see one, like the excellent 42f menu.

Map 3G

ST-WANDRILLE RANÇON (Seine-Maritime)
32 km from Le Havre

4 km from Caudebec is the hamlet of St-Wandrille, famous for its Abbey. The ruins are open from 10.15 to 11.45 a.m. and 3 to 7 p.m. Men only allowed in the cloisters so I can't report personally, but the ruins of the 14th-century nave are pleasant enough to stroll round and there is another walk to the St-Saturnius Chapel along the Abbey wall, to work up an appetite for:

Auberge Deux
Couronnes
(R)M.
(35) 66.11.44.
Closed
29/8–12/9;
1/2–23/2;
Sun. p.m. o.o.s.

A charming old Norman building in the village street, opposite the Abbey – quite small, full of flowers, colourful table linen, and oak beams of course. Excellent value menus from 50f.

Map 2F

SASSETOT-LE-MAUCONDUIT (Seine-Maritime) 55 km from
Le Havre

The coast road north from Fécamp, D 79, is altogether more attractive, with its valley indentations and wooded hills, than the rather dull countryside that lies only a few kilometres inland. Well worth a drive, especially to find, opposite the château:

Relais des Dalles
(R)M
(35) 27.41.83.
Closed
3/11–23/11;
15/2–28/2;
Mon. p.m.; Tue.
AE.

[There aren't many restaurants that merit both three crossed forks and a red 'R'* in Michelin for a 48f set menu. The Relais is the exception and is deservedly popular (so book)]. Attractively low beamed with a nice garden – well worth making a detour to this one.

'Whit Sunday lunchtime here was a great experience. Very busy but good food and service. Best moules à la crême experienced in a two-week Normandy holiday and excellent wine list.'

* Red 'R' removed since last edition.

La Suisse Normandie

A particularly attractive area of Normandy, roughly south of Caen; it bears little relation to Switzerland, not even claiming Normandy's highest peaks, but it does have a distinctive landscape of green hills and even greener valleys. The river Orne winds its way through rich pastureland or cuts into the rocks of the Armoricain massif.

The region is well-organised for the tourist and there should be something there for everyone, all ages. Even in July I did not find it over-crowded. I would wholeheartedly advise anyone who wanted to discover the heart of Normandy, with a variety of diversions, to take a holiday in this area. Here are some ideas for the hyper-active:

Canoeing is very popular, understandably when you see how attractive the river Orne is and picture paddling through its gorges. Canoes can be hired and courses for beginners arranged from: Base 'Lionel-Terry', Le Viaduc, 14570 Clécy. (31) 69.72.82.

Same address for rock-climbing organisation. Favourite destinations are Le Pain de Sucre, Le Faverie Cross or the St-Aubert Gorges, all with panoramic views. Bed and breakfast is available at the Lionel Terry centre; booking for all courses essential.

Watching the hang-gliders taking off from Les Rochers de la Houle near Clécy costs nothing; they give demonstrations every Sunday and *fête* days. If you too have Icarus ambitions apply to: Comité de Gestion de la Route des Crêtes. St-Omer 14220, Thury-Harcourt. (31) 69.70.32.

Probably the most popular pastime is fishing. Local restaurants benefit from the Orne's richness in trout, pike and perch. Permission has to be obtained from local societies: La Sociétie de Pêche, L-Orne Fleurie 14220, Thury-Harcourt.

While Dad goes fishing, the kids might like to hire a bicycle and explore the region on their own. Apply to 'Location de Bicyclettes', Clécy 14570. M. R. Letournel (31) 69.72.92. Or, for horse-riding, from L'Etrier de la Suisse Normandie, La Lande 14570, Clécy. (31) 69.70.06.

Scenic routes are well signed, and a day's car excursion need be no more taxing than to follow the arrows. An impressive example is the road to the Oëtre Rock, overlooking the Rouvre Gorges.

Sees.

Map 7E	**SÉES** (Orne) 152 km from Le Havre; 189 km from Cherbourg

For my money the most attractive little town for many miles around, perhaps because it is so obvious where its heart lies – in and around the early Gothic cathedral ('one of the finest examples of 13th and 14th century Norman Gothic' enthuses Michelin). The buttresses that had to be added to prop up the subsiding porch are a touch unfortunate, but otherwise it is a gem – not too vast, never crowded, seemingly always flooded with light. In summer evenings and weekends the floodlighting comes from the Son et Lumière spectacle; I have never managed to catch it, but it must be an uplifting vision, inspired by the 14th-century pilgrims who used to spend the night of the summer solstice in the cathedral, witnessing their contemporary version of 'alchimie des couleurs, magie des lumières'.

The cathedral is set in a pleasant cobbled market square hard by other ancient buidings, erstwhile seminaries, Bishop's Palace, convents, their functions changed perhaps, the town demoted from bustling Gallo-Roman provincial importance to drowsy backwater, but still with the priceless advantage of a centre, a hub, a heart.

I found a delightful little hotel, not in the main square but facing on to the gardens of the ruins of the Romanesque St-Pierre:

Le Cheval Blanc
(HR)S
pl. St-Pierre
(33) 27.80.48.
Closed Oct.;
1/2–15/2. Rest.
closed
1/10–15/2, Fri.
p.m.; Sat. o.o.s.
P. V.

All that one could wish for in a really simple country hotel. Black and white timbering, windows opening onto a vista of trees, flowery bedrooms, helpful proprietors, pleasant dining-room. And the cost? 53f for a double room, with excellent menus from 34f!

Situated as it is, about halfway in a southerly loop between Cherbourg and Le Havre, and about 2½ hours drive from either, I think Sées would make an ideal base from which to explore the region and that the undemanding comfort and quiet of the Cheval Blanc could not fail to please most British visitors. A potential arrow, I think, only awaiting some confirmatory reports.

To the south-west of Sées runs the Forest of Écouves, well-manicured, neat piles of logs, shade, quiet, good for shady picnics on benches provided, or for long walks down the avenues. Boar, roe and red deer are among its population. The road through the forest west of Sées, the D908, is very beautiful; it leads to the rather boring little town of **Carrouges**, but, unusually sited in a dip below the town, lies the enormous 16th-century castle, moated, chequered bricks, visitable for 8f from April to October from 9–12 and 2–6 except Tue. (See also Château d'O p.147, Medavy p.147 and Haras du Pin p. 109.)

Map 7C	**LE TEILLEUL** (Manche) 155 km from Cherbourg.

On the N 176 towards Domfront:

La Clé des Champs (HR)M *(33) 59.42.27.* *Closed 14/1–11/2.*	A modern and comfortable Logis. Rooms 90 to 190f. Menus start at 60f. *'Very well-appointed and reasonably priced. Restaurant excellent. – K. F. Buttall.* *'An extremely good small quiet hotel. The patron is chef and the food is outstandingly good. We stay there once or twice a year, sometimes just for one night on our way south, sometimes for four or five days. A little English spoken.' – H. R. Powis.*

Map 5D

THURY-HARCOURT (Calvados) 131 km from Le Havre; 150 km from Cherbourg

Disappointingly characterless after its post-war reincarnation. The elegance of its name and its situation in the heart of the Suisse Normande conjures up a picture of a more interesting town. This let-down continued when I visited the much-praised **Relais de la Poste** last year. I thought the meal over-rated and the bedrooms over-priced, and decided to omit the hotel this year. Now I hear that new owners, M. and Mme Engrand, have taken over and locals like them. More reports please.

See also Goupillières p.103.

The Poste, with its Michelin star and central position, has so dominated the town that other establishments have tended to be overlooked. Down by the bridge over the river is:

Du Val d'Orne (HR)S *(31) 79.70.81.*

An old-fashioned hotel, serving simple meals from 32f and with equally simple, but perfectly adequate, rooms; a double will cost around 100f. A good cheap base from which to explore the valley of the Orne.

Cornerwise on is a little restaurant that my local friends, Erik and Liz de Mauny, tell me is their favourite:

Suisse Normande (R)S *Closed Wed.*

Clearly popular not only with the de Maunys. In high season you should certainly book to get a place in the pretty, Norman-style dining-room. Excellent regional cooking on menus starting at 45f.

Map 2E

LE TILLEUL (Seine–Maritime) 26 km from Le Havre

2 km short of Étretat on the coast road. A discovery. If you take a sharp left opposite the church at Le Tilleul, you will find (eventually) a beautiful uncrowded beach. The narrow lane winds through cornfields, down a wooded ravine to a sign which says, roughly, 'No entry – road in bad condition'. I was meekly preparing to turn back when a friendly picnicking Frenchman urged me to 'Continuez'. 'Take no notice of the notice.' (I've often noticed that the French are far less law-abiding than are we – they can't tolerate a queue, nonchalantly abandon their cars on pedestrian crossings and regard any notice that starts 'Défendu' as a challenge.) I was grateful to this one because I found a group of other cars parked at the terminus, before a scramble down to a wide and wonderful beach. Like its neighbour, Étretat, it is enclosed by those

unique statuesque cliffs; no sand, alas, along this coast, and the cobbles are hard on the feet, but lots of flat rocks for picnic tables and only a scattering of families, in peak season. Good bathing from the steeply shelving beach.

I ate my picnic lunch on the grassy hill above the bay, listened to the counterpoint of soprano lark, tenor seagull, vibrato bass pigeon, and thought, 'If this is work, I like it'.

Le Tilleulerai
(R)S

At the crossroads is a little restaurant, favourite with many Havrais families, who drive out here to eat excellent seafood. Simple, cheap and good.

Map 1H

TOCQUEVILLE-SUR-EU (Seine-Maritime) 122 km from Le Havre; 127 km from Calais

Turn off the D 925 on to the V 2 and follow the sign towards the coast, to Tocqueville. Behind the church is:

Le Quatre Pain
(R)M
Closed
10/8–10/9;
Feb.; Mon.; Sun.
p.m. o.o.s.

I have been trying for three years now to eat at Le Quatre Pain, intrigued by the award of a Michelin star to such an exceptionally modest establishment. It still looks as unassuming as when I first discovered it. No outward sign of its eminence – just a 'Bar' sign above what looks like the village shop in a sleepy deserted hamlet.

This year, by booking weeks ahead, I made it – and was disappointed.

When M. Brachais's cooking started to draw the discriminating to his little shop I am sure I too would have enthused about the unexpected quality of the country-style food, but now, with all tables full, and signs of the interior being smartened up, it is neither one thing nor t'other, losing identity and character. The food is undoubtedly better than one would expect from a village café, but not good enough for a star.

The strain shows. Madame Brachais and her daughter were literally running from one table to another, still we had to wait over 40 minutes for the menu and a much-needed glass of wine. I don't think there is time for much tasting in the kitchen – everything was a shade under-seasoned. All good quality, but a shade boring, and I hate having to choose a pud at the beginning of the meal.

The menu is wisely limited and an average meal would cost around 120f. I couldn't help comparing it with Warin's in Rouen, where we had eaten incomparably better the day before. Here my hure de saumon looked better than it tasted and the sauce d'etrilles round the sole was thin and watery.

However, this was Sunday lunch, when most restaurants come under pressure. One reader reports very well and a critical local hotelier friend likes it, so perhaps my expectations were unreasonably high. I certainly admired some of the little touches, like the complimentary baby welsh rarebits and the miniature pancakes with the coffee. Open verdict, awaiting further evidence.

| Map 5C | **TORIGNI-SUR-VIRE** (Manche) 91 km from Cherbourg |

A useful stop on the N 174, a good fast road south. The nice little town is dominated and given character by the restored château, on whose terraces the market is held. Very pleasant wandering round here peering into the baskets of hens, speckled guineafowl and doves and feeling sorry for the rabbits stunned in the cramped runs. The surrounding park and lakes are pleasant places to stroll and the river Vire splashes agreeably through the town.

A most spectacular beauty spot is only 6 km away – the Roches de Ham. Park in a flat meadow and walk to the edge prepared to have your breath taken away. With no warning, the land comes to an end and hundreds of feet below, at the bottom of an escarpment of white cliffs, runs the river, through a panorama of Normandy. You can walk down a pleasant winding lane to the river and puff back up again to take tea and crêpes in the garden of the café by the car.

Hôtel de la Gare
(HR)S

For the hungry and hard-up, a Relais Routiers – the ultimate in simplicity, with paper cloths, bar, curious lorry drivers – in the station yard just north of the town. Marvellous value – four good courses for 35f including coffee and wine. And les routiers don't tolerate small helpings.

'To celebrate such an excellent meal we treated ourselves to Calvados with our coffee for another 2f! We were quite amused to see the lorry drivers tuck into avocado pear or cold salmon on the first course and a splendid vacharin for pudding.' – David Dunham.

A double room is 50f but I was not brave enough to look.

| Map 2E | **TOUQUES** (Calvados) 77 km from Le Havre |

Only three kilometres inland from Deauville, on the river from which it takes its name, lies the charming little medieval town of Touques. No longer an important port, as it was in the 11th century when some of its old houses along the river and the church of St-Pierre were built, it attracts few tourists now. That is a pity, since its mature charms contrast well with those of its more popular parvenu neighbour and its brassy *port de plaisance*.

Thomas à Becket built a church here and gave it his name and the Dukes of Normandy were regular visitors. A few small ruins of William the Conqueror's castle at Bourneville-sur-Touques are reminders of the town's early eminence.

A huge new hotel, **l'Amirauté**, bids to claim some of the tourist market for Touques, but I didn't like either its modern looks or its position on the bypass by the industrial estate, so can't report. Neither can I comment this year on **Le Relais du Haras**, favourite of Gault-Millau. Its prices have gone up to a level (170f cheapest menu) that I find incompatible with its charms. During its limited hours, best bet now is:

Aux Landiers
(R)M
*90 r. Louvel-et-
Briere
(31) 88. 00. 39.
Closed
15/6–30/6;
Tue.; Wed.;
Thur.*

A nice little Norman-style restaurant, good at charcoal grills, with a recommended 90f menu.

Map 3F

TROUVILLE-ALLIQUERVILLE (Seine-Maritime) 37 km from Le Havre

**Le Moulin à
Grains**
(R)M–L
*(35) 38.04.46.
Closed
15/7–10/8; Sun.
p.m.; Mon. P.
AE.*

Particularly useful because of its position (apparently in the heart of nowhere but in fact just a minute off the main N 15 between Bolbec and Yvetot) and because it is open in winter when there is not a lot of choice in this area.

A picturesquely timbered old Norman mill, with smartish meals served in the garden in summer and around the log fire in winter. Specialises in huge grills of really fresh fish and pig, with a new menu of 90f including wine and coffee.

Map 3E

TROUVILLE-SUR-MER (Calvados) 74 km from Le Havre

Where Deauville dies for part of the year, languishing at the loss of its colourful migrant visitors, its *demodée* neighbour, Trouville, just across the river, enjoys year-round vitality. Deauville is elegant, expensive, gaudy, effete, cosmopolitan; its sister town is bourgeois, cost-conscious, faded, gutsy and very French.

The parade along its *planches* may not be as chic as Deauville's but breathes the same sea air and benefits from the same view of vast beach across to the Le Havre headland. The best view of the town comes from the Deauville side, when the evening sun exploits the bright colours of the fishing boats along the quays and contrasts them with the old grey houses and shops rising steeply behind them. Back on the harbour the fish market stays open late, even on Sundays, and you can stroll along the stalls learning the French names for the many varieties. I even saw a dangerous-looking tray of oursins there.

Along the quay are several fishy restaurants; my favourite is:

Les Vapeurs
(R)M
*160 bd F.
Moureau
(31) 88.15.24.
Closed Tue.;
Wed.*

A real French brasserie, bustling, lined with mirrors and twenties posters, busy waiters in black trousers and waistcoats, open late. Well-known and popular, so book if you can.

They don't mind how little you order. I had their special moules – a great mound of 'em, which at 22f were more than I could eat. My husband chose turbot and got a great steaming hunk, patently fresh, plainly served with a few potatoes. Tarte Tatin wasn't special, but the atmosphere made up for deficiencies.

Chez Antoinette, Restaurant du Port at No. 142 (closed Tue.) also looked good and popular, and the upstairs restaurant has a better view of the port. For an altogether different cosy beamed atmosphere, try **La Petite Auberge** just behind the quay. Not cheap but very pretty, good fish and meat too.

Hotel Reynita
(H)M
29 r. Carnot
(31) 88.15.13.
Closed Jan. AE,
DC, V.

Nice welcome, quiet, central, good-sized rooms from 88f, double bed and shower, to 230f with three beds and bath.

Les Sablettes
(H)M
15 f. P-Besson
(31) 88.10.66.
Closed
15/11–1/2.

Well-kept, central but quiet. 184f double with bath.

Amienoise
(H)M
5 r. Bonsecours
(31) 88.12.23.

Old-fashioned, very French, clean, quiet side street. 132–169f double.

Hotel Carmen
(HR)M
24 r. Carnot.
(31) 88.35.43.
Closed 4/1–4/2.

The best choice if you like to eat in your hotel. *'A pleasant Logis, run by M. and Mme Bude, only 300 yards from the beach.'* – H. Cromwell. Rooms 100–210f. Menus 60–100f.

4 km outside Trouville on the D 74 is the **St-Gatien airport**, where many locals retreat to eat away from the holidaymakers.

'Whoever told you that the food at St-Gatien airport was some of the best in the area was not wrong. We lunched on the 78f menu – the salade du jour was strips of fried cabillaud, batavia, poached bantam's eggs still warm, delicious terrine maison, followed by chicken breasts in cream, ham and cheese, mixed vegetables like mushrooms in garlic, aubergines. Then very fresh cheeses and a great choice of puds. I had raspberry bavarois with strawberry sauce. The dining-room is very elegant – style Normande – overlooking the runway.' – Elizabeth Armstrong.

I had always meant to try this one – now I certainly shall do so.

Map 5B   **TRELLY** (Manche) 80 km from Cherbourg

Trelly lies between the D 971 and D 7 south of Coutances, but whenever I pass a sign towards it on these two fast roads it always takes me by surprise that anything so intrinsically rural should be even within striking distance of 'civilisation'. The lanes round the Verte Campagne, in the hamlet of Le Chevalier, are the heart of Normandy; best of all in the spring, when starred with primroses and the cowslips that are sadly so rare in England nowadays, and when the lambs look up in astonishment as the car edges its way between the high hedges, but green year round, if not with bud then with mistletoe. Aptly named, therefore is:

**La Verte
Campagne**
(HR)M
*(33) 47.65.33.
Closed mid-
Nov.–mid-Dec.;
Sun. p.m.; Mon.*

A member of the group of hotels known as 'Châteaux-hôtels Independants and Hostelleries d'atmosphere'. It certainly doesn't come in the first category but most emphatically in the second. It is a modest 18th-century farmhouse, grey stone, bright with white paint and climbing roses in summer. Inside are flagged floors, beams, flowers, chintzes, log fires in winter.

Mme Meredith, the widow of an English naval officer, runs it with a minimum of help – too minimal, some would say; there are reports of very poor service and long waits, but it would take a brave customer to complain. 'Madame Meredith can be a bit of a Tartar,' as one reader puts it. Chef's night off seems to be a bit erratic too. One couple found on a Wednesday night that a cold buffet had been laid on instead of the hot dinner thay had been looking forward to; when they told Madame M. they would rather eat out in that case, she 'carried on something rotten'.

However, even the doubters agree with me that they would go back. Praiseworthy details include tea by the log fire, bedrooms with real furniture, sheets matching décor, drinks in the garden, a general elegance hard to find nowadays, and the feeling of staying in a private house rather than an impersonal hotel. If you like a lot of fuss, forget this one. What you will get is a country-house atmosphere and every incentive to chat to your fellow guests in the intimacy of the tiny dining-room or round the fireside in the salon.

The eight bedrooms vary enormously; last time I got a minute double, very pretty, shaded from the aggressive sunshine with green creeper framing the lattices, and a sit-up-and-beg bath. 6 and 7 are the best rooms – twin beds, bathroom, separate loo. *'Quite the most delightful hotel room we've stayed in for a long time.'* – Commander A. J. W. Wilson.

Food, when the chef is in attendance, is good and imaginative. Not a lot of choice, but a range of prices from 60 to 110f. Rooms 110 to 230f.

(*Stop press.* I hear that Madame Meredith has taken on a new partner and changes are in the air.)

Map 1A   **URVILLE-NACQUEVILLE** (Manche) 11 km from Cherbourg

On the coast road west of Cherbourg. There is a little beach at Urville-Nacqueville, but not much else. However, this might offer a cheap overnight stop, near the port:

Beau Rivage
(HR)S
*(33) 03.52.40.
Closed Oct.;
Sun. o.o.s. Rest.
closed Sat. o.o.s.*

'Restaurant simple and pleasant; hotel on roadside in village, quiet and very rural feel.' – Rosemary Thorner.

'We have used this hotel for a number of years, as accommodation in Cherbourg itself is difficult and comparatively expensive. Rooms are comfortable and the menu at 40f is very good value indeed.' – R. O. Hooton.

Rooms from 70f. Menus 45–100f.

Map 2G	**VAL DE SAANE** (Seine-Maritime) 73 km from Le Havre

A market village, north of the N 29 Bolbec–Tôtes road. It is just 3 km south of Auzouville (see p.37); and it was Madame Lambert who recommended:

La Mère Duval
(R)S
pl. de l'Église
(35) 32.30.13.
Closed Tue. p.m;
Wed.

A pretty, beamed, rustic restaurant in the market square, flowers in copper pots, lots of locals, cane chairs, red cloths. Menus are straightforward and simple but ingredients are of high quality and readers have all been delighted with the meals they have taken there on the night when Madame Clamaron at Auzouville has been closed. Four substantial courses cost 51f (not weekends though) or 71f.

Map 2B	**VALOGNES** (Manche) 20 km from Cherbourg

Although the centre of this dairy-market town is sadly concrete modern, thanks to the events of June 1944, there is enough of the 18th century, when it was known as the Normandy Versailles, in the quiet back streets to give an idea of how it once must have been – the capital of the Cotentin peninsula. An enormous market fills the square on Fridays.

Hôtel de
l'Agriculture 👍
(HR)S
16r. L. de Lisle
(33) 40.00.21.
Closed Sun.,
Mon. p.m.
1/1–15/1, 15/9–
30/9.
Change of
proprietor

Everyone likes this attractive, creeper-clad old inn – the locals, the travellers and the regulars who make it a cheap base for a weekend. The value is amazing. Four-course meals are 50f, five courses are 65f and for 85f you get a gargantuan six-courser, including oysters and a vast fruits de mer. Not for the gourmet but for country tastes and appetites. Must book.

A few doors along the quiet road is another old house, being converted into an annexe. One double-bedded room, one single and bathroom, all well furnished and carpeted, for 120f. Rooms are smaller in the main hotel and cost 60–110f.

'I cannot too highly recommend the Hôtel de l'Agriculture, in a quiet street with ample parking space, just off the main Cherbourg-Bayeux road. The food is excellent.' – P. A. Thorne.

Mrs P. Millward offers a good tip here. She, like so many others, found the restaurant full (it does take coach parties, unfortunately) but saw tables being laid up in the bar and promptly bagged one of those: *'spotless linen cloths and cutlery quickly laid and excellent meal eaten for 48f. Moules and soupe de poissons arrived piping hot in huge copper pans – plenty for four people – followed by equally delectable meat course.'*

One reader, Mr B. R. Scholes, points out that many of the hotels in this ferry-convenient area are closed in September/October and recommends a new possibility, open year-round:

Hôtel Saint-
Malo
H(S)
7 r. Saint-Malo.
(33) 40.03.27 👍

Rooms 70–140f, no restaurant.

Map 1G

VARENGEVILLE-SUR-MER (Seine-Maritime) 100 km from Le Havre

A popular excursion from Dieppe, 12 km away to the east. Turn off the D 75 on to the V 13 for an area of unspoiled Norman countryside. Down the country lane stands the ancient church, buffeted by the sea gales, its graveyard running down to the very edge of the high cliffs. Braque is buried there and inside the church his Tree of Jesse, burning blue, brings a steady stream of tourists. Nearby is the Parc des Moutiers, an 'English' garden, surrounding a Lutyens house. The French are mad about it, but it's comforting for a *chauviniste* to discover that it's not really a patch on any self-respecting English equivalent.

I didn't think much of the well-publicised 15f-worth offered by the Manoir d'Ango either. This fascinating 1530-ish manor was built by Jehan Ango, a complete Renaissance man, developer of the ports of Rouen, Honfleur, Le Havre, a great shipowner, Governor of Dieppe, banker, explorer. Here he entertained François I and Diane de Poitiers; from a high window in the manor he showed the King a fleet of fifteen galleons riding at sea – a gift to support the King's projected attempt to seize Calais back from the English.

All fascinating stuff and the Italian Renaissance-style architecture is rare in France, but with a quick peep inside the courtyard to see the distinctively patterned dovecot, you can take it all in from the outside for free, even being cheeky enough to picnic in the shade of the avenue leading to the gatehouse.

La Terrasse
(HR)S
Vasterival
Closed
1/11–15/3. G.
E.

Modest, peaceful, set in the pine trees above the sea; readers have liked it and its proprietor, but demi-pension is obligatory and the menu has been criticised as 'ordinary'. A double room is 70–100f. Walks round here are good and there is an interesting little beach, so perhaps the hotel's shortcomings might be overlooked for a simple, undemanding weekend.

Map 2B

LE VAST (Manche) 20 km from Cherbourg

One of the prettiest villages in the area, on the D 26 St-Vaast road. Time stands still and the only rushing comes from the river Saire which flows alongside the main (and only) street. On the corner is the village shop, **Les Moulins du Vast**, where they make their own large buttery brioches. Madame Thonine will fetch one, all hot from the oven and sell it to you by weight. Sliced and dripping with Normandy butter and some cherry jam is the way to eat it, but don't forget that brioches, like croissants, are very dull fare indeed if they're not eaten the same day.

Map 6G

VERNEUIL-SUR-AVRE (Eure) 163 km from Le Havre

On Normandy's border, defined by the river Avre, and therefore fortified in the 11th century to hold the frontier against France. Lots of splendid old houses in the area between the Tour Grise, the 1120 drum tower, and the 15th-century church of La Madeleine, three stories high, crowned with a double diadem of lantern and Flamboyant tower. Notre Dame is another interesting church to visit in this fascinating little town, with wide market square full of colour on Saturdays, ramparts to explore and the river Avre nearby. An excellent choice for a weekend, particularly with the bonus of:

► Hôtel du Saumon
(HR)M
*89 pl. de la Madeleine
(32) 32.02.36.
Rest. closed
Wed. lunch. P.
AE.*

You're not going to believe this, but the name of the charming *patron* of the Hôtel du Saumon is M. Poisson. How tired he must be of the jokes. He is a director of the Hostellerie du Clos (see below) and between them the two hotels should well satisfy most tastes.

He showed me all round the Saumon and I liked it very much indeed; perfectly charming, perfectly French. There is a modern wing, comfortable and functional in the rear courtyard, but I preferred the older rooms on the square, spacious and full of character. A double costs from 74f to 172f with bath. The menus are excellent. The 65f version offered, for example, a specially interesting hors d'oeuvre, a poulet normande and good cheeseboard and desserts; the 45f was even better value.

Arrowed for a charmingly French hotel, helpful proprietor, good food, pleasant rooms, good value, in a delightful town.

► Le Clos
(HR)L
*98 r. de la Ferté Vidame.
(32) 32.21.81.
Closed
15/12–15/1;
Mon. P. AE, DC.*

This odd-looking, turretted, brick-patterned hotel is one of the more modest members of the Relais et Châteaux chain, and that is no slur. As far as the prices go, it's a definite advantage. At 256 to 350f for an extremely elegant and comfortable double bedroom and bath, they are good value.

The atmosphere is very *correcte*: dignified, calm, orderly, the discreet charm of the bourgeoisie. The efficient Madame Simon welcomes, while her son Philippe is in the kitchen preparing superb dishes like a terrine de langoustine et d'artichaut or l'agneau à la gousse d'ail, which anyone nervous of garlic should certainly try in order to prove that eaten like this in quantity, meltingly tender round the lamb, it does not deserve its unfortunate reputation. Menu at 115f highly recommended.

Arrowed for excellent value in the luxury category, with comfort and unusually good cuisine.

Map 5H   **VERNON** (Eure) 151 km from Le Havre

An appealing small town on the Seine; some attractive old houses still stand in tree-lined avenues near the 12th-century Notre Dame and there is an extensive and bustling Saturday market. The liveliness unusually extends into Sunday, when many of the shops stay open, making it a good base for a weekend.

There is plenty to see and do in the neighbourhood, following the convolutions of the Seine or exploring the banks of the two other local rivers, the Eure and the Epte. On the latter, **Fourges** is a pleasant destination for an excursion. You can picnic there, where a massive old waterwheel revolves hypnotically against the background of a picturesque old inn (the Moulin de Fourges, regrettably looking a bit too seedy to recommend further).

The dignified 18th-century **Chateau of Bizy** (closed Fri.) is another popular excursion and a drive in that direction, taking the D 52 through the forest, is particularly worth-while in the autumn, when the beech and chestnut leaves are at their most colourful.

But Vernon's best-known tourist attraction is, of course, the house and gardens at nearby **Giverny**. It is open from 1 April to 1 November, 10–12 and 2–6, except Mon., admission 25f.

I had thought that perhaps in late October the gardens might be disappointing, but the chrysanths, dahlias and michaelmas daisies, interplanted in usual French garden colour-blindness with gaudy begonias and busy lizzies made a blaze of colour in the autumn sunshine; although I missed the wisteria, the green bridge over the waterlily pond was as evocatively familiar as I could have wished. Plenty of customers even as late as this, so it could be over-trafficked in high season.

The autoroute runs very near and Paris is no distance, so the area is studded with restaurants, many of them expensive. Vernon itself seemed badly served both for food and beds. The most obvious hotel is the *Evreux* and I had had one glowing recommendation, but the very ordinary double room offered was 290f, and the po-faced receptionist said she was only prepared to let us have it if dinner were eaten in the hotel, so I declined on principle. The menu was long, printed, fairly expensive, fairly boring, so it was no wrench.

I crossed the road to:

Strasbourg
(HR)M
6 pl. Evreux
(32) 51.23.12.
Rest. closed
15/12–10/1;
Sun p.m.; Mon.
P. E, V.

In this old-fashioned hotel we got a similar double room with bath for 140f and, arriving mid-morning in a welter of vacuum cleaners and polishers, can vouch for the cleanliness. Breakfast was good, with freshly squeezed orange and croissants, the management friendly, and behind the hotel was a large private car park. There was no obligation to eat in, which was just as well since the large dining-room was gloomily empty (menu at 50f).

We drank a reviving beer at a little bar overlooking the river and asked for local eating tips. An avalanche of advice poured out from *patron*, wife, friends, fellow drinkers; maps and Michelin were seized and argued over and although the din was prodigious the votes proved unanimous. All good stuff. 'You must go *now*,' they said, 'or you won't get in – it's market day and everyone eats at:

Restaurant de la Poste
(R)S
26 av. Gambetta
(32) 51.10.63.
Closed Wed.

Proved to be just opposite the Strasbourg, so the two would combine very well, since the restaurant is excellent value too.

Small, comfortable, well-patronised not by the stallholders I had expected but by a solid bourgeois clientèle of shoppers. The five-course 55f menu had lots of variety, including good moules, onion soup (soups seem to be vanishing from French menus these days), steaks, pigeon, trout. Recommended.

Map 1G	**LES VERTUS, OFFRANVILLE** (Seine-Maritime) 108 km from Le Havre

Probably *the* place for a luxurious blow-out in these parts, 3.5 km outside Dieppe. Certainly the smart Dieppois think so. It's on the main N 27 Rouen road, past the Mammouth hypermarket, so if you feel you've deserved a treat after trolley-trundling, you could spend all the money you've saved at:

▶ **La Bûcherie**
(R)M–L
St-Aubin-sur-
Scie.
(35) 84.84.10.
Closed
20/10–10/11;
Mon. P. AE, DC,
V.

Outside smart, freshly-painted, inside ditto, with thick carpets, flowers, shining cutlery and glasses, cocktail bar. M. Delauney, the *patron* chef, is ambitious, dedicated, and, I am sure, up-and-coming. He insists that he will have nothing but the freshest of the market's produce and there is a rather nice disclaimer on the menu: 'nous sommes tributaires du temps et de la pêche'.

Good value menus, four courses for 90f or six for 140f.

Map 1G	**VEULES-LES-ROSES** (Seine-Maritime) 62 km from Le Havre

The cobbles (galets) on the beach of this attractive little flowery village give their name to a very special restaurant:

▶ **Les Galets**
(R)L
(35) 97.61.33.
Closed Feb.;
Tue. p.m.; Wed.
DC.

I don't know why I feel I have to apologise when recommending a luxury restaurant in France; the menu here is 160f, which, translated into English terms – around £14 – would be a rare bargain. Saved up for a treat (there I go again), I guarantee an experience to treasure from a meal here. The difference between the good and the great is perfectly illustrated by Gilbert Pleasance's inventiveness and attention to detail (he smokes his own fish, for example). Here is a Norman chef who is not content to rely solely on the reputation of the local produce, but is always ready to experiment, taste, improvise, improve. The best of both traditional and Nouvelle Cuisine, in fact.

His sole, for example, is cut into goujonettes delicately fried, their richness cut with a dash of truffle-flavoured vinegar. He makes fresh pasta to serve in restrained portions with a pearly salmon on a bed of sorrel. And his desserts are particularly outstanding, at a time when other restaurants are making economies here. Try his soufflé pancakes stuffed with a pear purée or the mousse of wild strawberries served with a fresh raspberry coulis and gilded with crème fraiche.

The menu is four courses long, including a wonderful cheeseboard, but if appetite were lacking, this might be the place to order only one superb dish (especially as a complimentary feuilleté de foie de canard comes with the aperitif and a selection of tiny tartes aux fruits with the coffee!). One word of warning, though. The wine list is neither cheap nor particularly exciting. They had a bad flood here not long ago, and the cellar suffered. Choose carefully.

Delightful at night, when the polished silver shines in the light of candles, or on a hot summer's day, when the terrace comes into its own. But book anyway.

Map 6B   **VILLEDIEU-LES-POELES** (Manche) 112 km from Cherbourg

"God's Town of the Frying Pans', where the streets are lined with shops selling the locally-made copper ware, is one of the most popular *French Entrée* destinations. It's a pleasant little town, particularly busy on Tuesdays, when its wide market square gets taken over from an early hour with colourful market stalls.

Hôtel St-Pierre et St-Michel
(HR)S
pl. République
(33) 61.00.11.
Closed
15/12–1/1, Fri.
o.o.s.

Too early an hour, writes one reader, whose sleep was shattered at 5 a.m. Traffic noise has been the most serious complaint about this well-known archetypally French inn, but the latest report is that double-glazing has been installed and not even the Tuesday lorries and market cries can be heard from the front rooms.

Earlier reports had it that the standard of service and food was falling. *'Are they resting on* French Entrée *laurels?'* asked one, but I believe all is now very well indeed, with the Michelin red 'R' well-deserved for good food at a good price. Rooms 60 to 150f, menus from 40f.

Le Fruitier
(HR)S–M
(33) 51.14.24.
Closed two
weeks in Feb.:

'We stayed here again for a week in June and found it as excellent as ever and Madame Lebargy was positively blooming. They have acquired the next-door premises and plan to extend into them. The hotel has a really beautiful new dining-room, reception and bedrooms. A double room with bath is 170f or with shower 150f, and a reduction of 20f per room will be made to the bill if the occupants eat in.' – John Halliday.

Map 3F   **VILLEQUIER** (Seine-Maritime) 45 km from Le Havre

From Caudebec take the D 81, following the Seine, and 3 km towards the Tancarville Bridge is the village whose doubtful claim to fame is that Victor Hugo's daughter drowned there. Turn left off the busy main road to find:

▶ **Hôtel de France**
(HR)S
quai Victor Hugo
(35) 56.78.70.
Closed Sun
p.m.; Mon.

 food

 rooms

Undiluted praise for a discovery that I am particularly proud of. I first wrote about the Hôtel de France in *F.E.1* and since then readers' enthusiastic letters have amply proved my praise was justified:

'Thank you for the very happy week we recently spent exploring Normandy! Our best meal (three of us always choosing different dishes) was, we all agreed, at the Hôtel de France.'

'The evening meal at the Hôtel de France was the best of our holiday. They were so imaginative – a little sorbet with Kirsch between the entrée and the main course. The lady of the house in constant supervision, the little restaurant packed and with good reason – a very well spent 55f.' – Mrs M. Rose.

Don't be put off by the un-smart exterior. The rustic dining-room is very pretty and the hotel sits on the very banks of the river, ensuring a bonus of watery interest. In summer the courtyard is pressed into service too. The rooms are very basic indeed but at 95f with shower and wc, and that marvellous view, a lot can be forgiven.

The charming and hardworking young owners, M. et Mme Loisel, have now come up with a *Special Offer*, which I hasten to pass on to my readers as a very good idea for a weekend in Normandy without a long drive, always provided that the hotel's undeniable simplicity is acceptable. For 450f you get: from Friday p.m. to Sunday p.m. i.e. two nights' room, breakfast, four meals, with M. Loisel's specialities *for two people*. Book by letter or wave a copy of *French Entrée*.

Otherwise a five course menu costs 51.50f and for 74f you get six courses. Unless of course you splash out on the bargain of the year – 102f for a whole lobster, sorbet au Calvados, carré d'agneau, pièce de boeuf flambée aux 2 poivres or Caneton Melly, salade aux 4 sauces, plâteau de fromages, baked Alaska or crêpes Victor Hugo. But be warned, the word is getting round and it is now advisable to book.

Grand Sapin
(HR)S
Closed
12/11–21/11;
15/1–6/2; Wed.
o.o.s.

Mixed reports here. Everyone agrees that at 85f for a double room and 41f for the menu, the value is exceptional, but there are criticisms of the management – *'impersonal', 'uncaring', 'inefficient'* – and of the bathwater – *'cold at 6 p.m. but hot in the morning!'* The position is splendid – right on the river bank, with extensive garden for summer sitting – but I suspect, as it is such an obvious choice, alongside the main road, it might get a bit over-run in summer.

I think the bedrooms are lovely. Old-fashioned but comfortable, with faded chintzes and flowery wallpaper, very spacious and un-plastic, and most of them with a wonderful view over the water. Ask for one with a balcony, if you can, for best appreciation.

The food is not outstanding and has been compared unfavourably with that of the little Hôtel de France, but it is certainly very adequate, with menus to suit all pockets.

Map 5D   **VILLERS-BOCAGE** (Calvados) 113 km from Cherbourg

On the main N 175 between Caen and Vire.

**Hôtel Les
Trois Rois**
H(S) R(M)
(31) 77.00.32.
Closed
25/6–2/7; Feb.;
Mon.; Sun. p.m.
o.o.s.

A friendly little Logis de France, providing a useful overnight stop. Set back from the main road, but could be noisy. Inside all is calm. Elegant dining-room serving well-prepared, imaginative food. Henry and Aline Martinotti are the proprietors and go out of their way to make their guests enjoy their stay. He cooks specialities like 'chausson de homard et sa mousseline aux truffes' and 'turbot farci vieille auberge', which won him a gastronomic concours first prize. Menus from 68f. Rooms 80 to 160f.

Map 5E   **VIMOUTIERS** (Orne) 160 km from Le Havre

The centre of the dairy produce area. A statue to Marie Harel, who gets the credit for having 'invented' Camembert, stands at the entrance to the little post-war town.

The hamlet of Camembert lies 3 km to the south-west with another memorial to the farmer's wife who is said to have neglected her cheesemaking one day and found it strangely and deliciously transformed the next. The farms along the *Route des Fromages* display signs offering their version of the local speciality. I couldn't resist that particular souvenir and followed a sign into a ridiculously picturesque farmyard full of hens, dogs, flowers. Fat cows continued their munching in the apple orchard, indifferent as to whether I bought their produce or not. I did, and with some innocent-seeming *cidre bouché* made by the same farmer, it made the basis of a perfect picnic.

Escale de Vitou
(R)S
Centre de Loisirs, rte Argentan.
(33) 39.12.37
Closed 15/1–30/1; Sun. p.m.; Mon. o.o.s.
V.

A few km out of the town on the D 916 lies this complex of sports facilities, with an excellent-value restaurant, all in most attractive surroundings – an ideal place for a family holiday. Vast open-air swimming pool, grass skiing, stables, tennis courts, fishing, pedalos on the lake. What with a well-equipped playground and sandy, well-swept beach, all the children there seemed to be having a splendid, never-dull-for-a-moment holiday.

There are eleven little Norman-style gîtes, varying in size, accommodation and price, but all bright and well-equipped. The permutations of season and length of stay etc. are so endless it's best to write for details. Weekend stays are also available.

The restaurant, unlike so many in such situations, stands in its own right as an attractive proposition. Overlooking the lake, it offers a very good menu at 38f (not Sat. p.m.).

Map 6C   **VIRE** (Calvados) 117 km from Cherbourg

High above the rolling Norman countryside, the site is attractive enough, but the town was annihilated during the war, and I can't say I find its reincarnation is one of my favourites. Its specialities are sausages – boudins and andouilles. Not everyone's taste, but this is the place to try them at least once.

One of my biggest disappointments in researching *F.E.2* was the Cheval Blanc; I found it noisy, gloomy, unfriendly and over-priced, and could not understand why every other guide book should recommend it so highly. Most of all I disapproved of its fierce *patronne*, who clearly considered a Michelin rosette a licence to be rude to her clients. But now there are changes afoot. The rosette has gone. We shall have to see what effect this harshest of penalties will have on the management's attitude, and can only hope that by the time the next edition appears, this old favourite of so many British travellers will have learnt its lesson.

Hôtel des Voyageurs
(HR)S
(31) 68.01.16.
Closed Sun.

Not much to look at either but what a difference in every other way that matters! Here is one recent experience:

'The owner/chef, Patrick Denian, has numerous certificates on his walls testifying to his excellent prize-winning regional dishes. We found it all quite charming and tasteful, and the food excellent. We chose the 60f menu (others at 42f and 120f) which offered their enormous cold buffet as a starter .Then a house speciality, a pavé of boudin and andouille combined, served with a steamed apple and salad. My partner's main dish was salmon trout marinaded in red wine and poached, served with delicious thick cream and mustard sauce. With sorbets, desserts and cheese, this one was a meal to remember, served by friendly efficient staff.' – Lance Berelowitz

How I agree that first essentials are to find a friendly welcome and a chef who serves unpretentious food based on local ingredients and time-honoured recipes. I have yet to stay there myself (perhaps when I do it will help to dispel my prejudice against Vire), but someone who has, writes: *'We had a clean comfortable room at a charge of 50f for two. Dinner was excellent, with plenty of choice on the cheapest menu, very convenient parking in an enclosed courtyard beside the hotel.'* – Diana Moorhouse.

Rooms are now 75 to 135f and menus from 46f.

Just outside Vire, on the Villedieu road is:

Le Relais Normand
(HR)S
Martilly.
(31) 68.08.67.
Closed Sat.
o.o.s.

The wife of the proprietor, Madame Goure, speaks good English, and I have several testimonials to her welcome and to the cleanliness of her establishment. M. Goure is the chef and cooks local specialities like rabbit in cider, veal vallée d'Auge and of course andouille de Vire.

I feel this would make an excellent cheap stop, with rooms from 50 to 70f and good menus starting at 35f, but I have not checked it personally yet.

Map 4G   **VIRONVAY** (Eure) 116 km from Le Havre

The autoroutes and *routes nationales* round Louviers look like tangled knitting, especially from the driver's seat, so try to have a map-reader you can blame. All the more welcome, then, is a surprisingly rural retreat of calm which would make a restful, if somewhat expensive, overnight stop, at Vironvay. Take the Louviers Sud turning off the A 13 and follow the signs to:

Les Saisons
(H)L (R)M
(32) 40.02.56.
Closed
16/8–31/8;
28/1–28/2.
Rest. closed
Sun. p.m.; Mon.
DC, E, V.

A very unusual arrangement of five cottages or *pavillons* each with double bedroom, sitting room and bath for 480f, or nine rooms from 210f. All very comfortable and serene. Meals are eaten in a very pretty pink and green restaurant or in the garden at elegantly-laid white tables.

Unfortunately there aren't many such respites of fresh air and tranquillity so near the autoroutes, and Les Saisons has been well written up, so it is always necessary to reserve well in advance.

Map 2F.   **YPORT** (Seine-Maritime) 38 km from Le Havre

The chalky white rocks of this little fishing port will be familiar from many posters. A fine view of them may be had from:

La Sirène
(HR)S
(35) 27.31.87.
Closed Mon.
o.o.s.

A nice little Logis right on the seafront, with steep steps up to the entrance, making it unsuitable for the less agile/more inebriated guest. All ten rooms cost 110f and menus start at 50f.

'We had twin beds, basin, shower and private toilet. Good breakfast for 10f, with croissants. Excellent food – four menus, even the cheapest having five courses with wide choice. – G. E. Waters.

Map 2G   **YVETOT** (Seine-Maritime) 51 km from Le Havre

A fair-sized market town centre, rebuilt, whose ferro-concrete St-Pierre church has a hard-to-miss free-standing belfry/scaffolding encasing Max Ingrand stained glass; I'm told it's glowingly impressive from inside. Not a lot of interest otherwise nowadays, and hard to believe that from the 14th century to the Revolution the town was an independent territory with its own King; However, lying as it does at the hub of several *routes nationales*, it might prove a useful overnight stop.

'Tartes citrons and indeed all the pâtissiers and charcutiers were better in Yvetot than any other areas visited.' – M. C. Wilson.

Hôtel du Havre
(HR)M
pl. Belges
(32) 95.16.77.
Closed
18/22–18/1;
Sun.

'Good busy commercial hotel in centre of town. Clean and pleasant rooms, interesting and very good typically French provincial food.'
Rooms 100 to 190f, menus from 60f.

Wine Hints from Jancis Robinson

HOW TO READ A WINE LIST

Wine lists in France, just like their counterparts in British restaurants, can be confusing – and sometimes even terrifying, with the only affordable bottles hidden below a stack of great names at even greater prices. There are certain ground rules in their layout, however.

The most basic of wines made in France are called *vins de table*, and may well be listed under this heading, to differentiate them from wines with some sort of geographical designation, either *Appellation Contrôlée* (AC) or, slightly more lowly, *Vins de Qualité Supérieur*. The 'house wine' in many French restaurants is of this simple *vin de table* sort and may be described as Vin de la Maison, or Vin du Patron meaning 'our wine'. There are many branded table wines too, the sort that carry a brand name, and these should be listed under a special heading, *Vins de Marque*. There is also a new breed of rather superior *vin de table* which is worth looking out for, and which may be listed under the heading *Vins de Table*, or the region where it was made, or under the general heading *Vins de Pays*. These are sound quality *vins de table* which are good enough to tag their provenance onto their name.

All other wines will usually be grouped under the heading of the region where they were made and, usually, split according to red wines (*rouges*) and whites (*blancs*). The following are the main wine regions of France, in the order in which they *usually* appear on a smart wine list (though there is, exasperatingly, no standard convention):

Champagne

Almost all champagne is dry, white and sparkling, and only the wines of the Champagne region in northern France may call their wines champagne. Other sparkling wines are Vins Mousseux, though they may boast on their label that they were made by the rigorous *méthode champenoise.*

Bordeaux

France's biggest and best-known region for top-quality dryish reds, wines that we call claret. Most of such wines are called Château This or Château That, which will vary from about 50 francs a bottle to the earth and then some. 1980, 1979 and 1976 are vintages worth drinking now. Bordeaux's great white wines are sweet (*doux*) dessert wines from Sauternes, though there are now some good value dry (*sec*) wines too.

Bourgogne

We call this small, highly-priced region Burgundy. Its dry whites such as

Montrachet are the greatest in the world; its reds can be lovely scented, smooth liquids, though there are many highly-priced disappointments. 1980 and 1978 were good years for reds, but good whites are produced with reassuring frequency.

Beaujolais/Mâconnais

This is the region just south of Burgundy proper that can offer some less expensive versions of Burgundy's white wines from the vineyards round Mâcon and some easy-drinking, gulpable reds from the vineyards of the Beaujolais area. Drink all these wines young.

Rhône

Mainly red wines and generally very good value. The whites can be quirky and heavy, but there has been a run of extremely good vintages of the meaty or spicy reds.

Loire

France's other great river is best-known, rather neatly, for its white wines – all with lots of acidity and great with food. Most Loire wines are designed for early consumption.

Alsace

France's most overlooked wine region, perhaps because it is almost in Germany. Fragrant, dry whites named after the Germanic grape varieties from which they are made. (This practice, varietal naming, is still uncommon in France even though it is gaining ground elsewhere throughout the wine world.)

Since *French Entrée* territory is so far from France's vine land, the visitor is offered a much more catholic selection of (French) wines than in wine regions further south. The French take chauvinism seriously and on a local scale. Remember that most dry white wines do not improve with age, so don't begrudge being asked to drink a very young vintage. Merely feel grateful that you can enjoy the wine while it's young and fresh. As for matching specific wines with food, I subscribe to the view that you should start by deciding what colour and weight you feel like drinking rather than following the choice dictated by the 'white with fish and red with meat' rule. If you want white with a rich meat dish, it makes sense to choose a full-bodied one such as white burgundy, while light-bodied, fairly tart reds like Beaujolais and Bourgueil make better fish partners than a rich Rhône would.

COMMON WINE NAMES – AN ALPHABETICAL GUIDE

The following are the words most likely to be encountered on labels and wine lists, with brief notes to help you towards the clues they give to what's inside the bottle. Especially good vintages are listed. If no vintage is listed, choose the youngest vintage available.

Alsace – Wine region, see above. 1983.

Anjou – Loire source of lots of medium rosé and a bit of safe, unexciting dry white.

Appellation Contrôlée – France's top 20 per cent of wine, named after the area where it is made.

Barsac – Sweet white bordeaux. Part of Sauterness so all Barsac is Sauternes but not all Sauternes is Barsac. 1983, 1979, 1976, 1975.

Beaujolais – Light, juicy reds. 1983, 1981, 1978.

Beaune – Southern town in the Burgundy heartland. Any wine carrying this name alone will be expensive, 1980, 1978, 1976.

Blanc de Blancs – Sounds fancy but means very little. Literally, a white wine made of white grapes, unusual in a champagne but obvious in a still white.

Bordeaux – Wine region, see above. 1983, 1982, 1981, 1979, 1978, 1976, 1975 for reds.

Bourgogne – 'Burgundy', a wine region, see above.

Bourgueil (Pronounce 'Boor-gurr-yeh') – Light red from the middle Loire.

Chablis – A much traduced name. True chablis (and the only sort of chablis you're likely to encounter in France) is steely-dry white burgundy from a village of the same name in the far north of the Burgundy region. 1981, 1979, 1978.

Champagne – Wine region, see above.

Châteauneuf-du-Pape – Full-bodied spicy red from the southern Rhône. 1983, 1980, 1979, 1978, 1977, 1976.

Chenin (Blanc) – The white grape of the Middle Loire, medium dry usually.

Corbières – Straightforward southern red.

Côte(s) de – 'Côte(s) de X' is usually better than a wine named simply 'X', as it means it comes from the (superior) hillsides above the lower ground of the X vineyards.

Coteaux de – Similar to 'Côte(s) de'.

Coteaux du Languedoc – Lightish southern red.

Coteaux du Layon – Small Middle Loire area producing some excellent but many unexciting medium dry whites.

Coteaux du Tricastin – Lightish version of Côtes-du-Rhône.

Côtes de Provence – Appellation for the dry white, herby red and, principally, dry pink wines of Provence in south-east France.

Côtes-du-Rhône – This big appellation with some new-style dry whites but mainly lightish spicy reds like Châteauneuf is usually good value.

Crozes-Hermitage – Convenient, earlier-maturing but still concentrated version of (almost always red) Hermitage. 1983, 1980, 1979, 1978.

Cru – Means 'growth' literally, *Grand cru* means 'great growth' and really rather good. *Cru classé* means that the growth has been officially classified as up to some definite scratch, and most of the world's best clarets are *crus classés*.

Doux – Sweet.

Entre-Deux Mers – Dry, and rarely exciting, white from Bordeaux.

Fleurie – Single-village beaujolais; superior. 1983, 1981, 1978.

Gaillac – Inexpensive white and sometimes red from south-west France.

Graves – Red and usually-dry white from a good-value area of Bordeaux.

Gewürztraminer – Perfumed grape grown in Alsace to produce France's most easily-recognisable white wine.

Hautes-Côtes de Beaune or Nuits – Affordable red and white burgundy from the slopes, high in altitude but not, for once, necessarily quality.

Hermitage – Long-lived tannic red from the northern Rhône. 1983, 1980, 1979, 1978, 1976.

Juliénas – Single-village beaujolais; superior. 1983, 1981, 1978.

Loire – Wine region, see above.

Mâcon – Southern end of Burgundy, source of good-value whites and some unexciting reds.

Margaux – Médoc village producing scented clarets.

méthode champenoise – The Champagne region's way of putting bubbles into wine and usually the sign of a good one.

Meursault – Very respectable burgundy, almost all white. 1981, 1978.

Minervois – Better-than-average southern red.

mis(e) bouteilles au château – Bottled at the Château (as opposed to in some merchant's cellars) and usually a sign of quality.

Moelleux – Medium sweet.

Monbazillac – Good-value country cousin to Sauternes.

Montrachet – Very great white burgundy. 1982, 1981, 1978.

Moulin-à-Vent – Single-village beaujolais which, unusually, can be kept. 1983, 1981, 1978, 1976.

Mousseux – Sparkling.

Mouton-Cadet – Not a special property, but a commercial blend of claret.

Muscadet – Lean, dry white from the mouth of the Loire. Very tart.

Muscat – The grape whose wines, unusually, taste and smell grapey. Dry in Alsace; very sweet and strong from places like Rivesaltes, Frontignan and Beaumes de Venise.

Nuits-St-Georges – Burgundy's second wine town. Bottles carrying this name are often expensive. 1980, 1978, 1976.

Pauillac – Bordeaux's most famous village, containing three of the five top châteaux. Very aristocratic claret. 1983, 1982, 1979, 1978, 1976, 1975.

Pomerol – Soft, fruity claret. Similar to St Emilion. 1983, 1982, 1981, 1979, 1978, 1975.

Pommard – Soft, fruity red burgundy. 1982, 1981, 1979, 1978.

Pouilly-Fuissé – Famous appellation in the Mâcon region. Dry, white and sometimes overpriced.

Pouilly-Fumé – Much tarter than Pouilly-Fuissé, made from the Sauvignon grape (see below) in the Loire.

Premières Côtes de Bordeaux – Inexpensive red and sweet white bordeaux.

Primeur – Wine designed to be drunk within months of the vintage e.g. from November till Easter. Beaujolais Nouveau is a 'Primeur'.

Puligny-Montrachet – Steely white burgundy and often very good. 1982, 1981, 1978.

Riesling – Germany's famous grape produces great dry wine in Alsace.

Ste-Croix-du-Mont – Inexpensive sweet white bordeaux.

St Emilion – Soft, early-maturing claret from many little properties, most of which seem to be allowed to call themselves *crus classés*. 1983, 1982, 1981, 1979, 1978, 1975.

St Estèphe – Sometimes rather hard but noble claret. 1982, 1979, 1978, 1976, 1975.

St Julien – Another Médoc village housing many great châteaux. 1983, 1982, 1979, 1978, 1976, 1975.

Sancerre – Twin village to the Pouilly of Pouilly Fumé, and producing very similar wines.

Santenay – Light red burgundy. 1980, 1978.

Saumur – Town in the middle Loire giving its name to wines of all colours, degrees of sweetness and some very good sparkling wine too.

Sauvignon – Grape producing dry whites with lots of 'bite'.

Savigny-lés-Beaune – Village just outside Beaune responsible for some good-value 'proper' red burgundy. 1980, 1978.

Sec – Dry.

Sylvaner – Alsace's 'everyday' light, dry white. Often the best wine you can buy by the glass in a French bar.

Touraine – An area in the middle Loire producing inexpensive Sauvignon and other wines.

VDQS – *Vin Délimité de Qualité Supérieure* (see above) – between AC and Vins de Pays.

Vin de Pays – Quality level at the top end of table wine. Many good-value inexpensive reds and some whites stating their region of origin on the label.

Vin de Table – The most basic sort of wine made in France. Very few excitements in this category. The blends with the name of a Burgundy merchant on the label are usually the most expensive.

Volnay – Soft red burgundy. Wine onomatopoeia? 1982, 1981, 1979, 1978.

WHAT TO BRING BACK

Provided you forgo any other liquor, and provided you make all the purchases in an ordinary (i.e. non-duty-free) shop, you may bring back seven litres of wine to Britain without paying any duty.

Nine 75cl bottles makes exactly this amount, as, of course, do seven of the litre bottles so common in French supermarkets. Ten 70cl bottles make so little more than seven litres that no Customs official is likely to complain. The label will state a bottle's capacity.

Excise duty is currently 78p on a 75cl bottle and 72p on a 70cl bottle (plus 15% VAT of purchase price abroad), and it is largely this that you are saving by importing your own wine. The extra cost of transporting a bottle from Bordeaux to London as opposed to Paris is negligible. Duty is the same on any bottle, however, regardless of the value of the wine. This means that savings are at their most dramatic – and most worth the effort – for the least expensive wines. You can buy seven litres of *vin de table* in France for around 30f, when the same amount of equivalent quality wine in Britain would cost almost as many pounds.

The corollary of all this is that you should bring back seven litres of the most ordinary wine you find you enjoy drinking, if your tastes and pocket are modest. Connoisseurs on the other hand should confine themselves to bringing back the odd bottle too obscure or rare to be found in this country. Many good mature wines are cheaper here than there – though this of course is dependent on the franc/sterling ratio.

Glossary of cooking terms and dishes

(It would take another book to list comprehensively French cooking terms and dishes, but here are the ones most likely to be encountered)

Aigre-doux	bittersweet
Aiguillette	thin slice (aiguille – needle)
Aile	wing
Aioli	garlic mayonnaise
Allemande (à l')	German style, i.e: with sausages and sauerkraut
Amuses-gueule	appetisers
Anglaise (à l')	plain boiled. Crème Anglaise – egg and cream sauce
Andouille	large uncooked sausage, served cold after boiling
Andouillettes	ditto but made from smaller intenstines, usually served hot after grilling
Anis	aniseed
Argenteuil	with asparagus
Assiette Anglaise	plate of cold meats

Baba au Rhum	yeast based sponge macerated in rum
Baguette	long thin loaf
Ballotine	boned, stuffed and rolled meat or poultry, usually cold
Béarnaise	sauce made from egg yolks, butter, tarragon, wine, shallots
Beurre Blanc	sauce from Nantes, with butter, reduction of shallot-flavoured vinegar or wine
Béchamel	white sauce flavoured with infusion of herbs
Beignets	fritters
Bercy	sauce with white wine and shallots
Beurre noir	browned butter
Bigarade	with oranges
Billy By	mussel soup
Bisque	creamy shellfish soup
Blanquette	stew with thick white creamy sauce, usually veal
Boeuf à la mode	braised beef
Bombe	ice cream mould
Bonne femme	with root vegetables
Bordelais	Bordeaux-style, with red or white wine, marrow bone fat
Bouchée	mouthful, i.e. vol au vent
Boudin	sausage, white or black
Bourride	thick fish soup
Braisé	braised
Brandade (de morue)	dried salt cod pounded into a mousse
Broche	spit
Brochette	skewer

Brouillade	stew, using oil
Brouillé	scrambled
Brulé	burnt, i.e. crême brulée
Campagne	country style
Cannelle	cinnamon
Carbonade	braised in beer
Cardinal	red-coloured sauce, i.e. with lobster or in pâtisserie with redcurrant
Charcuterie	cold pork-butcher's meats
Charlotte	Mould, as dessert lined with spongefingers, as savoury lined with vegetable
Chasseur	with mushrooms, shallots, wine
Chausson	pastry turnover
Chemise	covering, i.e. pastry.
Chiffonade	thinly-cut, i.e. lettuce
Choron	tomato Bearnaise
Choucroute	Alsation stew with sauerkraut and sausages
Civet	stew
Clafoutis	batter dessert, usually with cherries
Clamart	with peas
Cocotte	covered casserole
Compôte	cooked fruit
Concassé	i.e. tomatoes concassées – skinned, chopped, juice extracted.
Confit	preserved
Confiture	jam
Consommé	clear soup
Cou	neck
Coulis	juice, puree (of vegetables or fruit)
Cassolette or cassoulette	small pan
Cassoulet	rich stew with goose, pork and haricot beans
Cervelas	pork garlic sausage
Cervelles	brains
Chantilly	whipped sweetened cream
Cocque (à la)	i.e. oeufs – boiled eggs
Court-bouillon	aromatic liquor for cooking meat, fish, vegetables
Couscous	N. African dish with millet, chicken, vegetable variations
Crapaudine	involving fowl, particularly pigeon, trussed
Crécy	with carrots
Crême Pâtissière	thick custard filling
Crêpe	pancake
Crépinette	little flat sausage, encased in caul
Croque Monsieur	toasted cheese and ham sandwich
Croustade	pastry or baked bread shell
Croûte	pastry crust
Croûton	cube of fried or toasted bread
Cru	raw
Crudités	raw vegetables
Demi-glâce	basic brown sauce

Doria	with cucumber
Emincé	thinly sliced
Etuvé	stewed, i.e. vegetables in butter
Entremets	sweets
Farci	stuffed
Fines herbes	parsley, thyme, bayleaf
Feuillété	leaves of flaky pastry
Flamande	Flemish style, with beer
Flambé	flamed in spirit
Flamiche	flan
Florentine	with spinach
Flute	thinnest bread loaf
Foie gras	goose liver
Fondu	melted
Fond (d'artichaut)	heart (of artichoke)
Forestière	with mushrooms, bacon and potatoes
Four (au)	baked in the oven
Fourré	stuffed, usually sweets
Fricandeau	veal, usually topside
Frais, fraiche	fresh and cool
Frangipane	almond creme patisserie
Fricadelle	Swedish meat ball
Fricassé	(usually of veal) in creamy sauce
Frit	fried
Frites	chips
Friture	assorted small fish, fried in batter
Froid	cold
Fumé	smoked
Galantine	loaf-shaped chopped meat, fish or vegetable, set in natural jelly
Galette	Breton pancake, flat cake
Garbure	thick country soup
Garni	garnished, usually with vegetables
Gaufre	waffle
Gelée	aspic
Gésier	gizzard
Gibier	game
Gigôt	leg
Glacé	iced
Gougère	choux pastry, large base
Goujons	fried strips, usually of fish
Graine	seed
Gratin	baked dish of vegetables cooked in cream and eggs
Gratinée	browned under grill
Grêcque (à la)	cold vegetables served in oil
Grenouilles	frogs; cuisees de grenouille – frogs' legs
Grillé	grilled
Gros sel	coarse salt

Hachis	minced or chopped
Haricot	slow cooked stew
Hochepot	hotpot
Hollandaise	sauce with egg, butter, lemon
Hongroise	Hungarian, i.e. spiced with paprika
Hors d'oeuvre	assorted starters
Huile	oil
Île flottante	floating island – soft meringue on egg custard sauce
Indienne	Indian, i.e. with hot spices
Jambon	ham
Jardinière	from the garden, i.e. with vegetables
Jarret	shin, i.e. jarret de veau
Julienne	matchstick vegetables
Jus	natural juice
Lait	milk
Langue	tongue
Lard	bacon
Longe	loin
Macedoine	diced fruits or vegetables
Madeleine	small sponge cake
Magret	breast (of duck)
Maïs	sweetcorn
Maître d'hôtel	sauce with butter, lemon, parsley
Marchand de vin	sauce with red wine, shallot
Marengo	sauce with tomatoes, olive oil, white wine
Marinière	seamens' style, i.e. moules marinère (mussels in white wine)
Marmite	deep casserole
Matelote	fish stew, i.e. of eel
Medaillon	round slice
Mélange	mixture
Meunière	sauce with butter, lemon
Miel	honey
Mille feuille	flaky pastry, lit. 1,000 leaves
Mirepoix	cubed carrot, onion etc. used for sauces
Moëlle	beef marrow
Mornay	cheese sauce
Mouclade	mussel stew
Mousseline	Hollandaise sauce, lightened with egg whites
Moutarde	mustard
Nage (à la)	poached in flavoured liquor (fish)
Nature	plain
Navarin	
(d'agneau)	stew of lamb with spring vegetables
Noisette	nut-brown, burned butter
Noix de veau	nut of veal (leg)
Normande	Normandy style, with cream, apple, cider, Calvados
Nouilles	noodles

Os	bone
Paillettes	straws (of pastry)
Panaché	mixed
Panade	flour crust
Papillote (en)	cooked in paper case
Parmentier	with potatoes
Pâté	paste, of meat or fish
Pâte	pastry
Pâte brisée	rich short crust pastry
Pâtisserie	pastries
Paupiettes	paper thin slices
Pavé	thick slice
Paysan	country style
Perigueux	with truffles
Persillade	chopped parsley and garlic topping
Petits fours	tiny cakes, sweetmeats
Petit pain	bread roll
Piperade	peppers, onions, tomatoes in scrambled egg
Poché	poached
Poëlé	fried
Poitrine	breast
Poivre	pepper
Pommade	paste
Potage	thick soup
Pot-au-four	broth with meat and vegetables
Potée	country soup with cabbage
Pralines	caramelised almonds
Primeurs	young veg
Printanièr(e)	garnished with early vegetables
Profiterole	choux pastry balls
Provencale	with garlic, tomatoes, olive oil, peppers
Purée	mashed and sieved
Quenelle	pounded fish or meat, bound with egg, poached
Queue	tail
Quiche	pastry flan, i.e. quiche Lorraine – egg, bacon, cream
Râble	saddle, i.e. rable de lievre
Ragout	stew
Ramequin	little pot
Rapé	grated
Ratatouille	provencale stew of onions garlic, peppers, tomatoes
Ravigote	highly seasoned white sauce
Rémoulade	mayonnaise with gherkins, capers, herbs and shallot
Rillettes	potted shredded meat, usually fat pork or goose
Riz	rice
Robert	sauce with mustard, vinegar, onion
Roquefort	ewe's milk blue cheese
Rossini	garnished with foie gras and truffle
Rôti	roast
Rouelle	nugget

Rouille	hot garlicky sauce for soupe de poisson
Roulade	roll
Roux	sauce base – flour and butter
Sabayon	sweet fluffy sauce, with eggs and wine
Safran	saffron
Sagou	sago
St.-Germain	with peas
Salade niçoise	with tunny, anchovies, tomatoes, beans, black olives
Salé	salted
Salmis	dish of game or fowl, with red wine
Sang	blood
Santé	lit. healthy, i.e. with spinach and potato
Salpicon	meat, fowl, vegetables, chopped fine, bound with sauce and used as fillings
Saucisse	fresh sausage
Saucisson	dried sausage
Sauté	cooked in fat in open pan
Sauvage	wild
Savarin	ring of yeast sponge, soaked in syrup and liquor.
Sel	salt
Selle	saddle
Selon	according to, i.e. selon grosseur (according to size)
Smitane	with sour cream, white wine, onion
Soissons	with dried white beans
Sorbet	water ice
Soubise	with creamed onions
Soufflé	puffed, i.e. mixed with egg white and baked
Sucre	sugar (Sucré – sugared)
Suprême	fillet of poultry breast or fish
Tartare	raw minced beef, flavoured with onion etc. and bound with raw egg
Tartare (sauce)	mayonnaise with capers, herbs, onions
Tarte Tatin	upside down apple pie
Terrine	pottery dish/baked minced, chopped meat, veg., chicken, fish or fruit
Thé	tea
Tiède	luke warm
Timbale	steamed mould
Tisane	infusion
Tourte	pie
Tranche	thick slice
Truffes	truffles
Tuile	tile, i.e. thin biscuit
Vacherin	meringue confection
Vallée d'Auge	with cream, apple, Calvados
Vapeur (au)	steamed
Velouté	white sauce, bouillon-flavoured
Véronique	with grapes
Vert(e)	green, i.e. sauce verte with herbs
Vessie	pigs bladder
Vichyssoise	chilled creamy leak and potato soup

Vierge	prime olive oil
Vinaigre	vinegar (lit. bitter wine)
Vinaigrette	wine vinegar and oil dressing
Volaille	poultry
Vol-au-vent	puff pastry case
Xérès	sherry
Yaourt	yoghurt

FISH – Les Poissons, SHELLFISH – Les Coquillages

Anchois	anchovy	*Langouste*	crawfish
Anguille	eel	*Langoustine*	Dublin Bay prawn
Araignée de mer	spider crab	*Lieu*	ling
Bar	sea bass	*Limand*	lemon sole
Barbue	brill	*Lotte de mer*	monkfish
Baudroie	monkfish, anglerfish	*Loup de mer*	sea bass
Belon	oyster – flat shelled	*Maquereau*	mackerel
Bigorneau	winkle	*Merlan*	whiting
Blanchaille	whitebait	*Morue*	salt cod
Brochet	pike	*Moule*	mussel
Cabillaud	cod	*Mulet*	grey mullet
Calamar	squid	*Ombre*	grayling
Carrelet	plaice	*Oursin*	sea urchin
Chapon de mer	scorpion fish	*Palourde*	clam
Claire	oyster	*Petoncle*	small scallop
Coquille	scallop	*Plie*	plaice
St.Jacques		*Portugaise*	oyster
Crabe	crab	*Poulpe*	octopus
Crevette grise	shrimp	*Praire*	oyster
Crevette rose	prawn	*Raie*	skate
Daurade	sea bream	*Rascasse*	scorpion-fish
Écrevisse	crayfish	*Rouget*	red mullet
Éperlan	smelt	*St. Pierre*	John Dory
Espadon	swordfish	*Saumon*	Salmon
Etrille	baby crab	*Saumonette*	rock salmon
Favouille	spider crab	*Seiche*	squid
Flétan	halibut	*Sole*	sole
Fruits de mer	seafood	*Soupion*	inkfish
Grondin	red gurnet	*Thon*	tunny
Hareng	herring	*Tortue*	turtle
Homard	lobster	*Tourteau*	large crab
Huitre	oyster	*Truite*	trout
Julienne	ding	*Turbot*	turbot
Laitance	soft herring roe	*Turbotin*	chicken turbot
Lamproie	lamprey		

FRUITS – Les fruits, VEGETABLES – Les legumes, NUTS – Les noix
HERBS – Les herbes, SPICES – Les epices

Ail	garlic	*Basilic*	basil
Algue	seaweed	*Betterave*	beetroot
Amande	almond	*Blette*	Swiss chard
Ananas	pineapple	*Brugnon*	nectarine
Aneth	dill	*Cassis*	blackcurrant
Abricot	apricot	*Céléri*	celery
Arachide	peanut	*Céléri-rave*	celeriac
Artichaut	globe artichoke	*Cêpe*	edible fungus
Asperge	asparagus	*Cerfeuil*	chervil
Avocat	avocado	*Cérise*	cherry
Banane	banana	*Champignon*	mushroom

Chanterelle	edible fungus	*Morille*	dark brown crinkly
Chatâigne	chestnut		edible fungus
Chicorée	endive	*Mûre*	blackberry
Chou	cabbage	*Muscade*	nutmeg
Choufleur	cauliflower	*Myrtille*	bilberry, blueberry
Choux de Bruxelles	Brussels sprout	*Navet*	turnip
Ciboulette	chive	*Noisette*	hazelnut
Citron	lemmon	*Oignon*	onion
Citron vert	lime	*Oseille*	sorrel
Coing	quince	*Palmier*	palm
Concombre	cucumber	*Pamplemousse*	grapefruit
Coriandre	coriander	*Panais*	parsnip
Cornichon	gherkin	*Passe-Pierre*	seaweed
Courge	pumpkin	*Pastèque*	water melon
Courgette	courgette	*Pêche*	peach
Cresson	watercress	*Persil*	parsley
Échalotte	shallot	*Petit pois*	pea
Endive	chicory	*Piment doux*	sweet pepper
Épinard	spinach	*Pissenlit*	dandelion
Escarole	salad leaves	*Pistache*	pistachio
Estragon	tarragon	*Pleurote*	edible fungi
Fenouil	fennel	*Poire*	pear
Féve	broad bean	*Poireau*	leek
Flageolet	dried bean	*Poivre*	pepper
Fraise	strawberry	*Poivron*	green, red and yellow
Framboise	raspberry		peppers
Genièvre	juniper	*Pomme*	apple
Gingembre	ginger	*Pomme-de-terre*	potato
Girofle	clove	*Prune*	plum
Girolle	edible fungus	*Pruneau*	prune
Granade	pomegranate	*Quetsch*	small dark plum
Griotte	bitter red cherry	*Radis*	radish
Groseille	gooseberry	*Raifort*	horseradish
Groseille noire	blackcurrant	*Raisin*	grape
Groseille rouge	redcurrant	*Reine Claude*	greengage
Haricot	dried white bean	*Romarin*	rosemary
Haricot vert	French bean	*Safron*	saffron
Laitue	lettuce	*Salisifis*	salsify
Mandarine	tangerine, mandarin	*Thym*	thyme
Mangetout	sugar pea	*Tilleul*	lime blossom
Marron	chestnut	*Tomate*	tomato
Menthe	mint	*Topinambour*	Jerusalem artichoke
Mirabelle	tiny gold plum	*Truffe*	truffle

MEAT – Les Viandes

Le Boeuf	Beef	*Faux Filet*	sirloin steak
Charolais	is the best	*Filet*	fillet
Chateaubriand	double fillet steak		
Contrefilet	sirloin	*L'Agneau*	Lamb
Entrecôte	rib steak	*Pré-Salé*	is the best
		Carré	neck cutlets

Côte	chump chop	*Les Abats*	Offal
Epaule	shoulder	*Foie*	liver
Gigot	leg	*Foie gras*	goose liver
Le Porc	Pork	*Cervelles*	brains
Jambon	ham	*Langue*	tongue
Jambon cru	raw smoked ham	*Ris*	sweetbreads
Porcelet	suckling pig	*Rognons*	kidneys
Le Veau	Veal	*Tripes*	tripe
Escalope	thin slice cut from fillet		

POULTRY – Volaille, GAME – Gibier

Abatis	giblets	*Lièvre*	hare
Bécasse	woodcock	*Oie*	goose
Bécassine	snipe	*Perdreau*	partridge
Caille	quail	*Pigeon*	pigeon
Canard	duck	*Pintade*	guineafowl
Caneton	duckling	*Pluvier*	plover
Chapon	capon	*Poularde*	chicken (boiling)
Chevreuil	roe deer	*Poulet*	chicken (roasting)
Dinde	young hen turkey	*Poussin*	spring chicken
Dindon	turkey	*Sanglier*	wild boar
Dindonneau	young turkey	*Sarcelle*	teal
Faisan	pheasant	*Venaison*	venison
Grive	thrush		

Readers' Recommendations

Place	Establishment	Recommended by
Les Andelys	Hôtel Normandie (HR)S	Mrs J. Kirwan
Annebault	Le Cardinal (R)M	Martine Maubant
Arromanches	Le Mulberry (R)S	Michael Sibley
Auderville	Hôtel de la Hague (HR)S	Susan Leyden
Auffay	L'Aigle d'Or (R)S	Vi Dyson
Avranches	La Pomme d'Or (R)S	Debbie Comfort
	Hôtel du Jardin des	
	Plantes (H)M	J. L. Humphrys
Balleroy	Manoir de la Drôme (R)M	
Barfleur	Hôtel Phare (HR)M	Mary Cureton
Barneville-le-Bertran	Auberge de la Source (HR)S	
Bayeux	Hôtel Bayeux (H)M	
	Hôtel de Brunville (H)M	J.A. Boucher
	La Chaloupe (R)S	Mel Swales
Berny-Bocage	Hôtel de France (HR)S	
Bourg-Dun	Auberge de la Poste (R)S	
Brécey	Madame Gauchet,	
	La Blaitière (C)M	
Bréville	Le Mougins des	
	Moulins à Vent (H)M	Anne Bates
Caen	Le Boeuf Ferre (R)S	Pat Fenn
	Hôtel Cordelier (H)M	William Bennett
	La Mandarine (R)M	Pat Fenn
Caudebec-en-Caux	Le Cheval Blanc (R)S	Christine Sleigh
Cherbourg	La Soupière (R)S	G. Caron
Clécy	Le Site Normande	
	(R)M	P. Priday
	Le Pressoir (R)S	
	Mme Leboucher,	
	Le Vey (C)	
Coudeville	Mme Lechavilier	
	Le Herbert (C)	T. Belafield
Courseulles	La Cremaillière (R)M	Eric Sheldon
Coutances	Hotel Moderne (HR)S	Mme Perrin
La Croix-Avranchin	Mme Gerard Meslin,	
	'Mouraine' (C)	Mr and Mrs L. Watson
Duclair	Au Coq Hardye (R)S	Elaine Pavey
Ecouche	Hostellerie du Lion	
	d'Or (R)S	R.G. Johnson
Eu	Le Relais (R)M	

Fécamp	L'Escalier (R)M	
	La Marine (R)M	
	Les Gourmets (R)M	Jeremy Cockayne
Flers	Le Galion (R)S	Mel Swales
Grandcamp Maisy	Le Dugesclin (HR)M	Susan Leyden
Granville	Le Mangeoire (R)S	M. G. Horler
	Le Channel (R)S	D. Hallifax
Hanse du Brick	Le Brick (R)S	Mark Saxton
Le Havre	Le Petit Bedon (R)M	John Julius Norwich
	Le Celtic (H)S	Miss M. G. Stone
	Hôtel Gambetta (H)S	
	Le Boucaniers (R)S	Pauline Carder
	La Lorraine (R)S	H. Greenhowe
Hermanville-sur-Mer	Le Canada (R)M	Nigel Williams
Honfleur	Hôtel Monet (H)M	Joan Manning
	Castel Albertine (H)M	Mrs L. J. Rankin
Jumieges	M. P. Chatel,	
	Le Quesnoy (c)	Mary and Brian Day
Lisieux	Hôtel St Louis (H)S	John Curtis
	Le Club (R)S	John Curtis
	Hôtel des Capucines (HR)S	D.F. Joliffe
Louvetot	Auberge au Grand Méchant Loup (R)S	Mike Souter
Lyons-la-Forêt	Hostellerie du Domaine St Paul (R)M	
	La Halle (R)S	
Montmartin-en-Granges (nr. St Lo)	Le Rata (R)S	
Mont St Michel (N.B., on main road, not on Mount)	Hôtel le Relais du Roy (HR)S	Wendy Forrest-Webb
Montagne	Château des Caneaux (H)M	P. Fenn
Montreuil-l'Argillé (near Orbec)	La Goulafrière (R)M	Vi Dyson
Muids	Au Pecheur Matinal (R)S	Joan Taylor
Neufchatel-en-Bray	Hôtel des Airelles (HR)S	D.F. Joliffe
Nôtre-Dame-de Courson	Le Tournebroche (R)M	Martine Maubant
Noyers Bocage	Le Relais Normand (R)M	
Pont Audemer	Hostellerie Le Beau Rivage (R)S	J. Noel
Pont d'Ouilly	Hôtel de la Place (HR)S	Shirley Court
Pont l'Evêque	Auberge de la Hauquerie (R)S	

Pontorson	Au Vent des Grèves	
	(R)S	B. Hillier
Port-en-Bessin	Auberge St Simeon	Francis Gauthroy
(St-Honorine-des		
Pertes)		
Quettehou	La Chaumière	M. Saxton
La Roque	L'Auberge de Mesnil	
	(R)S	F. Couesnon
Rouen	St. Léonard (HR)M	B. Thompson
	Le Bois Chenu (R)S	B. Thompson
	Le Bourse (R)S	Mike Souter
	Le Bistro d'Adrien (R)S	R. J. Evans
		M. L. Adcorn
	Hôtel Quebec (H)S	Joan Wakeman Long
St André d'Herbertot	Le Prieuré (R)M	Martine Maubant
		Henry Brownrigg
St Aubin-sur-Scie	Coquille Fleurie (R)S	Roger Lushington
Ste Cecile (nr Villedieu)	Le Manoir de l'Archerie	
	(R)M	F. Couesnon
		Brian Hugill
St Germain-de-La	Hôtel Germain (HR)S	Heather Filmer
Tallevende (nr Vire)		
Ste Marguerite-sur-Mer	Les Sapins (HR)M	David Hale
St Martin-aux-	La Trinité (R)S	Doreen Horsley
Chartrains		
St Michel-des-Andains	La Bruyère (R)M	
(nr Bagnoles)		
St Samson	Domaine de la Brousse	
	(R)S	Martine Maubant
St Sylvain	La Cremaillère (R)M	Martine Maubant
St Vaast	Le Port (R)S	Barbara Watson
	L'Escale (R)S	N. Dyer
Sées	Le Dauphin (HR)S	David Cutar
Tapotin (nr Cherbourg)	Le Moulin de la Haulle	
	(R)S	M. Saxton
Teurtheville-Bocage	Le Moulin au Poivre	
	(R)S	Amanda Taylor
		M. Saxton
Thury Harcourt	Hôtel de La Place (HR)S	Bertha Barnardiston
Tourove	Hôtel de France (HR)S	R. F. Ash
Tracy (nr Arromanches)	Auberge de la Rosière	
	(R)S	Joan Maning
Trouville	Il Teatro (R)M	Michael Main
Valognes	Hôtel St Mâlo (H)M	B. R. Scholes
Veullettes-sur-Mer	Les Frégates (R)M	
Villedieu-les Poëles	Hôtel de la Gare (HR)S	Vi Dyson
Vire	Au Vrai Normand (R)S	G. Jeffs
Vironvay	Le Relais de Vironvay (R)M	
Vitré	Le Petit Billot (R)S	Lindsay Williamson

Index